ESCAPING

DELETE

A CEO in the Black Hole

JON BELLMAN

INTRODUCTION

Information Technology powers our lives and lifestyles. Our electric grid, air traffic control, healthcare, defense, communication, education, banking, public safety, entertainment, and food delivery systems are all computer-based. Information Technology or IT has helped to make our lives longer, more efficient and more interesting. We depend upon IT as we depend upon the other great human inventions of money, clothing, and language.

Yet, the IT needles may be stuck too deeply into our arms. When IT systems break down, tragedy looms. Troops wait for ammunition that is weeks late, a patient receives an improperly labeled drug during surgery and the fire department responds to the wrong address. At what point does the rush to computerize everything lower our living standards?

As our IT systems become increasingly connected to each other, we are more vulnerable than ever to a domino-style capability blackout. If we continue on our present path, technology-driven calamity becomes a question of when, and not if. We must acknowledge our risks and address them before a hijacker figures out how to shut down our public safety networks. The possibility is scarily realistic: spies have already gained access to our electric grid and banking network. Should we panic? If an online auction or a social media site is successfully attacked, it won't result in catastrophe. If the water purification system in Los Angeles County is compromised, it could.

A sure path to an IT-driven economic and social depression is reality repression. Our existence has become so connected to our technology that a few days of service interruption would permanently tear the paper-thin fabric of our societal security blanket. Our time can be likened to the economic one when pundits predicted Enron's stock price would rise to the heavens or real estate prices could no longer fall more than twenty percent.

Understanding the progenitor of a technology – the technology project – enables us to recognize and better manage technology risk. Like buildings, bridges, and airplanes, the technologies that power our economy are built with blueprints, tools, and great human energy. So what happens when blueprints are wrong, tools don't work, or human energy is misapplied?

Great waste results and risk becomes an unintended feature of what was built. On a technology project, unlike one that produces a building, a bridge, or an airplane, true progress toward completion is more difficult to gauge. Nor can we know what pressures will result in shortcuts taken or safeguards avoided in order to meet a deadline.

IT often fails because of the complexity of the human interactions surrounding its design, implementation, and use. There is no single recipe for doing IT right; rather, success depends upon a deep understanding of a technology project's objectives, costs and time constraints. One must consider the interplay among executives, consultants and vendors, and recognize that only with keen timing, effective operating disciplines and the flexibility to adjust to highly fluid situations does a project have a good chance of birthing a working system.

Project environments can be fraught with human frailties and battling egos. A penchant for covering up mistakes from a foundering few often will waylay the purposeful efforts of the many. Business people blame the technology people, but technology projects fail when business people don't mind the store. Good technology is the servant of good business and not the other way around. Executives must take responsibility. Vendor promises ought to be scrutinized, not celebrated. By employing common sense, sobriety and simple control mechanisms, failures could be reduced and executives would have less to stew and sue about.

On a personal level, technology has profoundly changed our lives. The late 20th century worker learned computers on the job, but the 21st century worker comes to work with computer skills, social media knowledge, and smartphone savvy. We create online content with far greater ease than our parents programmed their VCRs. Do these skills translate into business and organizational effectiveness, or do they produce a thick din of productivity-retarding and psychically deafening noise?

It is a large and contentious question. But one thing is clear: as technology capability grows, so does the variety, frequency and cost of its abuse. We are fighting a losing war to preserve privacy. Warned against indelibly placing personal information online, we do it anyway. Religious affiliations and sexual proclivities are advertised on social media websites with no more restraint than comments about a favored rock band or sports car. Last names are used as passwords and pictures of drunken antics are uploaded without hesitation.

We compulsively bang at our mini-sized keys. We can't step into an elevator without pushing past technology's prisoners, their attention to safety and courtesy drowned out by electronic blather from their smartphones. On the way to work or school, we blast music through our devices' ear buds at deafness-inducing levels, not pausing to consider the obvious, long-term harm. Instead, we leap to read this text or that email instantly, even though the instancy of the experience dulls its impact.

Foolhardiness is costly. Employers find videos posted by pranksters and rescind job offers. Cyber-bullies torture classmates. Stalkers build repositories of personal information to keep closer eyes on their targets. Identity thieves wreak havoc on victims and on their creditors. Fringe groups amass infrastructure information needed to launch terrorist attacks. IT provides nearly unlimited power, and the enemies of good are limited only by their creativity in wielding that power.

Hope can triumph over fear. Doing technology right is achievable, but the challenge is paradoxical. It requires balancing a myopic perspective of what is being sought with a holistic understanding of how the technology will impact its intertwined neighbors. Benefits must transcend complexity. The learned seeker will find that clarity is essential, while the expert techno-chef is on a never-ending journey to simplify.

Responsible technology behavior must come from the individual too. To harness technology's might, we must establish personal disciplines and learn to recognize when incremental capability, albeit sexy, consumes too much attention. IT should be leveraged to extend the limits of our lives, not steal time, increase unhappiness and scatter personal clarity. ESCAPING DELETE will enable its readers to recognize when too much of a good thing becomes a very bad thing.

ACKNOWLEDGEMENTS

To honor my wonderful dad, Berny Bellman, who passed away in 2016.

Enjoy, learn well, and prosper,

Jon Bellman

CAST OF CHARACTERS

Biff Harper	CEO of PNP
Big-Box	PNP's largest customer
Broadway	The IT system linking PNP and Big-Box
Buck Roscoe	Head of private equity firm
Earl McCweeg	Plant worker
Fred Namath	Pro-Con consultant
Gary Gibson	Jailed software executive
Horace Green	Merchant from Big-Box
Jack Bluto	Maverick consultant
John Flynch	Pro-Con's lead consultant
Lars Lanugo	CEO of Big-Box
Meyer Steadman	Director of Manufacturing
PNP	Pots & Pans Company
Pro-Con	IT consulting firm/systems integrator
Rona Sims	Senior Vice President - Sales and Marketing
Stanley Chmeat	CIO of PNP
ThickWare	Software vendor

PART I - THE SITUATION

THURSDAY, JULY 7TH 5:50 PM

Jack Bluto's white knuckles tore into 25D's seat bolster. Smoke burned his eyes as he jammed his head between his knees. The first pop – and it was merely that – occurred twenty minutes ago. Jack had been toying with his smartphone, looking for a ground signal to download his email as MidPoint Airlines Flight 101 descended below 10,000 feet. The pop came five seconds after the two gentle chimes signaled final approach. Jack and the guy across the aisle in 26B picked up their heads and looked at each other. Neither knew what happened, but a mutual glance reassured them both. A minute later 26B was asleep and Jack was reading his emails.

The second noise came from below. A rolling, low-pitched burst of thunder, it was more forceful than deafening. Gray smoke leapt out of the passenger service units as the starboard wing dipped low. Jack's smartphone flipped out of his hand and slid like a hockey puck along the aisle until it hit the snack cart in the rear galley. *What the hell is happening? I don't give a damn, I just want to live!*

Ten seconds later the third explosion blew open the starboard lavatory doors, expectorating the toilet tanks' contents into the passenger compartment. The overhead bins shook open, lobbing laptops across the aisle. *Why no announcements? Where are the flight attendants? Why didn't I say something when the TSA let those two scary looking guys through without checking them? They boarded the flight at the next gate, didn't they? Why didn't I pay more attention?*

The pilot's cabin door opened. Two flight attendants came out. *I can't hear what they're saying! I can't do anything. Wait, one of those guys is grabbing the flight attendant. I can't see. Oh please, please, don't let them be terrorists. Please god, I'll do anything you want. Anything!* The oxygen mask dropped down above Jack, and the retainer string from the mask brushed his lips. He put it on and took a deep, shaky breath.

The plane rolled back to center and steadied. The toilet tanks' contents that hadn't landed in laps or pant cuffs settled in the aisle. Jack looked up. *Finally! Maybe god listened. Damn it, I hope so.* Jack saw a flight attendant straddle the aisle as she climbed atop the armrests of 1C and 1D. Steadying herself with one hand on the roof of the cabin, she pulled a portable megaphone to her lips.

"Stay calm," she barked. "The pilot is going to make an emergency landing at O'Hare. There was an explosion in the cargo bay. The pilot assures me that we will land safely. Assume the crash position and brace for impact."

My god, she knows nothing! How does the pilot know we're going to land safely? Where's Sully when we need him? Just let me see those houses once we get under the clouds. My head is going to explode. The stench from the flotsam in the aisle was unbearable.

Jack heard the loud "click" of the landing gear locking into place. He squinted through the window and saw cars on the ground. *We'll land in less than two minutes.* He held his breath. He always held his breath once he saw the cars and kept it held until the wheels touched.

We're coming in too hot, too fast. He gasped and ripped off his mask. The wheels hit. They swerved as he gulped the plane's filthy air. The brakes squealed wildly and the passengers were thrown back and forth. Finally the plane slowed. Whoops and hollers came out of every row. *I will live tonight. Thank god!*

"Stay in your seats and remain calm," a voice boomed across the plane's PA system. "We are awaiting further instructions from ground control. We'll have you off the plane momentarily."

Why delay now? Where are the evacuation slides? Damn it! I can't breathe this air. Is that my smartphone? Jack reached down into the murky pool covering the aisle. His hand closed around it too easily. "Shit!"

THURSDAY, JULY 7TH 9:12 PM

Jack disembarked via the front door. His legs shook as he slowly walked down the stairs onto a runway full of flashing emergency vehicles. The last ray of summer evening sunshine slunk from the sky.

FBI agents and TSA dogs sniffed the plane for nearly three and a half hours before releasing the passengers. There had never been a bomb. Rather, five Fujohara 24" 3D laptop computers were loaded into the hottest section of the cargo hold. The lithium batteries in those laptops caught fire in the plane's underbelly, causing a leaky oxygen canister to explode beneath the toilet tanks. The explosion punched a fist-sized hole through the plane's hull.

Jack was led past the airport's chapel to the Incident Recovery Area. Moments later, a man was examining Jack's hair across the urinal divider in the IRA men's room. When Jack realized he was being stared at, he looked up and the man cleared his throat uncomfortably and said, "I'm amazed that the plane didn't blow."

"Why didn't it?" Jack yelped, jumping back from the urinal, realizing this was one of the scary-looking guys.

"Because the explosions happened below suck-out altitude," the man answered while zipping his fly and fumbling to show Jack his sky marshal identification badge.

✳ ✳ ✳

THURSDAY, JULY 7ᵀᴴ 5:50 PM

Biff Harper read the text from MidPoint and frowned.

"Finish your beer and let's go. We need to run to Gate D37 to catch our flight," he said to Stanley Chmeat. "The next flight isn't for two hours and it's always full."

Stanley nodded and started gulping his Sam Adams.

"I can't believe Atlanta switched gates again. How could a town with such great weather have such a fucked up airport?" Biff asked, his voice rising.

Stanley, still chugging, said nothing.

The words seemed awkward in Biff's mouth; anger and profanity were uncharacteristic for him, but he was swimming in blackening waters. His long sought-after millions had been in sniffing distance, until a few hours ago. A day of angst, subterfuge, and Stanley's incessant commentary had moved Biff closer to his rarely reached "losing it" threshold.

His loud complaints brought approving glances from nearby passengers. PNP's forty-seven-year-old CEO was used to attracting stares in airports, sometimes inappropriately long ones. He was a man who never had to approach women; they approached him. With an ever-so-slight swagger, a strong chin, deep blue eyes, and the wide shoulders of a professional athlete, his presence was formidable. Despite his age, Biff's well-styled sandy blond hair had only a touch of gray at the temples. Even today, Biff's pressed Royal Dornoch golf sweater and perfectly tailored khakis disguised his troubles to the casual onlooker.

He and Stanley, PNP's Chief Information Officer or CIO, were returning to Chicago after a long day of meeting, first with Big-Box Stores and then with ThickWare Software Systems. Big-Box, headquartered in Macon, Georgia, sold PNP's pots and pans its stores. ThickWare, in Atlanta, supplied business software to both PNP and Big-Box.

Big-Box mandated that all of its suppliers were to be fully integrated with its Broadway system and PNP was working toward connecting its computers to Broadway. Big-Box's global chain of four thousand retail stores developed Broadway to inform suppliers when products were selling either faster or slower than forecasted. Once PNP was connected to Broadway, Big-Box would be able to adjust its order flows in a moment's notice, saving millions in inventory expenses annually for both PNP and Big-Box.

Earlier that afternoon, John Flynch, a consultant from Pro-Con Partners had left Atlanta to fly back to New York. Flynch had been spending four days a week with PNP managing the Thick-Ware IT project and he joined Biff and Stanley for the meeting at ThickWare's headquarters in Atlanta.

Flynch's team of twenty-seven consultants included four from Pro-Con, three from ThickWare, two from Bajupta, a firm based in Bangalore, India, and two from a small independent firm. Bajupta also had another dozen consultants operating offshore in India. Biff had been nervous about going offshore for such a critical project, but Stanley had assured Biff that Bajupta was Level 5 certified. Biff didn't understand what that meant or how it made up for nine thousand miles of physical separation, but he felt that he needed to support his CIO's decisions.

The meeting with ThickWare was downright unpleasant. PNP had already paid more than three million dollars in software license fees and was on the hook for a perpetual 21% annual maintenance fee, entitling PNP to receive periodic ThickWare upgrades. PNP chose ThickWare from a pool of a dozen software vendors after a three-month selection and evaluation process managed by Flynch. Flynch's college roommate just happened to be the lead sales guy on ThickWare's team, but Flynch was up front about this and tried hard to avoid any appearance of impropriety. ThickWare won the beauty contest after site visits, product demos, and a compelling response to PNP's one hundred and eleven page Request for Proposal, or RFP. ThickWare's response included a business case showing that PNP would likely receive approximately $100 million in benefits once the technology was operational.

Biff flew to Atlanta to express his displeasure with the buggy software code ThickWare had supplied. It was, however, a two-faced move as he and Stanley drove to Macon to assure Big-Box that PNP's implementation was right on track. Big-Box's fiery, white-haired CEO, Lars Lanugo, issued an edict that any vendors not up and running on Broadway by December 31st would be dropped by Big-Box. Biff was annoyed about having to lie, a practice he'd normally avoid.

Biff was worried about his relationship with Big-Box, and Stanley wasn't helping. The private equity firm that owned most of PNP had pushed Biff to hire Stanley. Before joining PNP, Stanley put in a company-wide IT system at a sheepskin prophylactics manufacturer. A post-mortem of the project, lauding Stanley's contributions, appeared in *Tektanic*, one of the industry's most well-read trade periodicals. Biff didn't realize that Stanley built the system around the outdated business processes that the prophylactics company had been running for years.

Stanley had largely ignored the business process refinements suggested by King-Con, the international consulting giant, in its ten million dollar project with the prophylactics company; Stanley was happy just to get the massive system working without losing his job. Perhaps he resented not being part of the decision to hire King-Con or felt that their suggestions would be too difficult to implement. Nevertheless, he walked out of the prophylactics manufacturer with a handsome bonus. Although Stanley received an excellent reference, it was unclear whether the prophylactics manufacturer was actually using the new system.

✷ ✷ ✷

Founded in Toledo by Marv Schwartz in 1936, PNP soldiered on for nearly six decades as an independent company until the threat of bankruptcy forced Schwartz's bungling, big-spending descendants to sell out for pennies on the dollar to a large manufacturing conglomerate. After passing through the balance sheets of other uninspired and indifferent suitors, PNP was eventually sold for twelve million dollars to a Lower Wacker Drive private equity firm, Roscoe & Lauer. Twelve million dollars on eight hundred million in sales was so repugnant that one had to wonder if Marv's remains were curled up in a fetal position inside his coffin.

✵ ✵ ✵

Biff grew up with an intensity that shone through in his unrivaled work ethic. It had been that way since Biff was in his early teens. Biff studied hard, but performed better in brawn than in brain, lettering in four sports at Newtown High School in New York City's Flushing neighborhood.

He detested his father, Harry, a hard-drinking Marine Corps colonel who was overseas most of the time. Biff's mother Sally raised Biff and his sister. Biff couldn't afford college and started working full-time at seventeen. An aunt in Chicago's Naperville suburb with a job lead brought Biff to PNP.

Biff was assigned to the #6 Ingerand machine, used to manufacture aluminum trivets. For nine hours a day minus lunch and two coffee breaks, Biff loaded heavy aluminum ingots into a tilting barrel furnace. From there he directed the molten aluminum into the trivet molds. After the trivets solidified, he cleaned the molds with lye and then loaded the excess aluminum into a buggy. Biff pushed that buggy along the factory floor to the smelting department.

Biff's pluck and willingness to take on any dirty work or injury-prone assignment enabled him to move up swiftly. For the next fifteen years, Biff worked harder than anyone at PNP. His star rose via stints in manufacturing, marketing, and sales. Selling was Biff's forte: people liked buying from him. The sale that made him was the one to Constance Ophelia, an older woman descended from an iconic Chicago family. Cash-rich Constance was prim, slim, and attractive in a statuesque way, and a regular in Chicago's society pages. Biff enjoyed having other people gawk at his well-known wife.

They had a sixteen-year-old daughter from Constance's previous marriage. Amelia dated voraciously, often asking Biff's advice. He found her questions terribly embarrassing, inspiring him to spend more time at the office. Constance had the time to raise Amelia on her own, and this arrangement was more than fine with Biff.

Constance had no idea that Biff stopped off almost nightly at a seedy strip club near O'Hare. Biff wasn't sure what drew him to the strip club, as he rarely felt satisfied, even when once or twice per month he would pay a hundred dollars for "VIP service." He always closed his eyes and let his mind wander elsewhere.

Biff had risen to Vice President of Sales at PNP when Roscoe & Lauer took over. Two other candidates turned down Roscoe & Lauer before Biff was finally offered the CEO's job.

Buck Roscoe, the former Ohio Senator who converted his Capitol Hill relationships into millions of dollars, felt Biff lacked the finance skills required to run a company. Biff won the offer from Buck after begging Mrs. Roscoe. Buck agreed that Biff could make up in desire what he lacked in depth. Roscoe had a reputation for brutality toward those whose performances fell short, and Biff realized that he had to quickly rise to the challenges of his new position.

Biff charged hard into his new responsibilities and stretched his limits. His responsibilities were overwhelming his athletic constitution. Biff developed the dark circles and paunch indicative of chronic exhaustion. He started drinking most weekdays after the promotion, and his blood pressure and insulin cycle were going awry. The drinking, combined with the more-than-occasional Ambien, helped him get to sleep at night. This routine had worked for him until recently, when he rediscovered a large bottle of oxycodone in the old golf bag in his garage.

One evening, while Constance was yelling at him from upstairs, Biff took a nearly empty, pocket-sized Midol bottle from the downstairs bathroom. He flushed the contents down the toilet and filled the small bottle with the painkillers, after putting two pink pills into his mouth. *My god, this is like my father's hip flask*, he realized. Biff bit down on the pills, closed the small bottle, and slipped it into his pocket.

Still, Biff's stick-to-it-iveness and superior concentration enabled him to stay focused at work. But when Biff attended IT project meetings, his tired eyes quickly glazed over when one of Stanley's direct reports gave the details of some arcane aspect of the Broadway project.

As a first-time CEO in a weak bargaining position, Biff's jackpot would come if PNP could clean itself up and Roscoe & Lauer could sell PNP. Finally Biff would have his own millions. Not his wife's. Not bad for a hardworking kid who grew up down the block from the Corona Ice King in Queens.

✵ ✵ ✵

SUNDAY, JULY 10TH 7:15 AM

Jack woke to find his replacement smartphone waiting for him at the Palmer House's front desk. Feeling naked these past three days, he was relieved to have his trusty sidearm back in its holster.

He walked north nearly a mile to a bagel joint on Rush Street. In the newspaper pile he found a mostly complete main section of the Tribune, shmeared with cream cheese. His eyes widened when he saw the Tribune's coverage of his tumultuous MidPoint flight:

> *The FAA determined that Thursday's incident on MidPoint Flight 101 from Kansas City to Chicago O'Hare was caused by improperly stored cargo in the plane's baggage compartment. Anthony Maraschino, spokesman for the FAA, announced in his press conference, "It is unclear whether an explosion or multiple explosions took place, but we can confirm that there was unauthorized activity in the cargo hold. Our incident response team is investigating whether an intruder tampered with the cargo or if a defect in MidPoint Airways' recently implemented Vision Cargo Sorting System caused baggage to be inappropriately loaded.*

> *Stuart LaSalle, President of Baggage Handler's Local 17, released the following statement: "MidPoint Airways has a checkered safety record. We are saddened that MidPoint put its economic motives ahead of passenger safety by rushing ahead with a technology that was not ready. Members of our brotherhood and sisterhood repeatedly informed management that the system had not been properly tested and could cause cargo loading errors resulting in catastrophic in-flight failure."*

> *Ryan Sears, Vice President of Customer Relations for MidPoint Airways reported that MidPoint has been recertified by the FAA to immediately resume full operations. When asked whether passengers would be safe, Sears replied, "Absolutely. MidPoint is reviewing concerns regarding its Vision Cargo Sorting System*

with the representatives from Pro-Con who developed the system. Pro-Con's internal audit team already determined that any potential bugs in their system could not have caused the Flight 101 incident. When asked whether MidPoint's management was aware that Pro-Con was one of the contractors that worked on the failed Denver Airport Baggage Handling System in the mid '90's, Sears responded, "I am aware that they were one of several contractors involved. That project had nothing to do with us."

Jack grimaced. MidPoint's system was probably very broken, but an airline's livelihood depended on its implied safety guarantee. If an airline suspended its flights to address safety concerns, it would be admitting that those safety risks existed while its planes flew. *There's so much hyperbole and hypocrisy out there,* Jack thought. *Why can't they just do the right thing?*

Jack knew that this problem was like a myriad of others that went unreported. Like global warming, technology failure was as pervasive as it was confusing, and it was ripe for obfuscation by profit-seeking opportunists. Whether balancing a runway for planes, a prison for inmates, or a nuclear waste dump for spent fuel rods, the risks were huge and the failure costs were daunting.

When would a problem like this cause a plane to explode? Or ten planes? We are too dependent on a massive interconnected network of systems. No one lives "off the grid" anymore, and everyone is at risk when portions of that grid fail. A tree falling on a power line started the Great Blackout of 2003, and it brought down half of the United States in under an hour. What happens the next time when we can't recover so quickly? Who cares about a retailer's 90,000 lost job applications? What happens if the credit card clearing network that we rely on for our 21st century lifestyles fails beyond recovery?

Jack knew that 'existence-critical' systems failed for the same reasons that technology failed at individual companies. He'd also learned that the same set of good practices could be applied at any size or complexity level and that bigger-than-life problems generally required the same solutions as the mom and pop-sized ones. Despite the amazing advances in technology, the problems persisted. *Are we already doomed or is there a way out of the IT Black Hole?*

☆ ☆ ☆

Stanley Chmeat was PNP's forty-year-old CIO. Stanley's job description, according to Buck Roscoe, was to make sure that PNP's computers didn't screw up PNP's business. Buck didn't know computers and he didn't want to know them. Buck, like Stanley's father, Congressman Chmeat, knew money, and all were expecting a big payday from a turnaround at PNP.

Congressman Chmeat had retired after two terms on Capitol Hill and joined Franken & Mershow, a Washington D.C. lobbyist. Chmeat lobbied hard for the military to buy 3D laptops from Fujohara, even though those laptops heated user's laps up to one hundred and forty degrees Fahrenheit. Franken & Mershow sued the testing firm and got a gag order preventing publication of the results and their release to the FAA.

The former Congressman didn't know that five prototype 3D Fujohara laptops were checked on MidPoint Flight 101 by drug reps who had just presented to urologists at ED-World, the national erectile dysfunction conference. The Vision System generated a loading schema guiding the baggage handlers to load the Fujohara laptops into the hottest part of the cargo hold. Those drug reps didn't know to power down their computers and the laptops' sizzling sleep mode temperatures were enough to trigger the fire and explosion.

☆ ☆ ☆

Stanley Chmeat was pear-shaped, with thinning black hair and a tired-looking face. He earned an engineering degree and an MBA from the University of Virginia. He was a local western suburbs of Chicago boy, and like his dad, knew all about money. He was used to having favors done for him; it was part of his upbringing. Born with a flair for bargaining, Stanley did as well as he could to resist being scorned as the chubby kid in his class. But he couldn't avoid the handle 'Lunchmeat,' a nickname that came back to haunt him when he returned home after earning his MBA.

Stanley and his fleshy wife Stacey were fixtures at the new fourteen million-dollar House of Worship in Niles. Like a hulking Disney World attraction, the House of Worship was built in the shape of a glass pyramid with neon strip lights running along its four bottom edges and four side edges. Stanley had recently been assigned as commissioner of the House's family council, despite having no children. Rumors abounded that Stanley had won the coveted position, which enabled him to give media interviews, by arranging a job for the son of the church's largest benefactor.

Stanley established a well-known presence in technology, and made the cover of *Tektanic* three times. He was a fixture on the speakers' dockets of *Tektanic*'s technology conferences, often held at the world's most luxurious golf resorts. Stanley shared Biff's passion for golf, but Biff was a much better player. Stanley's golf shirts and sweaters were emblazoned with technology or consulting vendors' logos while Biff's sported PNP's tired crossed frying pans.

At the conferences and on the course, Stanley courted vendors like a champion, and they sought to be his friend. His drawers bulged with vendor-supplied pens, his bookshelves were stuffed with leather-bound portfolios from dozens of consulting firms, and one wall of his office was covered with selfies taken with professional golfers.

In Stanley's department, dissent was never considered because it would result in the dismissal of the dissenter. He didn't like interference from the business people and enjoyed giving complex answers to simple questions. Executives learned to curtail their questions after a few befuddling answers. So while Stanley was well-networked and respected outside of PNP, darling status had eluded him within PNP's leadership team.

Still, Stanley remained approachable to his fawning subordinates, many of whom he had handpicked from recruiters. As warm as he was toward his people, Stanley was tough on his vendors. Stanley felt that since PNP was a leader in its market, vendors should consider themselves privileged to deal with him. Vendors greatly coveted a reference from PNP and Stanley was willing to give references at a price. This meant modest discounts for PNP and personal favors for Stanley.

Stanley felt that using consultants was the only way to complete large projects and he enjoyed relationships with many of Pro-Con's competitors. Pro-Con knew about these relationships and was always on guard, working to protect its PNP revenue. Stanley was responsible for signing off on all the bills submitted by Flynch, and usually did so without reviewing the charges. Four days before the Big-Box meeting in Atlanta, Flynch treated Stanley to dinner at Gene & Georgetti, the famed Chicago steak house.

SUNDAY, JULY 3ᴿᴰ (1 WEEK EARLIER) 7:30 PM

"Stanley, are you making progress on ThickWare?"

"We've killed ninety or ninety-five percent of the bugs."

"I've seen this problem with our other clients. ThickWare was so rushed to come out with their latest software release after Compuzila came out with theirs. It seems the entire market has forsaken quality in lieu of speed," said Flynch.

"Right now my biggest question is just...how can ThickWare survive? I'm already charging them back at least $250,000 in our contractors' time that we spent fixing the software," said Stanley.

"You must recover that money from them," Flynch said, pausing as he surveyed the menu. "Stanley, try the pork-chop. It's outstanding."

With the waiter hovering over the pair, Stanley looked up and nodded. It would be the pork this evening.

"Bring another round when you get back," Stanley said, touching his Wild Turkey as the waiter retreated from earshot.

✳ ✳ ✳

FRIDAY, JULY 8TH 11:55 AM

The day after his return to Naperville, Biff Harper lunched with Rona Sims. Rona was the hard-charging Senior Vice President for Sales and Marketing at PNP. It was her job to grow the business. Rona had been a stockbroker for six years and left the profession to marry at age thirty. She got a divorce at age thirty-two; soon after, she met Biff in the airport in St. Louis. They dated briefly and spent a mostly sexless weekend in Acapulco. After realizing she wasn't attracted to him Rona gently broke things off, but they remained close friends and Biff convinced Rona to join him at PNP. Rona was now Biff's go-to employee when he needed to get things done, or just to work out a problem.

"I am so pissed off," Rona said hotly. "Lunchmeat is going to wreck our business. The guy is an idiot. He goes on vendor junkets when he should be finishing projects. Do you realize how much time I am spending on the phone apologizing to our best customers because TWERP keeps delaying their orders? Big-Box is our largest account and we are going to lose them too. TWERP should not take a year."

Biff looked at Rona. He had already asked her not to call the ThickWare ERP project by that nickname, but she didn't care.

"I absolutely refuse to waste another Monday afternoon in a TWERP status meeting!" Rona continued angrily. "This guy is really interfering with our business. How could the private equity firm be so stupid not to see this coming and why didn't they do anything after that data loss we had a few months ago?"

Biff shook his head and sighed.

"Come on, to allow our Homemaker's Club email and home addresses to get stolen by a spammer! I deal with this every day. Master Borscht will never include any more of our products on his show because his booker is still pissed at us," Rona exclaimed, her voice rising in frustration.

"Rona, I understand. But what can I do? I told you what Buck said. All along I hadn't scrutinized Stanley for what he was doing because he came in here with such strong credentials. But now we are months into this technology project and not only am I not seeing results, I think we're worse off now than before we started. We're hemorrhaging cash because we've got twenty-seven consultants and I have no idea what they're doing."

"They're jacking off and not getting anywhere," Rona said.

"I need to know where we are but I'm not sure how to find out. I can't ask Stanley because he's deluded himself into thinking the project is on track," Biff responded.

"Or he is trying to cover up his failures," Rona said.

"Maybe. Stanley's department is so loyal to him and no one from our other departments knows enough about the project to ask intelligent questions."

Rona frowned. "What are we going to do? This technology project is on a road to nowhere."

"I know Rona, I know, that's obvious," replied Biff.

Rona's smartphone rang. She mouthed "Big-Box" to Biff as she stood up. Biff acknowledged with a weak smile that wasn't reassuring. Rona started toward the door and spoke confidently into her phone, "Rona Sims, how may I help you?"

✵ ✵ ✵

Rona spurned MIT's acceptance and became a University of Illinois math major because her dad was a particle physics professor there and she attended for free. Dr. Sims was a former Israeli army officer who had met Rona's mother the day of his first interview at U of I, and they'd been together ever since. Rona's mother's family owned the largest BMW dealership in Chicago and Rona grew up understanding that she ate because customers paid the bills. She also inherited her mother's sense of feminine, style-powered charisma.

A 5'3" brunette with wide eyes and an electric smile, Rona stood out from the cream-colored, cubicle-lined, middle America hallways of PNP. She had a curvy build and her waist was tightly cinched at the middle like a Barbie Doll's. Rona preferred Prada to the polyester pantsuits worn by other ladies at PNP's headquarters. While those ladies were shopping at the Walmart in nearby Aurora, Rona went to Fendi on Fifth Avenue every time she had a customer trip to New York, and paired her designer pieces with unusual vintage-store finds. She never tried to show anybody up; she was just being herself. The PNP ladies loved Rona's flair, and she was always getting compliments in the hallway.

Second only to Biff in hours worked, Rona easily earned her customers' confidence and respect. Slack or shiftless behavior irked her, and failing to deliver on a promise to Rona was a mistake few would chance. Rona's word was her most valued asset and when someone she dealt with didn't measure up to her standard of integrity, she could lash out with nearly every expletive ever heard in a truck stop restroom.

Rona was all that a confident man could want: dramatic, passionate, athletic, and loyal. But most men couldn't please her and relationships were one of the few areas in which Rona didn't excel. She specialized in finding men who were too weak, too selfish, or too full of themselves to handle her. Few men, even the smart and confident, were as motivated or as excellence-oriented as she was.

At thirty-nine, Rona was hungry for that full life. To her, that meant kids and a big house. She had even considered moving out of her Naperville townhouse to an apartment in Chicago's yuppy-ish Lincoln Park in order to tap a better flow of eligible men. There were so few good men out there, and seemingly none in Naperville.

As Senior VP at PNP, Rona made sure that PNP's customers were happy. It was easy in one sense: PNP's brand was the strongest in the industry. Rona's problem was on the order fulfillment side; frustrating, because it was largely out of her control whether PNP could build and ship its products on-time.

She usually impressed Roscoe & Lauer, but they also blamed her when inventories swelled with slow-moving styles. Inventory was a curse because it cost money, and Rona typically over-ordered because she had low confidence in PNP's ability to meet its customer delivery dates. Better to spend a few thousand dollars on extra inventory, she reasoned, rather than risk a few hundred thousand in lost business when a frustrated customer switches a big order to a nimbler supplier.

✳ ✳ ✳

SUNDAY, JULY 10TH 11:15 AM

Jack Bluto and Biff Harper crossed paths in the locker room at the Hollow Hills Country Club as Biff walked toward the showers.

Jack followed Biff into the common shower area. Before Biff could turn on the water, Jack extended his hand and said, "Excuse me Mr. Harper, I'm Jack Bluto." Biff looked at the hand and hesitated a moment. Naked, Biff had already hung his towel on a distant rod. He was cornered. Glumly, Biff looked up and with an uncomfortably clenched posture, took the hand and quietly asked, "Do I know you?"

"No, but you may want to. I think I can help you," Jack proclaimed loudly and confidently.

"What are you talking about? Are you the new golf pro here? Oh, wait a second. You work in the parking lot, don't you? Is my car okay?"

"No, I run a business in New York called Reality Check."

"What are you doing here?" Biff said uncomfortably, waiting for Jack to let go of his hand while looking around for a partition to hide behind.

"I taught a class at Northwestern this weekend and I recognized you from the Tribune's business section. I heard you are having some technology challenges."

The last sentence shocked Biff, who took a deep breath. This issue had weighed on Biff's mind during the entire forty-five minutes he had just spent on the treadmill. As he finally felt Jack's grip loosen, he yanked his hand away, turned his back to Jack, and grasped for the hot water handle.

"Were you the guy I read about in the *Wall Street Telegram* who did the homeless babysitting deal?" Biff said, jumping back at first from the heat of the shower.

"Yes."

"Let me finish my shower and then we'll talk."

"I would like to, but I'm already late for my tee time and my group is waiting."

"Whom are you playing with?"

"I'm a guest of Fleggum's and a couple of his partners from Metal Bank."

"Oh, Fleggum's a good man and a decent golfer," Biff said, impressed by Jack's connections, and now curious about whether Jack could help. "Enjoy the round and call me in my office tomorrow morning. Speak to Gertrude, my assistant, and tell her that I asked you to come in."

Jack nodded.

"You were right, we need help," Biff said.

Flustered, Biff returned to the shower. While confident in his appearance, Biff was a man who walked around the locker room wearing two towels, and Jack didn't even wear one. But Biff was desperate, and he hoped this locker-room tête-à-tête would pay off, even though it seemed so weird.

No going home tonight, Jack said to himself, as he walked toward the first hole on a cloudy, cool summer morning. *I'd better cancel my 7 PM MidPoint flight.*

✵ ✵ ✵

MONDAY, JULY 11TH 10:30 AM

Jack introduced himself to PNP's receptionist. "Is he expecting you?" she asked.

"Yes," Jack responded, "he asked me to come by today. Please call his assistant Gertrude and let her know that I'm here." Jack noted the signboard next to the reception seating area. It said: "Welcome Our Friends From The Naperville Chamber Of Commerce." The date on the sign was four days earlier. There was no mention of Jack's visit.

Within fifteen minutes, Jack was ushered into Biff's office. Biff was finishing a phone call and Jack's eyes had the time to wander across the spines of the business books in Biff's sizable collection. Jack had read two of the books recently. The first was written by the mercurial CEO of an old conglomerate, a bulldog who posited that charisma is necessary for strong leadership and that only a certain type of person can effectively lead a major organization. The second was written by a young Chief Operating Officer of a furniture company. She asserted that a company with the right processes and metrics and a deep bench of interchangeable well-trained managers was more effective in creating shareholder value. *Structured confusion,* Jack mused, *just like a technology project.*

Biff put down the phone and looked up.

"Biff, ever read James Allen or Dale Carnegie?"

"Why?"

"James Allen and Dale Carnegie said a lot about behavior. Maybe PNP's challenges are more behavioral than technical. ThickWare probably has bugs in it, but I know their software mostly works. Maybe your people need to change their thinking about the technology and how to use it?"

"Keep going," said Biff, outwardly courteous but inwardly skeptical.

"I need to give you a history lesson first, okay?"

Biff nodded.

"Think of the last sixty-five years of business computing in terms of five waves. For the first thirty-five years, companies wrote programs to automate specific business functions like billing, inventory management, or payroll. Building systems required mainframe computers and teams of internal programmers. During that first wave, software vendors emerged to write programs or applications to sell to a variety of businesses."

"But those applications didn't talk with each other, right?" Biff asked.

"Exactly. When a business bought one of those applications, programmers had to adapt the code to the business. Making these customizations required specialized knowledge, and this encouraged the growth of the technology consulting industry. Consulting or contracting companies emerged to help businesses to augment their internal teams on large projects."

"Go on."

"The second wave of business computing started in the early eighties and accelerated fantastically toward the end of the millennium. This was the wave of the integrated applications. Software companies realized that in order to lock their customers into long-term contracts, they had to cross departmental lines and tie these islands of software functionality together."

"ERP?" Biff asked.

"Yes, Enterprise Resource Planning. ERP is a brilliant tool and it helped power the productivity boost of the last generation, yet ERP's contribution to our present quality of life is ignored by nearly everyone."

"Okay."

"Biff, the impact was huge. ERP enabled businesses to computerize their Order to Cash cycles, which cover all of the activities from receiving a customer order, scheduling production, purchasing the components and raw materials, manufacturing the product, shipping it, billing for it, collecting funds, and then tracking all of the accounting."

Biff nodded for Jack to continue.

"Nearly all large and medium-sized businesses implemented these second wave systems. A driving catalyst for these technology implementations was the Y2K-related paranoia."

"Was the paranoia justified?" Biff asked.

"Not really. Businesses were concerned that their hodge-podge systems wouldn't take money on the first day of the third millennium, so they binged and bought the most modern ERP systems and hired armies of implementation consultants. Billions were paid out in fees. Unfortunately, many of these systems were jammed in by freshly minted consultants who didn't understand their clients' needs."

"Go on."

"Rather than leverage the new productivity-enabling capabilities of the software, most businesses customized the software to make it look like their old systems."

"Why did they do that?"

"Because it was easier to mimic yesterday rather than think about tomorrow, especially when it was widely believed that Y2K was a ticking time bomb."

"Okay, Jack, but at what cost?"

"It was immeasurable because the suboptimizers indelibly engineered mediocrity into their operations. Once these ERP systems became live, the shareholders of these companies were sentenced to owning mid 70's Jaguars."

"How's that?"

"Because these systems had fancy nameplates, but they didn't run very well."

Biff nodded.

Jack continued, "Virtually every organization uses ERP to help govern and conduct its processes. A movie studio pays employees and tracks assets, a government collects taxes and issues purchase orders, and a university manages staffing and janitorial supplies in its campus buildings. These make up a tiny portion of the processes conducted by these enterprises."

"Does your ERP advice work in these other organizations?" Biff said.

"Absolutely. Hospitals, airlines, manufacturers, and municipal governments all screw up technology projects in the same ways and Reality Check's techniques apply across the board," Jack said.

"Okay, go on."

"Twenty years ago we entered the third wave," Jack said. "Simply put, the third wave joined organizations together via the Internet, blurring traditional boundaries."

"But you have to be cautious about what you share," Biff said.

"Yes, but your walls can't be too high. A misconception about this third wave is that as those organizational walls came down, security and propriety would be compromised. Despite some well-publicized break-ins, data is relatively safe because of advancements in data security."

"Okay," Biff said.

"The third wave hit stride as new inter-company optimization algorithms smoothed variability across the supply and demand chains. These algorithms balanced production and inventory more effectively, increasing overall economic productivity. Better information known as Analytics or Business Intelligence allows companies to examine trends and data quickly, enabling them to focus their products and services to smaller and smaller market segments."

"ThickWare claimed we'd be able to do that." Biff said.

"Yes, providing customers with exactly what they need quickly, even in the smallest lot sizes. No one wants to be burdened with inventory. Your customers will want to place smaller and more targeted orders, and your production systems must deliver these orders efficiently and profitably," Jack said.

"Agreed. We need to increase responsiveness while decreasing costs, and that's not easy," Biff declared.

"Right. Fueled by easy capital, thousands of new technology companies came into being to ride that third wave."

"But it created victims, too," Biff added, sighing. "I lost so much money when the first Internet bubble burst."

"Biff, when everyone is enchanted by noise, they all miss the signal. NASDAQ dropped by two-thirds from 2000 to 2003 and washed out a lot of rickety, ill-conceived technology companies. Now, years later, Internet technology has become more important than ever."

"But even though we now use the Internet at PNP, our processes have stayed the same."

"The third wave didn't introduce a new concept to business; rather, it greatly improved upon previous options. Companies communicated with phones and fax machines for years; the new software applications are different. Rather than a customer faxing a Purchase Order to a supplier, that supplier now can look into a cordoned-off section of its customer's production schedule, right through the Internet. This allows that supplier to better plan its own production. Companies farther upstream can better plan their production. These efficiencies show up both in our Gross National Product and in the quality of life we enjoy."

"Good, go on," Biff said.

"Challenges emerge when organizations try to partner with one another electronically. The third wave is still breaking toward the beach and surfing it involves risk but not as much risk as waiting for it to crash over your head and drown you."

"Does that bring us to today?" Biff asked.

"No. The world changed again. In 2004 or 2005 we entered the fourth wave, the wave of the user. Users grabbed the reins on technology's power from corporate IT and their influence grew geometrically."

"I agree," Biff said.

"Users cross-connect outside of their traditional organizational circles with few barriers, and they have the knowledge and the power to create great value for their organizations. We are in the new world. Interestingly, until the fourth wave, users were exposed to computing primarily at work. Now, their greatest exposure comes outside of work. Today everyone uses computers, from toddlers to seniors."

"True."

"And it's not only that. Who doesn't have a smartphone? There are more computers than televisions in people's homes, and the television is merging into the computer."

Biff nodded.

"The fourth wave overlaps the third and is just beginning to crest. Instant messaging, navigation systems, smartphone video, and countless other technologies have changed the nature of our interpersonal interactions and experiences. Ripple effects include the trend of working from home and the fifth wave, Big Data, is...""

Biff cut Jack off. "This sounds interesting Jack, but how does this help me?"

"Despite the amazing pace of change, IT projects fail for the exact same reasons that they did forty years ago."

"Go on," encouraged Biff.

Gertrude buzzed in, "Rona is here for her sales review."

"Send her in," Biff called out.

Rona hurried into Biff's office and unloaded a mound of reports on his desk.

"Rona, meet Jack Bluto. Jack is a consultant I met at the country club."

"Nice to meet you, Jack," Rona said, extending her hand. "Hmmm. Hollow Hills. What a perfect place to meet a consultant."

The barb was not lost on Jack. "It's really tough to find any CEOs to play with any more," Jack said slyly. "They're so busy trying to fix their companies' IT projects."

Biff turned toward Jack, but Jack's gaze lingered on Rona's turquoise pleated dress. Eye-catching, yet tasteful, it fell just below her knees. Jack watched Rona's large eyes turn toward Biff.

They were the same Caribbean turquoise. He examined Rona's noticeably toned bare folded arms. Turquoise bands on her ring fingers accentuated Rona's slender, but capable hands.

Looking at her, I feel like I'm outside a Greenwich Village café on a Friday evening, instead of in dowdy Naperville, Jack thought. Jack noted the 4" heels of her beige, Italian stilettos. He looked up, concerned that he'd been caught staring.

"Rona is tied up in the ThickWare mess. She owns the Big-Box relationship and she's done a great job with it despite our technology problems," Biff said.

"And now I feel like I've been thrown into a freezing ocean with no life preserver." Turning to Biff, Rona continued, "Has he met Lunchmeat yet?"

"Not yet," Biff responded, frowning. "Not helpful!"

"You mean the nickname?" Rona smirked, slipping a stick of gum into her mouth.

Biff nodded.

"Sorry. So how can Jack help? Why is he here?" Rona asked impatiently.

"I want PNP to understand how to approach a project like this," Jack responded calmly.

"How do we do that?" Biff asked.

"First, be realistic about your business. If you divide the world of companies into five tiers, ranging from best to worst, where would PNP lie?"

"Probably in the second tier."

"Let me tell you a little secret. Four out of five companies think they're in the second bracket. Why do you think that is?"

"I guess it's like most people believing that they are better than average drivers," Biff said.

"Exactly. When you believe you are near the top, you become complacent and stop striving for excellence. In order to improve, you must be keenly accurate and sober in assessing where you are today."

"With respect to technology, we are in the third or maybe the fourth fifth," Biff said.

"Okay then," Jack said. "I can help you."

"Jack, I like this, but I'm going to have to ask you to come back. I have a full schedule today and then I'm off to France for two days to visit with a customer. What are the next steps? What do you propose?"

Jack was impressed by Biff's directness. He responded in kind. "I need to spend seven to ten work days finding out what's going on here and then I can report back to you. During those two weeks I'll educate you on how to do technology right."

"Good. What do you typically charge on a job like this?"

"A helluva lot less than the cost of a failed project."

"What do you need to be successful?"

"Access to your project team, its leaders, your suppliers, and your customers. Also, unfettered access to your technology vendors and consultants. In these projects, I find that even though people are overworked and harried, they try to be helpful. Occasionally, I come across a guy who is looking to cover up what is going on. This guy can represent the greatest threat to the project. I also need full access to you, if you are the true owner of the project."

Rona listened intently as Jack answered. *He's confident and his voice has a melodic ring to it. But what's going on with his strange-looking hair?* She looked at the open collar of Jack's well-starched white shirt set off against his meticulously tailored black two-piece suit. Her eyes fell upon Jack's left hand. *No wedding ring.*

Biff's phone rang. He picked it up and motioned for Rona and Jack to step outside his office. As they were walking out, he put his hand over the microphone and said, "Jack, tell Gertrude to call Stanley and set you up to see him later this morning. I'll consider your proposal, but I'll need the numbers." With that, Biff put his head into a pile of papers and began his call. Jack only heard a few words of the conversation. He guessed that Biff was talking with his accountant.

Gertrude had gone to the ladies room, and Rona and Jack were suddenly alone in the anteroom outside of Biff's office.

"I want to learn what's happening here Rona. Can you spare a half hour at some point today?"

"Listen Jack, this damn project has been such a headache for us that you can't imagine. I'd like to help you, but I'm booked solid until 7."

"Well, then," Jack said, looking at Rona with an easy smile, "Are you free for drinks tonight?"

"So that's how you consultants work these days. You don't even bother with the interviews. Just get the clients drunk and let 'em talk," Rona shot back, smiling.

"Something like that," Jack said.

"Jack, I'm too busy, but if I don't get involved in this we're going to be dead when Big-Box needs us to go-live with Broadway."

"What time works for you?"

"7:30. Come by my office and we'll go to Dante's. There aren't many options around here."

Gertrude returned from the ladies room and cheerfully called Stanley to arrange for Jack's meeting. Before Jack realized it, Rona was gone. Gertrude pulled out a copy of an office floor plan and highlighted the path between Biff's office and Stanley's office, pointing out the men's room along the way.

"Thanks so much for your thoughtfulness," Jack said.

Gertrude smiled broadly and Jack set out on his journey.

✡ ✡ ✡

Little did Biff Harper realize that he and Jack had grown up two subway stops away from each other and eleven years apart.

Jack, 5'7", had a fast mind, a gifted tongue, and a knack for endearing people. Jack wasn't handsome, but he drew attention with a resonant voice and an engaging gaze. Dressing sharply was an unnatural skill that he spent many years honing. People tended to see him as theatric, sometimes aloof, but always friendly. His listening skills were unmatched and his ability to articulate simple solutions to complex problems was his *raison d'etre.*

As a boy, Jack roamed the same schoolyards that Biff lorded over in Queens, playing a barely passable game of stickball. Jack's batting average with girls paralleled his stickball numbers. He asked for many more dates than he got, but this just motivated him to keep asking. Jack aimed for the most sought after girls, astutely realizing that a rejection from a beauty was somehow more tolerable.

Great test taking earned him a spot at Princeton, a dramatic change from the easy life at Jamaica High School. While Jack's parents scrimped and saved and made it possible for him to attend college loan-free, there was never any extra. Jack's part-time job selling PCs enabled him to sample the golf, ski trips, and fancy vacations sported by his new friends. Those friends opened Jack's eyes to the business world. After Princeton, Jack chose to start his career at Pro-Con.

Pro-Con was heaven at first. Jack was meeting with senior client honchos on day one. At twenty-three it was fun to travel to Topeka or Toledo to implement IT systems at factories that made pencil leads or chicken wings. Jack's computers enabled mattress manufacturers, yarn spinners, and artificial crab leg extruders to organize their business information. He saw the world from a MidPoint center seat and a rental car. He loved the work and dug in for seven years and two million frequent flyer miles.

Life on the road catches up with everyone, and Jack was no exception. By thirty, Jack was rapidly losing his hair and his patience. The hypocrisy of the consulting business grated on him, especially as he focused on developing client relationships versus doing the nuts and bolts work that he had enjoyed.

There was always snow covering the technology; it was often unclear whether it worked or what risks it posed, and Jack knew that many of the clients he took on were past the point of no return. His bosses at Pro-Con discouraged Jack from telling clients how far off track the projects were, because the bosses feared those projects would be cancelled if their clients lost hope. Jack knew these projects would fail while continuing to divert critical management attention away from more promising opportunities. He saw Pro-Con collect millions in fees by perpetuating these undoable projects. Jack's disdain for this chicanery outgrew any desire he once had to settle into the field for the long haul. He needed a fresh start.

Rocco's Babysitting Services, a.k.a. RoccoLink, started as a joke in a bar off Union Square. Jack was drinking with his Princeton friends in the days when money was chasing internet versions of traditional brick and mortar businesses. The friends were competing to invent a business model that could get funding from the dumb money venture community. The game was to come up with a plausible sounding plan that was actually absurd. One friend pitched his internet Laundromat. Robot controlled, funnel shaped buggies would drive slowly on the sidewalks next to New York City apartment houses. A site registrant would receive a text five minutes before a buggy would be under his window. The registrant would then throw his dirty laundry out the window and into the buggy. The clothing would be laundered in a central processing plant and delivered back to the registrant.

As Jack listened, he looked through the bar's window and noticed a young mother with a stroller walking past Rocco, a neighborhood homeless person. Jack started to explain the connection to his friends, but they gave it drunken guffaws without paying attention to the details.

Jack correctly identified two growing demographics: first, working mothers needing daycare for their young children and, second, homeless people looking for self-improvement and quick cash. Jack decided to marry the excess demand of the working mothers and the excess supply of the homeless. RoccoLink was born to provide low-cost babysitting services.

The venture was perfectly timed: by then, Jack's friends from Princeton ascended into decision-making positions in the major venture capital firms and private equity shops. The world was awash in capital and Jack was looking to score. He closed twenty million in funding within four months and became a darling of daytime financial gossip television. Living in a swanky Greene Street condo in New York's SoHo, Jack felt like a player. He dated as often as possible, but never connected with anyone seriously. *Who needs depth when I can have breadth,* his Princeton-honed reasoning skills concluded.

Five months after Jack resigned from Pro-Con, RoccoLink launched its feature-packed site. Demand rolled in. RoccoLink rigorously background-screened every homeless applicant and excluded those with felony convictions. The cost for a Rocco's babysitter was less than half the market rate. Supply was problematic. The homeless had poor Internet access so Jack struck a deal with a handful of wine, cigarette, and snack food companies to subsidize the placement of Internet terminals in homeless shelters and soup kitchens. The steel-footed, urine-proofed, and theft-hardened RoccoLink terminals displayed ads to the homeless while enabling them to secure permanent RoccoLink email addresses, a meaningful step along the path of dignity toward a physical address.

RoccoLink's calendar program enabled the homeless to schedule their babysitting appointments. The babysitters built up reputation points over time and families had to bid to secure the services of RoccoLink Blue-Ribbon providers. Those babysitters with high reputation points and the most hours billed agreed with RoccoLink to mentor homeless 'probies' on their first few jobs. RoccoLink gave its providers vendor sponsored smartphones with directional locators so parents could find their children on a live map, continuously refreshed on the Internet.

By the end of its first year, RoccoLink had fifty-five employees, and a fancy Silicon Alley office complete with Ping Pong tables and Cappuccino machines. RoccoLink was heavily promoted in the media and Jack spoke with bankers about going public. Revenue was running at three hundred thousand per month, mostly in the New York, Chicago, and Miami markets when a handful of lawsuits started to roll in. They were all for petty matters like loitering with strollers for eight hours at a time in bookstores, and none were related to the quality of the childcare.

On the last bright day of the high times, Jack closed the sale of his company to a large roll-up of Internet businesses. He insisted on a cash deal and got nine million after taxes. The markets crashed and the acquiring company went belly up after ten months, leaving no way for needy mothers and homeless people to connect. Jack took a long beach vacation but had trouble reconciling his newly acquired wealth with the absurdity of the method used to obtain it. He decided to put his energies toward a more laudable objective: to help companies put troubled technology projects back on track. He came back to New York and put out a shingle for Reality Check. Jack bought designer suits and set out to meet people with problems he could solve. Reality Check immediately resonated with frustrated executives and Jack built a backlog of clients needing lifelines out of the IT Black Hole.

Jack took two million and bought the rest of the now-available Greene Street building, installing a state of the art office on the lower floors. He moved into the top two floors, and hired a Meatpacking District decorator to help him outfit his pad with hip furniture.

At thirty-six, Jack had career clarity and stability, but his revolving-door dating life was frustrating. He occasionally dated beautiful women and regularly dated smart, interesting women, but hadn't found the overlap. Last year, on his thirty-fifth birthday, he impulsively purchased a do-it-yourself hair transplant kit that he had seen on an infomercial while staying in a Toledo motel.

The hair transplant kit arrived the next day. Jack hurried through the instructions and didn't realize that only slight pressure needed to be applied with the scalp awl to prepare his crown for the donor roots. Bleeding, he called 911 and by the time he arrived at the Toledo airport for his flight back to New York, his head was covered with Mercurochrome.

The next day he showed up for work on Greene Street wearing a ball cap. The red staining from the topical antiseptic leaked down his forehead, and even though the stain was gone in a week, it took Jack several months to lose the "Mercurochrome Dome" nickname. It was a rare slip-up.

Jack enrolled at a pricey Park Avenue hair restoration center in an attempt to reverse, or at least cover up, his self-inflicted scars. Progress was slow, and Jack had recently completed the second of his three planned hair transplantation surgeries.

☆ ☆ ☆

"Come right in," Stanley Chmeat offered.

Stanley looked back at his computer screen. When Jack sunk into the high-backed leather chair in Stanley's office, he could see the reflection of Stanley's screen in the window behind the credenza. Stanley was completing a putt on an interactive golfing website. Jack didn't recognize the hole.

Jack gazed at the framed trade magazine covers on the wall in Stanley's office. Stanley's initials peeked out of his French cuff on a large blow-up of the *Tektanic* Man of the Year cover. SUC. Jack wondered what the middle initial stood for. Jacks eyes moved to the left. He saw Stanley's prized picture, with George W. Bush, taken at a fundraiser breakfast. The picture with the former president was atop a triangle of two other pictures; one featuring Stanley posed with Bill Gates and the other with Neil Armstrong.

"I'm so glad you're here," Stanley said, finally looking up. "This project is important to us and it's going better than Biff and the senior team realize. We just finished testing a major new piece of code that our consultants built to help connect our systems to Big-Box. Their system wasn't properly passing pricing information through to our system, but now that it's resolved, we're in good shape."

Jack nodded reassuringly, and Stanley continued.

"This is a modest implementation for me; I built the billing system for Diabetic Colas Corp. That project took two years and they're still using the system today, ten years later."

Jack noticed the golf pictures on Stanley's wall.

"Are you a golfer Stan?" Jack asked.

"Stanley, please and yes, I am. That's from a Pro-Am tournament I played in last year."

"Who sponsored the tournament?"

"Uh," Stanley paused for a second. "CompuSquat."

"Is PNP a CompuSquat shop?"

"No, we use whatever technology best fits with our business. Do you mind if I ask you a question?"

"You mean another question," Jack quipped, hoping to lighten the mood.

Stanley didn't smile. "I'm not sure what you're looking for. My team is well trained. In fact, I sent all of our systems engineers to Brussels for three weeks for ThickWare Platinum training."

Leaning closer to Jack, Stanley said in a lowered voice, "I heard that you never actually implemented ThickWare yourself.

I'm not sure why we're speaking about this unless you're doing some general research on our industry. I don't think my team members would appreciate you looking over their shoulders, especially someone who doesn't know our business. My people are working hard and they get touchy when they feel like their time is being wasted."

Jack was silent. Stanley continued, "You have to understand that these types of projects are very complicated. You can't pull out all the wiring that makes a business like this run and replace it overnight. It just doesn't work that way. This is a big project and it takes a lot of resources." Stanley leaned forward, pulling up the adjuster lever of his supple, leather desk chair, allowing its straining bladder a few hurried gulps of air. He then leaned back, clasping his fingers together behind his head. "Most of the business managers here aren't qualified to get involved in a project like this."

Jack remained silent.

"That's why we brought in Pro-Con. Despite what Biff might think, they're doing a decent job. I negotiated very aggressively and we're paying sixty percent of their normal rates. You show me another CIO that gets deals like that."

Jack knew this was the kiss of death: a big project being run by the technology people with an army of cut-rate consultants. Adding little top management involvement to this mess was a sure-fire recipe for failure. Jack surmised that Stanley probably knew his business but had a common tragic flaw. Simply put, Stanley couldn't recognize what he didn't know and this posed an unacceptable risk to PNP.

Jack was experienced in dealing with the Stanleys of the world. The more Stanley spoke, the more Jack committed to staying silent.

"Look, I know it's no secret that Biff thinks this project is in trouble and that I am the one screwing it up. Well, I have to be honest with you; I think I'm the only person in this company who doesn't have an ego to bruise. It doesn't bother me that Biff is upset," Stanley continued as he rolled his eyes, "and that Rona, that," Stanley lowered his voice, "that witch." He picked his voice up again, "I mean that assistant of his, she stirs up a lot of trouble. She's the type that gets angry for the sake of getting angry. That really annoys my team because she criticizes us without having the courtesy to attend the status meetings to find out what's really going on."

Jack nodded, but remained expressionless; surprised that Stanley would criticize a co-worker to him after they had just met.

Stanley continued, "Now you are here. I don't understand why my team needs another distraction. I'm sorry, but I have to meet with several of my team members today and I'm late for my next appointment." Stanley rose and remarked in a gratuitous tone, "I'm sorry I haven't been more helpful but if you can assist our company in any way, I'm sure we would all appreciate that."

"Thank you for your help, Stanley."

"My pleasure," Stanley replied with a patronizing smile. He stood and held out his right hand in an unusual manner. Jack noticed the open palm, but Stanley's palm was pointing up, and did not beckon a handshake. Gazing downward, Jack saw Stanley's thick, meaty fingers, the middle finger gently wagging to and fro.

Stanley continued, "Do you have any Reality Check pens?"

Jack smiled uncomfortably, shook his head no, and left. He once had Reality Check pens made up, but they were the bargain type and they broke easily. Jack looked up, but Stanley was already locked onto his computer screen and fingering his mouse.

Jack realized he had lost the map Gertrude had given him. He asked directions from a tall man in the hallway who pointed Jack in the direction of Biff's office. Biff and Gertrude had both gone. Rather than hang around, Jack found his way to the parking lot and jumped into his rental car. He always chose a Tapir, maroon when possible, his ultimate 'I never want to be noticed' consultant's car.

MONDAY, JULY 11TH 1:15 PM

He headed toward the local ChumpRoast for the Mega Chump coffee and two chocolate crullers special. He sat town at a table outside for a few moments of reflection. After a massive sugar and caffeine blast, he drove back to the plant.

✲ ✲ ✲

In his office, Biff mentally attacked the project and the decisions he had to face. Was it worth paying Jack, this assertive man whom he had just met? PNP had spent months selecting the technology and so much money trying to get it to work.

Biff's eyes fell upon on the family portrait on his desk, and his thoughts shifted to his marriage. It had been a long time since Biff felt happy at home. Before their wedding, Constance seemed so appealing. Now, thoughts of intimacy turned his stomach. She satisfied all of the requirements he'd had prior to meeting her. *Why is having less joyful than wanting? It doesn't make sense.*

The headaches that had been plaguing him for the past few months weren't letting up. He went into the private restroom attached to his office suite, stared into the mirror and gently arranged his hair. He felt so confused sometimes, especially when he recalled his days in Amsterdam, during occasional breaks from work. His hiking trip with Martin, a pot-smoking euro-tripping personal trainer and part-time aroma therapist, kept peeking out of the back of his mind. He hadn't been hiking in so long – Constance avoided anything involving the outdoors, except the walk from her car's parking spot to the mall entrance.

Biff wondered where Martin and their old friends were now, and what they were doing.

Biff looked again in the mirror and saw his father's carved chin and steady round eyes. For a moment, it seemed as though Harry was staring through the mirror. Biff leaned away, his headache intensifying. He read the quote that was taped to his mirror from Otis' Offerings, a weekly email of homespun wisdom sent around by one of his employees:

> *"Everyone in life has a clear path to happiness; only the courageous follow theirs while most get too caught up in the mediocrity of other people's trappings."*

Biff popped two round pink pills, his fifth and sixth of the day, and went back to his desk to find a blood pressure pill. He bit his lip and thought about the cold shower he would take later that evening.

Biff barely noticed when Jack entered the room a few moments later.

"Hi Biff."

"Hi," Biff said slowly. "Well, what have you found out so far? Did you talk with Stanley?"

"Yes, and I left with more questions than answers. I just don't know enough yet."

Biff shook off his frustrations from earlier. He dug down and found his clarity. He was usually able to do this when others were around; being by himself was the hard part. Biff cleared his mind, as another might clear his throat. It was a baseball pitcher's technique that he had learned in order to muster concentration in a game's-on-the-line moment.

"Jack, I'm not someone who always needs all the facts to solve a problem, but when I try the cowboy approach, I'm wrong more often than I'm right. We're dealing with a complex situation and though Stanley says most of our problems are with the hardware,

I think it's the software. Honestly, I'm not sure whether our consultants understand the software even it were working properly."

Jack was impressed. Biff's observations were dead on, and he seemed to possess that rare form of sense that was erroneously deemed to be common. Was Biff the plucky, "poor, smart, and hungry and no feelings," Gordon Gecko-type from the movie *Wall Street*? Jack couldn't tell. He had observed over the years that fast-climbing managers who could glibly articulate a perspective didn't necessarily understand cause and effect.

"I think you'll get the hardware and software working and the consultants will move up the learning curve, but let's consider the larger issues."

"Okay."

"Biff, all projects must be optimized within three interrelated dimensions or constraints: cost, quality, and time. These three dimensions form what is sometimes referred to as the golden triangle."

Biff nodded.

"Project management strives to ensure that the three legs of the triangle are controlled properly, enabling the desired outcome. Ideally, your project has infinite quality, consumes zero cost, and takes no time. Quality is also known as scope."

"You mean the work to be performed?" Biff asked.

"Yes. In PNP's scenario, you are seeking to optimize the balance of cost and scope, because Big-Box has fixed the timeframe."

"Good points, Jack, but how does this help?" Biff asked.

"How do you know that your project is off track?"

"That's easy. We're behind schedule on every module. Thick-Ware is full of bugs and critical hardware is twelve weeks late."

"Why?" asked Jack.

"Why," Biff repeated. "There are a thousand reasons why—"

Jack cut him off. "You have to know why in order to fix it. This project is taking up more time and money each week, am I right?"

"Yes, and it's getting more and more off track."

"It sounds like PNP needs to escape the classic IT Black Hole," Jack said.

"What's that?" Biff asked.

"First, your time and money get sucked in. Soon you are spending so much on consultants and internal staff that you literally feel like a heroin addict who can't rip the needle from his arm. Your customers can't get your attention because you are so focused on fixing your project and then all your reputation and customer goodwill gets sucked in as well."

"Then we're out of business?"

"Right on. You go supernova, with a big flash o'light and then you are deleted."

Biff pushed back from his desk. Jack sensed that Biff was getting ready to ask for his help.

"You must see a lot of organizations like us," Biff said.

"When I worked at Pro-Con, I couldn't get past my frustrations about how inconsistent our results were. Some IT projects were successful, others were total failures, but results were most often mediocre."

"That's consistent with my experience."

"Consulting is a great concept, but so often the consultants and the clients end a project with bitter tastes in their mouths. Even though our consulting firm tried to be objective, it experienced the same conflicts of interest that challenged stock analysts at the investment banking firms a few years ago."

"What do you mean?" said Biff.

"Remember how those analysts promoted companies that their colleagues courted for investment banking services? It was a win/win for the investment bankers and their clients because the banks earned substantial fees and their clients saw their share prices rise. People made money hand over fist."

"Yes," said Biff, "but someone always gets screwed."

"Right. And you know who: the public, more often than not. Average Joes thought analysts were honest brokers, so the public climbed over itself to bid up the price of stocks that had little inherent value. This led to the big crash that we talked about earlier."

"But how does this relate to technology?"

"There is a pervasive but relatively unrecognized technology sub-economy that mimics those banking relationships."

Biff nodded for him to continue.

"The big software companies need the consulting companies and the consulting companies need the big software companies. A client like PNP is the analog of the stock investor. The client is led to believe that with a pile of money and a few short months, some great new technology will enable that client to become a big winner. The sales pitches are designed to convince you that you'll fall behind the pack unless you boldly lead it."

"Why are you only discussing software? What about the hardware?"

"The hardware's capability is typically way ahead of the software's. Hardware is like buying commodity construction materials. You draw up a shopping list, find your best deals, and technicians do the installation. So much happens in the cloud today that you may not need to buy any hardware. Software is the limiting factor because it has to capture the design, theme, and substance of the changes you are trying to make at PNP."

"What happens when things fall apart?"

"You know what happens. The consulting companies blame the software companies and vice-versa, but it's all grandstanding. In the back room, they are sipping scotch together and laughing about these projects that are generating way more fees than they originally quoted to you. They know that once you are deep into it, you can't pull out. You become addicted to spending. You've been sucked into the Black Hole."

"Why aren't there laws protecting against this?" Biff said.

"There's no public outcry because the problem isn't well understood. Only when a failed IT project explodes into the media, usually involving lost lives, does anyone notice."

"The six o'clock news would rather carry a story about how a little guy gets screwed by a big corporation. It's not news when companies screw each other," Biff said.

"You're right," Jack said. "It takes the Justice Department or a motivated Attorney General to get involved. Also, what big executive wants to publicize that he made such a boneheaded mistake? And lose his vendor-supplied ticket to next year's Super Bowl? No way!"

"I get it."

"Reality Check's goal is to help you have a great project, not create extra billable hours for ourselves. Look, Biff, understand the consultants' game. Sometimes they bid jobs with very little profit margin because they are trying to break into a new industry or roll out a new service offering. That's okay. What's not okay is when they bid on a job and represent more success in their portfolio than they actually have. That hurts everyone. You ought to be doing reference checks on each and every consultant assigned to your company. Like Reagan used to say: 'Trust, but verify.'"

Jack looked at Biff. Like a couple considering a first kiss, they were feeling each other out, furtively probing for weakness, doubt, or fear. Jack knew it was time to propose his fee and he did so. Biff listened, motionless. Jack thought he saw a small palpitation at Biff's Adam's apple. Long seconds passed.

Jack spoke first. "I would like to charge more because I think it's worth more. The bottom line is that if you make significant course corrections because of Reality Check's guidance and this results in the project meeting its objectives, then this work will be worth tens or hundreds of times our fee."

"So, what are you saying? You want some sort of kicker?"

"Sure. Let's have an agreement in which your action is fully discretionary. If PNP gets up and running on time, then I propose an additional success fee. My sense is that you're a straight shooter who takes the high road. In my business, I'm betting on my clients. We're all partners. How many consultants would take on that challenge?"

"Interesting proposal, Jack," Biff responded. "I like the way you think, but that's a big number. You are right though; it's not a lot if we are successful. Of course, you assume that we won't be able to turn this around by ourselves. I could argue but I don't have the time. Let me sleep on it and I'll get back to you tomorrow. Also, shoot me an email with a couple of references."

"Will do. Please understand the devil in one of these projects is not the ideas and observations that I'll have; that part is easy. Implementing the fixes is where this game is won or lost, and that's mostly in your domain. I become a coach in the implementation. You're the on-the-field quarterback and captain."

"Now you're putting it back on me?" Biff asked.

Jack nodded, raising an eyebrow.

"Fair enough," Biff said. "I guess I can't outsource the success of this company to a consultant. By the way, are there any deliverables from our engagement, or we paying solely for your rhetoric?"

Jack smiled. "You'll receive our Reality Check Assessment Letter, which describes the observable symptoms, their root causes, and Reality Check's action recommendations. The letters are usually seven to ten pages long."

"How many tens of thousands of dollars is that per page?" Biff asked with a sly grin.

Jack laughed nervously. "During the first week I'll meet your heads of sales, marketing, finance, production, IT and any other employees you deem appropriate. My team will review the project's progress to date, the project management plan, and meet with the consultants and technology vendors."

"That sounds like a busy week."

"It is, but the process is designed to produce meaningful results quickly."

"And then?"

"In the second week I'll deliver a draft of the Reality Check Assessment Letter. Once you've reviewed it, we will reconvene with the leadership team, and they'll have the chance to rebut any of our findings. We'll modify the letter on the fly in this Decision Oriented Meeting."

"What's that?"

"You'll see. As we finalize the Reality Check Assessment Letter, we'll also conduct seminars with all of the project team members to help instill a can-do, success oriented operating environment."

"How many folks do you bring with you?" Biff asked.

"Expect to see at least two or three of our people here during the two weeks."

"And at the conclusion of the two weeks?"

"Up to you whether to retain us to implement the recommendations and guide your project back on track."

Biff raised both brows and nodded silently. "Jack, I need to go. Can you come back in the morning? I need to sit down with both you and Stanley before I decide whether to move forward."

"Sure," Jack replied. *Another night in a hotel.*

Biff excused himself. He had to go to Amelia's school; she had been caught smoking again, and Constance insisted that Biff handle it this time.

In his office, Stanley was speaking by phone to a recruiter about a new opportunity in a related industry. Stanley had a great fiefdom of recruiters who had helped him get his two previous jobs, and he knew how to return a favor. He paid hundreds of thousands of dollars in recruiting fees for the various employees he had hired over the years. An unspoken policy of never hiring anyone without paying a fee was Stanley's safety net. Those recruiters always had one or two openings that Stanley could parachute into.

MONDAY, JULY 11ᵀᴴ 3:30 PM

Jack walked out to PNP's parking lot. PNP would be a slam-dunk, no different than many Reality Checks. Yet Jack felt uneasy. Drinks with Rona were four hours away and he had no other appointments. He didn't want to hang around at PNP with no plan; it would make him appear too available and too weak.

Jack started toward his Tapir. He touched his forehead and examined the red blotch on his fingertip. It was not the image he wanted to project, especially not to Rona. She was refreshingly appealing and sexy, an appearance matched with her brash attitude. Definitely a New York girl, not a Naperville gal. But was she off-limits? *Well*, he mused, *it's not like I would be fishing off of my own dock. I'm no employee, just a consultant.*

Jack drove out of the parking lot, his attention flipping between PNP and Rona. *Will Biff buy? Could she like me? Is Broadway past the point of no return? How do I act cool?* Jack recalled what he learned in Buddhism 101 back at Princeton,

> *"The most important time to clarify your direction is at the beginning of a journey. While there will be inevitable course corrections along the way, the energy required for the trip goes down considerably when you push off in the right direction."*

It had always bothered Jack that his professor for Princeton's Introduction to Buddhism had refused to grade on a curve and typically failed the bottom fifteen percent of the class.

Jack's smartphone kept buzzing and each time he scrolled to read the message, he hoped it was from Rona. No such luck, only social media e-noise. He received one message that made him smile: his roommate from Princeton announced the birth of a son, attaching a picture of the adorable newborn, Noah.

MONDAY, JULY 11ᵀᴴ 7:20 PM

Jack was back at the plant and thirty feet from Rona's office when she appeared in the doorway. She flashed a friendly smile and beckoned him to follow her as she turned down the hall. She was finishing a conversation on her smartphone as she walked out of the plant into the parking lot. Rona kept talking, but smiled apologetically and mouthed, "get in your car" to Jack. His excitement mounting, he complied.

Jack followed Rona out of the parking lot and to the Dante's less than a mile from PNP. Her silvery BMW convertible was easy to follow. When Rona opened her car door, time slowed as her legs reached out to the pavement. Her muscular calves were small and elegant, yet well defined. Her painted toenails strained against the leather straps of her stilettos. Jack wasn't sure if this was for his benefit or if it was just her natural flair. Jack grabbed the handle on Rona's door as she stood up and gently closed it. "Thank you, I guess chivalry isn't dead," Rona said. "I like a man who's not afraid to be one."

Cool, Jack thought. *Maybe she had something more than shop talk in mind, too.*

They entered the bar portion of the restaurant and sat down. Jack wasn't too fond of chain joints trying to pass themselves off as fine dining, but he played it cool and kept quiet. The waitress came over and looked at Rona. Rona looked at Jack and said, "You first."

"I'll have a Heineken," he requested, raising the emotional bid of the situation.

"I'll have a Diet Coke," she responded, passing on the bid.

Jack tried to shake off the prick of rejection as they took seats at a high table in the bar area. The waitress returned with the drinks. The silence was long and Jack weakly filled it.

"Rona, do you know that more than three trillion dollars is spent every year on IT?"

"No," she said, looking annoyed again as she put two sticks of gum into her mouth.

"Yes, it's tremendous. Companies drown themselves in technology. Most CEOs don't realize what their IT departments are spending. That's the problem. Companies rush to install new IT systems without understanding risk. New systems interact with ones already installed, creating larger houses of cards. An organization can only tolerate so much information, and with each new system added, there is a multiplier effect with respect to complexity. The most common reason for project failure is the presence of too many independent variables that can't be balanced simultaneously..." Jack blathered nervously.

"I was a math major," Rona said flatly, cutting him off.

"Then you'll remember from school that the way to solve multivariate equations was one variable at a time, rather than all at once."

"Look, Jack, I'd like to go through this in detail but I have an appointment tonight and have to cut out in twenty minutes."

Jack scratched his forehead, irritating a tender pore into which a repurposed hair follicle had been recently planted. He quickly pulled his hand away. *How come hair transplant ads never deal with uncertainty? On infomercials, the bald guy never gets the girl and the guy with the new hair always does. God, my head must look so corny. Rona is giving me no opening whatsoever. Maybe I misread her earlier.*

"Here's the problem," Rona began. "PNP has really great products. Customers love us and our styles rule the business. Our design team came up with our Bridgehampton line and it's huge. If you know anything about cookware, our pots perform at restaurant quality and yet they're priced within reach of most retail customers. We've had great reviews from *Gassy Vegans*, *My Loving Souse*, and about twenty other cooking and ladies publications. Demand is greater than supply and we haven't had a sale or a markdown in two years. Sounds great so far, doesn't it? Except that we can't meet customer demand. We have two factories that produce Bridgehampton. There's no shortage of raw materials or labor. The problem is we have a warehouse full of the 12" pots with 14" lids. Manufacturing produced the wrong stuff and no one caught it."

"Wow!"

"TWERP screwed up the customer demand for the last quarter."

"Twerp?" Jack said, then realized what she meant.

"Yeah. Just look at Big-Box. They ordered five hundred pallets of Bridgehampton 8"-10"-12" frying pan sets. So far we have shipped them only one hundred and fifty pallets, which means that most stores have only a handful of product to sell. And it only gets worse.

"How?" Jack said.

"Because Big-Box paid for product placements on *Fricassee Fest* and *Turkey in the Slaw*. The hosts of both shows talked about how great our frying pans performed. Come on now, how awesome is that! Demand has been incredible. Do you know how much grief Big-Box gives us each time they turn away a customer because of a stock out? Now they're charging us back for a portion of the advertising costs they incurred. Frankly, they're being generous because they lose a tremendous amount of customer loyalty every time they turn away business. Nothing is worse than when a customer asks for a product she saw on TV that morning and gets bupkus."

"How did it get so bad? Didn't anyone see the problem coming?"

"Listen Jack, I'm not sure I should phrase it this way to you, but the truth is that we fucked up. Royally. Inexcusably. Big-Box asked to connect their buying system to our selling system so they could save inventory costs as well as have their orders processed faster. Sounds reasonable, doesn't it? Big-Box is the gorilla in this space and we owe them more than they owe us. PNP is a pimple on their behind."

"Okay," Jack said.

"What I'm most concerned about is that if our Chief Information Officer doesn't get off his fat ass, we will get dropped. We've worked too hard on this account to have that happen."

"Why has it been so difficult to fix?"

"Because PNP has this huge corporate-wide systems project going on. We might as well be playing Russian roulette with a six-shooter containing five bullets."

"Rona, I've been there," Jack said. "I hate to say this, but I've seen these things blow up before, just the way you are describing it."

"Jack, I've gotta go," Rona said, pushing back her bar stool.

"Rona, this has been great," Jack exclaimed, struggling to regain his professional voice. "I know you have to leave, but is there anything else you can tell me? I have a meeting with Biff tomorrow morning and I need to understand how I can help PNP."

"If you want to help, you can do three things for us: first, get our backorders with Big-Box shipped out as quickly as possible. Second, fix our relationship with Lars and their other executives. Third, connect us to Broadway," Rona responded.

Jack listened carefully, but didn't nod.

"That's a tall order right there," Rona said. "If you have anything left over, find a resting place for Lunchmeat."

"Well….I'll do my best," Jack said uncomfortably.

"Nice to talk to you. See you tomorrow…I'm outta here," Rona declared. She took a loud swig of her Diet Coke and flashed him a parting smile as she stood up to leave.

"Go ahead, I'll get the check," Jack said, but Rona was already out of hearing range. Jack turned his head, looked out Dante's window and observed for a half-second the natural recoiling of Rona's skirt as she sat down in the Bimmer's driver's seat.

"Wow," Jack said softly, as Rona closed her car door.

Jack sat back down. Two beers later he felt confident that he could close Biff tomorrow. Jack remained in Dante's for another hour, munching on tepid Buffalo wings and sobering up before the two-mile drive to the BigEight in Naperville. Jack checked in, quickly undressed and still burned out from last week's airplane misadventure, sat down in bed and opened the latest issue of *Tektanic*. Thirty seconds later, he was dead to the world.

TUESDAY, JULY 12TH 8:00 AM

Jack fought the local morning traffic but arrived at the PNP parking lot in time to watch Rona get out of her car. Jack walked up to her. "Hi!"

"Morning, Jack. How's it going?"

"It's still going. I see Biff in a few minutes. We'll see what happens. How are you?"

Rona made some comment about the traffic, accompanied by an endearing shrug of the shoulders. It wasn't much, but she gave off a friendly vibe. Jack decided to go for it.

"This may seem a little out of left field but I'd like to take you to dinner tonight, if you're available. I enjoyed our conversation last night and I'd love to finish it."

Rona hesitated. *Am I being asked out?* She looked at him carefully. He re-wore yesterday's black suit but with a blue shirt and a bright orange and red hounds tooth Hermes tie. Rona looked again. Jack's head looked far less scary this morning, and she was impressed by his forwardness.

Rona had planned to stop at the hospital that evening to visit her best friend Gladys. Jack wasn't exactly Rona's type, but he seemed nice, and she recalled her mom's sound advice to make a habit of accepting first dates – "a date never hurt anyone, and you never know what might happen," she would always say. "Okay," Rona said, glancing at Jack's tie again. "I guess it could be fun. What did you have in mind?"

The next moment was a slow walk through hell for Jack. He hadn't thought about what to do with Rona; he only knew that he wanted to see her. He sensed Rona wanted a man with a plan, a guy who could make decisions, and he was racking his brains for a good restaurant. Jack hoped his shaking knees weren't obvious.

"How about Le Maxwell?" he blurted out, naming the trendiest place in Chicago. He had drinks there one night and the bill was eighty dollars after twenty minutes.

"Sounds great. Are you staying near here or in the city?" Rona said.

"Right around here, at the BigEight."

"Good, I'll swing by there at 7:30 tonight and you can follow me. I have an errand to run after dinner so I can't stay out late."

"See you then."

Rona turned toward the building and walked quickly to her office.

Why won't Rona ride downtown with me? Maybe she plans to spend the night at her usual guy's house after I take her out for a $300 dinner. Wouldn't that stink, Jack thought. *Why Le Maxwell?* He could kick himself. *Why do I sully clarity with complexity whenever I meet a hot woman?*

TUESDAY, JULY 12ᵀᴴ 8:10 AM

Jack met Biff in his office and Biff immediately suggested they walk through the plant to the cafeteria. The shop floor buzzed with machinery and teemed with activity. Half-filled parts buggies with Toyota-style *kanban* cards were being pushed around. As they rounded a corner into the foundry area of the plant, Biff suddenly yanked Jack back as a large forklift sped by with a load of aluminum coils.

"Sorry about that, Jack. I should have warned you about our production floor. The drivers have the right of way and the pedestrians have to fend for themselves. It's a safety issue, but it boosts productivity."

"Whose idea was that?" Jack asked, his heart pounding.

"A consultant's," Biff replied.

Biff and Jack pushed through the swinging doors that led to the cafeteria. There were several long tables filled with the plant's workers on break. Biff nodded for Otis Jackson, the food server, to come over. Otis had gray hair and a kind, wrinkled face with a friendly, toothy smile. Fifteen years earlier, he had lost three fingers and an eye while operating a PNP screw machine without a safety cover. As a screw was being ejected, a piece of excess steel trim was shot into his right eye, tearing through his optic nerve. While blindly staggering backward and trying to right himself, Otis inadvertently grabbed Earl McCweeg's spinning slitter blade. The blade instantly sliced off the three middle fingers on Otis's left hand. In a moment of circumstantial cruelty, Otis's wedding ring popped off of his severed finger, and clinked along the floor across two production stations and into an open drain. Nothing could be done and Marv Schwartz, mostly acting out of sympathy, put Otis in charge of food serving. He wasn't very good at it but Biff kept him on.

"Otis, what's on tap for breakfast?" Biff asked.

"Bacon, eggs, and my super special chili," he replied.

"You mean the turbo chili?" Biff asked.

"Yep, that's it," Otis said gleefully. "It'll make a man out of you! Your friend too!"

"We'll stick with coffee for now," Biff said.

At PNP, Biff was seen as a man's man, and his people liked him. He drank beer with the employees and never wore a tiny bathing suit at the annual beach party. As Jack and Biff approached the coffee machine, Biff dug two quarters out of his pocket. "Sorry, it's no ChumpRoast. Regular or decaf?"

"Regular, with milk," Jack responded.

"No milk. There's creamer over there on the table."

Biff handed the cup to Jack. It was one of those poker cups with four cards printed on the outside and one on the bottom. *Eight high,* Jack noted to himself. *Not very impressive.*

The cafeteria was clean but smelled old. Even the fresh coat of paint it received each year couldn't mask the spewage from the deep-fat fryer. Jack examined the condiments table. Packets of ketchup, very yellow mustard, sweet pickle relish, sugar and non-dairy creamer. *Would it be such a burden for Biff to buy an eighty dollar refrigerator and keep some fresh milk and half-and-half? And the plaque in the lobby says* 'Our Employees Are Our Most Important Asset.'

Biff and Jack sat down at one of the long tables. Biff typically sat among his employees. He introduced Jack as a consultant helping out with the technology project.

"Not another one!" Earl McCweeg joked.

"These guys multiply like hamsters," Eunice Goldberg chimed in.

"Well, he looks a little smarter than the rest of them," Roosevelt Van Buren added.

Biff smiled. So did Jack. Jack enjoyed the banter; it would have been worse if they were silent. That would mean that they were either hiding something or they were too fed up with what was going on to have any interest in sharing information about the project. Instead, the production workers were focused on their everyday issues.

"Biff, we've got a problem on the #3 line," Earl said. "The tool that we use to make the 12s is busted again. It's the third time we've been shut down this month. Our guys don't have the right equipment in the tool crib to resurface it, so we have to send it over to Jenkin's Tool & Die."

"How long has the line been down?" Biff inquired.

"Two days now."

"Have you missed any shipments?"

"Not yet, the line has been running the double 18s."

"Don't we already have at least a dozen skids of double 18s sitting in the warehouse?"

"I'm not sure."

Eunice chimed in, "No Biff, those double 18s were shipped out last night. I checked with sales and one of our bigger customers, er, I forgot which one, ordered fifteen skids of double 18s for a promotion."

"Great," replied Biff.

As the large wall clock approached 8:59 AM, people started to return to their machines. There was no 9:00 AM bell but everyone knew to be back at work. As he rose, Earl said to Jack, "Stop by slitting when you get a moment and say hi."

"You got it," said Jack.

The rest of the coffee break was non-business. Biff spoke about his golf game and last winter's family ski vacation to Aspen, hoping to elicit similar personal details from Jack. Jack was tight lipped as his mind wandered to Rona. *Does she think it's a date?*

Jack sipped his weak coffee and looked at Biff. The silence lulled on and Biff motioned for Jack to rise. As they walked through the plant's plating area toward Stanley's office, Jack noticed that Biff was tensing up.

"Any chance of getting a plant tour?" Jack asked.

"Do you need one? Will it help your analysis?"

"Yes. Touring the plant will give me insight into PNP's business processes. A company's information flows are usually about as organized as its material flows."

"No problem. Otis usually gives our plant tours. Ask Gertrude to set it up."

"Thanks."

Biff still looked tense when the pair arrived at Stanley's office. This time Jack recognized the hole on Stanley's golfing website. Biff didn't seem to notice. Stanley stood up immediately and said to Biff, "I need to see you alone for a few moments before we start this meeting."

Biff was annoyed but wanted to avoid a confrontation.

"Jack, would you excuse us for a few moments? Wait back in my office and I'll call you there."

Jack sensed what would happen once he left, but he had no option. "Of course," Jack responded.

TUESDAY, JULY 12TH 9:30 AM

Jack walked to Biff's office. When Jack opened the office suite's door, he was surprised to see Rona seated in Gertrude's chair. Rona was looking at Biff's calendar, but she looked up at Jack calmly when he walked in, not as if she had been caught with her hand in the cookie jar.

"Hi, Jack!" Rona said.

"Hey, stranger, what are you doing?"

"Waiting for Biff. Just like you are."

Rona sat down at Biff's conference table and Jack went over to examine Biff's book collection more closely.

"Look at all these books," Jack said. "I wonder if they make the slightest difference in the way a reader approaches business problems. You don't get to be a good golfer by reading golf books or a good businessperson by reading business books. You need a coach to help you to lower your golf score or a mentor to teach you to make better business decisions. You learn by trying, failing, getting up, and trying again."

Rona seemed to nod, but Jack wasn't sure.

"Like diet books," he continued. "What a waste of money. People already know how to lose weight. Eat less and exercise more. When people spend twenty dollars on the book, they do it to feel good and because it's easier than pushing that cheesecake away."

Is he just showing off? I hope he doesn't think that tonight's dinner is a date. "Don't mention that to Biff – he takes his business books seriously," she responded.

Meanwhile, in the mist of Stanley's office's heavily cologned air, Biff and Stanley were having it out. Stanley was venting because Biff had cancelled several of Stanley's purchase orders. "How can we connect to Broadway if you won't give me the resources I need?"

Biff fought his tension and quietly responded, "You are well over budget and despite what your reports show, I don't think Broadway is anywhere near completion."

"Biff, you have to give us the additional resources. This is a make it or break it point for us. How can you think of sabotaging the project now?"

Rather than responding with a vitriolic burst to Stanley's accusation, Biff absorbed the tension, gathered himself and did not reply. He was not going to descend to Stanley's level. *A CEO has to maintain control.* Instead of yelling, he would use charm and reason to solve the problem. He always remembered how Robert F. Kennedy responded to Nikita Khrushchev's letter during the Cuban Missile Crisis. Rather than react to Khrushchev's inflammatory accusations, RFK addressed only the issues for which he could provide a helpful response. He responded to animus with calmness, to antagonism with logic. Even Fidel Castro admitted, years later, that RFK's tact had averted Armageddon.

It took discipline for Biff to mute his frustration with Stanley, but he managed. "I'm going to call Jack in now," Biff said as he reached for the phone on Stanley's desk.

When the phone rang in Biff's office, Rona answered it, surprising Biff. "If Jack Bluto is there, please send him over right away," Biff said stoically, his lips touching the microphone. Stanley observed this and his hand instinctively gripped the cylindrical container of disinfecting wipes that he kept under his desk.

✲ ✲ ✲

Jack surveyed the scene as he entered. A vein on the left side of Biff's forehead was bulging. Stanley's large neck was splotched with red.

"Okay, Jack, ask your questions," Biff said.

"Thank you, Biff," Jack said. Every Reality Check project unearthed tensions and Jack had learned that grace was a critical tool when digging through the symptoms to find the problems.

"Please tell me about your approach to managing this project," Jack said, turning to address Stanley.

Stanley responded slowly, "This is a large and complex undertaking, akin to building a bridge or a factory." He paused. "We are implementing electronic business connections between our customers, our suppliers, and ourselves. These connections will link directly to our new ThickWare ERP system. In addition, we are installing a Customer Resources Management or CRM system. By better understanding our customers' requirements, we will be able to make better Supply Chain decisions."

Stanley pressed a few buttons on his keyboard and a PowerPoint slide appeared on his wall screen. Jack looked up and recognized the Fujohara industrial-strength projector, professionally mounted to Stanley's ceiling. *Twenty grand including the installation and the service contract,* Jack estimated.

Stanley pressed the pocket clip on his pen and a red dot appeared. He aimed the laser at the screen. "We originally planned for three simultaneous projects: Broadway, ERP, and

CRM. We decided to update our Supply Chain software to take advantage of all the new information we are getting from our other systems. So we actually have four technology projects in process."

"How do you manage all that?" Jack asked.

"We have four Project Leaders. Three are director level and the fourth is a VP. These people all report to me."

Big mistake, Jack thought.

Stanley continued, "Each project has an administrator responsible for updating his or her project plan, maintaining the project budget, and managing the issues lists. Each Project Leader holds a weekly status meeting to resolve major issues. The resolution of the issues on the list is everybody's highest priority...."

"...and the issues lists are available online?" Jack asked.

"Exactly," Stanley said. "The Project Leaders hold coffee breaks at fixed times each day to surface new issues, build camaraderie, and facilitate communications. I hold one-hour meetings on Fridays with each of my four Project Leaders. At these meetings, we resolve issues for which the rest of the team needs my input."

"Good," Jack said. "What about staffing? Are the team members dedicated to individual projects?"

"Some team members are assigned full-time to one project and others are part-time or may have their time split among multiple projects."

Jack nodded.

"Also, our consultants helped us to institute a PMO or Program Management Office to ensure that we would remain on schedule with each project."

These were the sorts of professional-sounding responses that Jack had expected. *Lunchmeat was no dope, but his approach was a recipe for structured, organized failure,* Jack realized.

"How about interfaces?" Jack asked.

"Glad you asked," Stanley rose and walked over to the screen. He pressed a button on the wall and the screen retracted toward the ceiling.

Pretty neat, Jack thought.

Pretty wasteful, Biff thought.

The screen recoiled into its storage bay, revealing a large, multicolored wall map. It looked like a wire and pipe diagram for a nuclear submarine.

"This is our company-wide business process map," Stanley said proudly, his chest rising. "Everything that goes on in our company is represented here."

Jack and Biff both studied the map. It was too complex to understand.

"This diagram shows all the business processes superimposed upon all of the business systems that support these processes. The processes are depicted by the thick brown lines and the systems are shown by the blue dashed lines. The interfaces are in pink."

"Is this as-is or to-be?" Jack said.

"To-be," continued Stanley. "This is what our business will look like when the four projects are finished. The processes were refined as a result of a yearlong Business Process Reengineering project conducted by Pro-Con. This led to a detailed requirements analysis. By the way," Stanley said, "I was brought in by Roscoe & Lauer to design and manage this effort." Stanley spoke defiantly, looking right into Jack's eyes as he moved close to Biff, purposely crowding his personal space. Reflexively, Biff inched back, Stanley's cologne jabbing mercilessly at Biff's nostrils.

Stanley continued, "Once we developed the business requirements, we drew up RFPs or Requests for Proposals for each project and sent them to the vendors that we thought would qualify. We streamlined our approach by deciding that both the ERP system and the Supply Chain software would come from the same software vendor."

"ThickWare? Was that dictated by Big-Box?" Jack asked.

"No, Pro-Con helped us make that decision. It had nothing to do with Big-Box or with our use of older ThickWare software. We have to do what's right for our organization and not allow our independence to be compromised by a customer."

"Okay," Jack said, barely audibly.

Stanley continued, "We examined the vendor responses and then invited the top vendors to do day-long detailed presentations. We encouraged the vendors to simulate our business processes on their technologies, in other words, to run our data through their systems. For each project, we had three finalists. We narrowed this down to two vendors per project and then we made the decisions based on the quality of their references and the prices we were quoted. By going through this process, we assured ourselves of getting the right technologies for the best prices."

Jack knew Stanley was giving textbook answers. In reality, it was an overly meticulous, cover-your-butt-while-the-ships-are-sinking approach. It was peacetime mentality, totally inappropriate for projects in dire straits. If you dotted all your i's and crossed all your t's when implementing software, the world would pass you by. Jack realized that Stanley was trying to mask his own confusion with complexity. The level of obfuscation was almost obscene.

Biff sat quietly as Jack focused his attention on the peacetime lieutenant before him. "So PNP chose ThickWare for ERP and Supply Chain, right? And we know you're using ThickWare to connect to Broadway. So who are you using for CRM?"

"CustHug," Stanley replied.

"Does CustHug interface with ThickWare?" Jack inquired, leaning forward.

"No, but the next version of ThickWare, 3.5, will be fully Cust-Hug certified."

"Is 3.5 out yet?"

"Not officially, but we're using it. We're in the ThickWare beta program. Their engineers are building the software based on our needs."

"I see," Jack said.

Stanley continued, "We are on track to have two of our four major systems live by the end of this year. I know you are concerned about the Big-Box Broadway situation. That is totally under control and will be completed on time."

"I heard Big-Box is using ThickWare Version 2.4," Jack said.

"They are, and 3.5 will be compatible with 2.4. Once they synchronize the versions, we plan to virtualize our servers," Stanley said.

"Why virtualize?" Jack said.

"Because the ERP, Supply Chain, CRM, and Broadway projects require us to expand our server farm and grow our database from eight to three hundred terabytes."

"I see," Jack responded quietly. Biff looked helplessly at Jack.

"Now if you will excuse me," Stanley continued, "I have to meet with one of our hardware vendors off-site. If you have any questions, you may want to send them to me in advance via email so I can prepare more helpful answers."

Stanley rose without offering his hand to either Biff or Jack. The meeting was over. As Biff and Jack walked down the hallway, Myron, Stanley's network administrator, nodded hello to Jack. With his 6'4" height and rippling muscles nearly bursting through his tight white Oxford shirt, he looked like a male version of Pamela Anderson, except Pamela Anderson would never carry three Sharpie markers and two Bic Pens in her breast pocket. Jack stared; Myron's looks were magnetic. Biff avoided eye contact with Myron; instead, he watched Jack's eyes scanning Myron's Tarzanesque frame.

"Jack, give me a half hour and then join me in my office," Biff said after Myron turned the corner.

"Sounds good," Jack answered.

Jack stopped in the hallway and then wandered back toward Stanley's office. Solutions to PNP's problems were coalescing in Jack's mind. Now he had to work backward to create the persuasive arguments to legitimize his conclusions.

Stanley wasn't in his office, so Jack stood in the doorway, waiting. Looking around, Jack noticed three four-inch binders entitled ThickWare Requirements Document for PNP, Volumes II, III, and I. Jack hesitated for a moment, but Stanley's door was wide open and bare of any materials that Jack could be criticized for rifling through. He walked toward the bookshelf. Jack picked Volume II off the shelf. He winced at the book's weight. Jack opened the cover and started flipping through what seemed like dozens of section dividers. This document explained the multicolored map that Stanley had shown to Biff and Jack earlier. It listed each business process and the process owners, customers, suppliers, cycle times, and described the interrelationships among the processes.

Jack couldn't believe the level of detail. This expensive, to-be vision of the business was laden with assumptions about PNP's future business, scripted by consultants and PNP's technology team. *I bet Rona and Biff didn't attend a single one of these meetings.*

✲ ✲ ✲

Biff sat in his office, peering at his bookshelf. *How could Stanley accuse me of sabotaging the company? What could I do without angering Roscoe & Lauer?*

He got up from his desk and went looking for Jack, who was rounding the corner just outside Biff's office. Jack saw him and stopped.

Biff said, "Okay, Jack, you've got the job. Can you start in the morning? I am canceling my trip to France so I can be available for you."

Jack grinned. "Biff, that's great to hear. Two of my associates are standing by in our New York office with their bags packed. Annie and Marcus will be here in the morning."

"You guys really hit the ground running, don't you?" Biff asked.

"It's the nature of our business. We've got to be able to deploy in a moment's notice."

"And you'll be staying in town, right?"

"Yes, we'll all be at the BigEight."

Biff nodded. "Thanks, Jack, I'm not used to anything involving a technology project happening so quickly."

"No worries Biff. Please do me one favor?"

"What's that?"

"Send an email to everyone in your organization explaining Reality Check's presence here. It will help our team get going more quickly with your people. I'll send you a generic memo that you can modify."

"Thanks."

"No sweat. By the way, I'll probably stay in town this weekend, in order to make sure we finish the Reality Check Assessment Letter by next Friday."

"Good, I'll have your first payment ready by close of business today."

Jack smiled as they shook hands.

TUESDAY, JULY 12TH 4:45 PM

After spending the balance of the day sending emails and making phone calls to clear his schedule for the next two weeks, Jack drove to the BigEight. He booked the table at Le Maxwell, put on his shorts, T-shirt, and running shoes and went downstairs to the fitness room. After three sets on the dumbbells, he decided to jog around the neighborhood.

Naperville seemed to be a typical suburban American manufacturing community. From the outside, the plants all looked the same. They had nearly identical buildings, parking lots, and signs, but each company produced radically different goods. *Were their outward similarities creating efficiencies,* Jack wondered, *or was there a "stay in the pack" mentality and most managers gravitated toward some mediocre mean because it was the way things had always been done, similar to the screwed-up thinking that surrounded big technology projects?*

Jack finished his run and went back to the room. He turned on the TV and while watching the news, the in-room movie guide caught his glance. "$16! That's what it costs to buy a DVD," he muttered to himself. Jack hadn't heard of these movies and wasn't interested. He clicked the remote and the adult movie guide appeared. It reminded him of the Heart-Stopper breakfast menu at DoubleWide's, the fast-growing chain restaurant. These shapely, full-lipped women on the BigEight's 52" plasma were being served up like a tasty meal ready to be devoured.

His lusty thoughts about Rona combined with the opportunity for instant gratification overpowered Jack's need for an incremental sixteen dollars. Jack pressed the purchase button on the remote and drew the shades. *What the hell,* he rationalized. *It's not like Biff or any accounts payable clerk from PNP is going to review the hotel invoice.* He wondered whether the Pro-Con partners had a way of checking what movies their staffers watched. *Maybe a few of the partners were too busy watching those same movies themselves?*

✲ ✲ ✲

Ninety minutes later, Jack awoke from his movie-induced nap and got dressed. As Jack drove to PNP for his rendezvous with Rona, he thought about the movie, DoubleWide's, and technology. *Why are people so easily seduced by perceived features and benefits without understanding the investment they need to make to obtain them? I feel so disgusted after I inhale a Heart-Stopper and I feel sleazy after watching the porn.*

When a CIO signs that multi-million dollar technology purchase order, she just crested the biggest hill on the roller coaster. Too often it's a screaming plunge from there. It's the nature of wants and desires, Jack mused. *When we feel the pangs of hunger, the drives of sex, or the fear of a competitor, we often bite off way more than we ought to be chewing.*

TUESDAY, JULY 12TH 7:30 PM

Rona was on time. She pulled into the BigEight's parking lot, waved gaily, and summoned for Jack to follow. He did and they drove the twenty-two miles to the restaurant, with Jack never slipping more than fifty feet behind. When they arrived, they parked side by side in Le Maxwell's lot.

Rona was ravishing in her tight but tasteful blouse-less gray Armani suit and her Manolo Blahniks. Before he had time to lose his courage, Jack held out his arm, looked Rona in the eye and said, "May I?"

"Of course," Rona responded, and took his arm.

The maitre'd escorted them to the rear of the restaurant. Jack looked at Rona and said, "Wine?"

"You decide."

The waiter came over as Jack finished reading the menu.

"Cakebread Vine Hill," Jack said, without taking his eyes off of Rona.

Jack hated to waste money on expensive wine but felt that he had to impress. *Does Rona always dress so appealingly?*

"Great choice, Jack – dark, tannic, and absolutely lovely. I'm impressed," Rona said.

I'm in, Jack figured.

"Sorry if I was grouchy yesterday," Rona said. "You were just doing your job and this stupid project drives me crazy."

"I understand," Jack said.

"You have to realize something about me. I would kill for my customers. I learned that from my mother and grandfather, both auto dealers, and pots and pans are no different than cars."

"Are things that bad?" Jack asked. "Stanley says that the project is taking a turn for the better and now it's a matter of cleaning up a few bugs," Jack said, trying to stoke multiple passions within Rona.

"Let me tell you something about Lunchmeat," Rona began spiritedly, as the waiter took too long to dramatically uncork the Cakebread. When he finally finished, Rona continued speaking. "Two years ago, maybe three weeks after he was hired, Stanley offered to take me to lunch and tell me his plans for the new project. He seemed nice enough. He came across like a businessman, not a computer geek."

"Sounds like a good meeting."

"Not in retrospect. My instincts were right about him. Lunchmeat is in the self-enrichment business and to hell with the company. I can't be certain that the guy is a blatant criminal, but Stanley believes his position entitles him to gifts and favors provided by every vendor trying to do business with PNP. He controls millions in spending and has way too much power."

"So if his daughter had a wedding, his vendors would be bringing him gifts like in the opening scene of *The Godfather*," Jack said.

"Something like that, except he and his wife Stacey have no kids."

"Stacey?" Jack said.

"Yeah," Rona said. "I bet Stanley wasn't too nice to you."

"You're right," Jack said.

"You have nothing to offer him. You threaten his empire."

Jack nodded and took a sip of the Cakebread. Rona watched Jack and then did the same.

"Let's talk about you," Jack said.

"What would you like to know?" Rona responded, smiling.

"Where are you from? What do you do for fun? Ever been married?"

"Those are forward questions Jack. I thought you asked me here to discuss PNP."

"I did, but let's just say that I'm open minded."

"Aaah, I see. Clever...but fair enough."

Jack unclasped his arms, resting both hands on the table.

"I'm from around here," Rona said and paused briefly. "And I used to have a lot of fun, and then I got married," she said, chuckling. "We divorced a few years ago. I wanted a family and my ex-husband got more focused on his hedge fund business and less on me. We used to play tennis, ride horses, and play polo together, and then everything faded. Our marriage soon followed."

"Marriages and technology projects have the same failure patterns: incompatibility among the parties, unrealistic expectations, inadequate problem solving mechanisms, and tempting quick-fix offers from third parties," Jack said.

"So are you saying that a good technology project is like a good relationship?" Rona countered, smiling flirtatiously.

"Now you get it! Are you having more fun now that the marriage is broken up?"

"Perhaps...but I work too hard. When I'm not working, I'm working out or teaching yoga, you know, sort of a fitness nut." Rona said coyly.

Jack smiled.

"Tell me more about you," Rona encouraged.

"What do you want to know?" Jack said.

Rona remained silent, waiting for Jack to choose the next topic. Maybe it was that New York thing, but Jack seemed a little quicker than the guys she was used to. Earlier, she had read several of Jack's social media profiles, hoping that she had set her privacies so that Jack wouldn't know she'd checked him out.

"Okay, work. I love technology and I want it to create a better existence for all of us," Jack said.

"What do you mean?" Rona replied.

"Look how we rely upon our smartphones, our computers, and the content on the Internet. It's amazing."

"No question."

"But what happens when they don't work?"

"Like PNP?"

"Sure," Jack nodded. "PNP is a microcosm of a risk that we all face."

"How?" Rona asked.

"I learned a lot from building my Internet company and from working with Reality Check's business, healthcare, and government clients. The key point is this: our existence has become inseparable from the technology we've developed to support it. We're more vulnerable than ever and no one seems to realize it."

"You sound like Al Gore talking about global warming."

"I don't mean to be an alarmist, but our technological risks are daunting. At least with the climate issues, we may have years to solve the problems. Given the unbelievable pace at which technology embeds itself into our lives, I think we have to address the risk immediately."

"Are computers taking over, like in *The Terminator*?" Rona asked. "It reminds me of that crazy MidPoint flight last week."

"I was on that flight."

"No way." Rona stopped smiling and leaned closer, concern clear in her voice.

"I was, and I was scared to death."

"Oh, I am so sorry. It must have been terrible." Rona's turquoise eyes widened.

"It was. The proverbial weakest link almost broke that day."

Jack examined Rona's expression, looking for passion, but he wasn't sure what he saw. *I am really digging this girl*, he thought. "It won't be like in *The Terminator*," he continued. "It'll be something much more mundane that shuts us down. No government agency is truly responsible for defending the health of our technology. Like a weapons system or nuclear power, technology can be an enabler and a destroyer, but technology's destructive potential has not yet been fully seen."

"Will it be more like *Live Free or Die Hard*, when the fiend shuts off the power switch to our existence?" Rona asked.

Jack continued, "So you're an old movie addict, too." Jack leaned in closer, "The doomsday clock is ticking close to midnight and we are moving nearer to a technological holocaust."

"Come on, Jack, aren't you exaggerating? There are checks and balances."

"Are there?" Jack shook his head. "Not like you might think. Intertwined IT systems have boosted our living standards but also threaten us the most. That which generates the greatest benefit also creates the most risk. We are precariously close to leaping too far ahead and landing on something akin to what's depicted in the *Planet of the Apes*."

"You remind me of that movie with Dustin Hoffman and the virus," Rona said.

"You mean *Outbreak*?" Jack said.

"Yeah. Not a great movie, in my opinion," Rona said.

"But a great example. What I'm talking about is similar. Until the past few years, we never had the technology vectors to transmit the virus, but now in the wired and Wi-Fi world, we do."

"Are you talking about computer viruses?"

"Not necessarily. I am talking about a magnification of a problem like you are having at PNP. If PNP fails to connect to Broadway, what happens? The ecosystem self-corrects. Within a few weeks, Pots Unlimited takes up the extra volume and Big-

Box has pots and pans to sell its customers. Demand shifts from one supplier to the next and no harm is done to the economy. The supply chain lives."

"I don't like that outcome, but I guess I agree."

"The real challenge comes when you have inadequately designed technologies combined with catastrophic events. 9/11 was a clear example. It was a crazy, frantic situation. The firefighters couldn't connect with the cops and 343 firefighters died because they never heard the evacuation order. That was unacceptable."

"Were you near there that day?"

"I was and the only way I could communicate was via email. My phones all failed, but hey, who cares? I was fine. It was the guys in the line of fire who needed to communicate."

Rona nodded.

"The risk is bigger than people want to realize. Think about the availability of gas after Katrina. I was stranded for three days in Atlanta before gas was delivered. Or how about when Enron fell apart?"

"I think Enron blew up because no one really understood what it did until it was too late," Rona said.

"Exactly. Now suppose Enron's trading partners were as badly off as Enron was during the last hours of its meltdown. When Enron stopped paying its bills, its suppliers may not have been able to pay their suppliers. At that point you would have a chain reaction that would gravely damage the economy. You would have the China syndrome."

"You mean a core meltdown that travels through the earth all the way to China?"

"Good guess, but that's not what I meant. The China syndrome will be when we suffer a catastrophic technology outage and China moves past us to become the world's new superpower."

"Come on, Jack, that can't happen so easily."

"Can't it? No country is more dependent upon technology than we are. Suppose our Social Security system shuts down, people don't get checks and they can't buy food?"

Rona nodded.

Jack continued, "Technology has lengthened our supply lines. If those supply lines are cut, it is harder to jerry-rig a solution. Did you see *Soylent Green* with Charlton Heston and Edward G. Robinson?" Jack asked.

"Yeah, that's the movie when the world runs out of food and they turn people's corpses into crackers."

"That's it. No one likes to think about it, but we need to better protect ourselves against a massive technology cataclysm. Say Avian Flu breaks out and PNP is the only supplier of the medicine. The Flu spreads on the airplanes, and like the plague in old England, the vectors are so ubiquitous that the spread is nearly instantaneous."

Rona nodded solemnly.

"Suppose PNP's systems have been cyber-attacked and you couldn't ship the medicine. Thousands would die every day. People would hoard resources. they'd run on the banks. It would get ugly. Panic would mushroom into chaos. What would that do to the world markets, given the instancy of information today?"

"It would spread fear like the plague, I guess."

"Exactly. And while the Internet may be self-correcting, people are not. Don't be seduced into thinking that our way of life is backed up somewhere and ready to be restored following a catastrophe."

"So what do we do?"

"Technology needs to help prevent or recover from catastrophes rather than create or accelerate their impacts. The bottom line is that we can't tangle our technologies beyond the point where they can be untangled. The same design controls, methods, and techniques that PNP needs for its IT project are similar to those that we need to leverage on a much grander scale."

"Reminds me of the financial crisis in 2008," Rona remarked.

"That was a great example of how interlocking systems can bring down a worldwide core system," Jack said.

"A computer system?" Rona said.

"No, I'm talking about the banking system. Do you think that the big credit rating agencies understood and cautiously stewarded the health of our interlocking financial system?" Jack said.

"Probably not."

"They should have. Responsible people and good companies can't be apathetic. Apathy can choke the human condition faster than a noose. In a technology driven world, we all have to be aware of our obligations. If Broadway's lights go out, we'll all be scrambling to hide under the boardwalk," Jack exclaimed.

"Okay, Jack. That's enough," Rona said, smiling.

Jack looked up, surprised. *I am on a roll,* he thought.

Rona stood up. "I'm going to the ladies room."

Rona opened the door to the ladies room at Le Maxwell. She stared in the mirror. *Wow, she thought, this techno-goober is interesting. He's kinda' shrimpy, but I like his energy. I'll go with it for now,* she decided.

Jack wondered whether his rap was working as he absentmindedly fingered the still-sensitive donor roots at the back of his head. Rona returned, her red lipstick glistening and her brown hair shining.

"So what about you?" she said. "Ever been married?"

"What's to tell? Like you, I'm trying to find my place."

Rona listened carefully.

Jack continued, "I never have been married, but I've been close a couple of times."

"Okay."

"After 9/11, I adopted a different attitude toward life. Now I feel at peace. I still set big goals but I'm more focused on the shorter achievable steps. It's terrible to worry about what you can't control. As we say in the world of technology implementation, life has too many independent variables. If you try to control all of them you're guaranteed to control none."

Rona pursed her lips slightly. She took an unopened gum packet from her purse, held it for a moment, and then put it back.

At this moment, Jack realized that he should no longer compliment Rona or go out of his way to be overly polite. He could tell that Rona was interested and he decided to back off and let her take the lead. Like selling, he knew that the more anxious he appeared, the weaker his position. Rona was establishing herself as the buyer. Jack tried to determine his BATNA, or his Best Alternative To a Negotiated Agreement with Rona. This was one of the more useful concepts he had learned at Princeton. Jack realized his BATNA was another in-room adult movie, a poor alternative.

Dinner came and was excellent. They laughed heartily throughout the veal and shrimp. When the check arrived, Rona made the perfunctory grab for her wallet and then Jack, unable to think through the calculation quickly enough, seized the moment and said, "Allow me."

"Thank you, you're too kind." Rona said.

How many women have I seen feign that wallet fumble on a first date? Where do they learn that scam? She had no intention of paying.

Jack stood up first and pulled out Rona's chair. They left the restaurant. Rona was moving purposefully toward her car. *Maybe I miscalculated,* Jack thought.

Twenty feet before she reached her car, Rona turned around, "Jack, I have to say good night now – I have to run that errand I mentioned before. I had a great time, though."

Jack didn't flinch and didn't break his smile. He reached forward and kissed her gently on the lips. He leaned away for a moment and then Jack went in for a second kiss. Rona pursed her lips again and opened her mouth, making room for Jack's tongue. After several memorable seconds, she moved away, smiled, and softly said good night.

Does anyone really check those hotel invoices? Jack wondered.

PART II – THE SEVEN KEYS TO ESCAPING DELETE

KEY 1: PROJECT – COMPLETE SMALL, SHORT-TERM, HIGH VALUE PROJECTS

WEDNESDAY, JULY 13TH 7:10 AM

The hotel phone rang. Jack sat up in bed and smiled smugly, expecting Rona was calling to thank him for last night's dinner. Instead, it was Gertrude, Biff's assistant.

"Good morning, Mr. Bluto. Mr. Harper would like to meet with you in his office at 9:00 this morning. Plan to spend the day with us."

"Thanks, I'll see you then," Jack responded cheerfully. He was excited about helping PNP. As with any Reality Check, he knew that there would be those who would try to thwart his efforts. It would be a tough couple of weeks, but Jack had been through this many times and was prepared for the challenge.

Jack met with his associates that morning for breakfast at the BigEight. Marcus had brought Jack an extra suitcase of his clothes that he kept in the lobby of Reality Check's Greene Street office.

By the time Jack arrived at PNP, Biff had been in his office for four hours, fielding calls from Asian suppliers and European customers.

WEDNESDAY, JULY 13TH 9:00 AM

Biff motioned for Jack to sit down at the conference table in Biff's office. "Okay, Jack, let's make this happen. We need this scattered band marching to the beat of one drum. I'm that drum and you are going to direct me. What is our first step?"

"You just took it," Jack responded. "By making this your number one priority, you pumped up the urgency level of this project in the eyes of your people. You know what they say about leaders – they just lead. It makes my job easier."

"Good. Let's go."

"The second step of the Reality Check is to measure the results of this project to date. Do you remember your high school physics or calculus?" Jack asked.

"Somewhat. I actually enjoyed them."

"Great. It's helpful to think about a project in terms of position, displacement, velocity, acceleration, and time. We know what our desired ending position is. In order to figure out how to get there, we have to know our current position. Let's talk to the Broadway project administrator, the one who updates the project plans and timetables. This will enable us to get a fix on our current position, and then we can determine the displacement, or how far we've traveled since the starting position. Since we know the desired finishing position, and we're constrained by a specific timetable, we can calculate the velocity—the number of units of progress per time period required to get to the finish line. If the required velocity is greater than the average velocity since the beginning of the project then we know that we have to accelerate our pace by adding additional resources, improve the efficiency of our current resources, or move the finish line closer by reducing scope."

"Okay, I think that makes sense," Biff said. "How does the calculus fit in?"

"Calculus gives us equations that explain the interrelationships among position, displacement, velocity, acceleration, and time. Projects can be thought of as complex functions of time. The optimal function produces the most displacement per unit of time. This is what we are looking to achieve," Jack said.

Paradigm Paralysis

"This whole argument about project physics sounds plausible, doesn't it?" Jack continued, after a pause.

"Yes," Biff said.

"Well, it's a bunch of unadulterated consulting bullcrap."

Biff squirmed uncomfortably as Jack continued, "What I said makes sense academically, but not practically. Managers are easily seduced by nifty paradigms. Sometimes this stuff is interesting, but it tends to confound while appearing profound. Six Sigma, ERP, and CRM are all temptresses targeting your corporate soul. There are more than a few Tokyo Rose terminology salespeople out there looking to draw you in to the dark side."

Biff smiled, amused. *Jack is full of himself, but he knows what he's talking about.*

Jack continued, "Organizations fail when these paradigms become the ends instead of the means. The ends should be the same goals that merchants in the marketplace sought a thousand years ago: better customer service, lower costs, higher quality, and more reliable delivery. Unless these goals dominate the project environment, the team gets torpedoed by paradigm paralysis, a nasty cousin of analysis paralysis. Your customers care very little about your paradigms."

"But the world has changed so—" Biff said.

"Has it?" Jack replied, cutting him off. "I disagree. Technology has compressed transaction times, optimized transportation routings, and greatly increased service expectations, but weigh these against the extra time it takes to make the additional decisions we're now presented with."

"What do you mean?"

"Now rather than picking the apple growing outside your cave for your dinner, you have a supermarket of options for your every meal, and it takes time and energy to choose."

"Okay," Biff said.

"Remember when you had five channels on TV to choose from? Now you have five hundred. Is the experience better than it used to be?"

"No, but what's your point?"

"You need to automate for value, not technologize for technology's sake. Once you opt for the latter, you lose touch with what your customers care about."

"Which is what?"

"Getting what they want efficiently and easily, and these so-called paradigm-shift projects tend to retard your ability to deliver that."

"Why?"

"Because you never finish anything," Jack said.

50/50 Properties Of The Law Of 98/2

Biff thought for a moment then responded, "What you are saying sounds intuitive, but how about the statements that a project manager always seems to make as a project is approaching its deadline? He tells you that the project is 98% done. Well, I've been around the block once or twice and I know that the last 2% of the project consumes 50% of its resources. At 98%, I'm only half done!"

Jack laughed heartily, "Absolutely right! Splendid! Remember George Bush on the USS Abraham Lincoln in 2003?"

"You mean when he stood in front of the Mission Accomplished banner?" Biff asked.

"Exactly."

Biff nodded, "That's relevant. Rona talks about that all the time. Ask her and she'll pull your ear off about how she hates war," Biff paused. "Two of our employees lost their sons over there in the Iraq War."

"I'm terribly sorry, but that's exactly my point," Jack said somberly. "Executing a successful military campaign is like properly managing a complex technology implementation."

"What do you mean?" Biff asked.

"Projects, like people, behave non-linearly and must be managed accordingly. Traditional analysis methods are useful but if we rely on them too closely, we will manage ourselves into an abyss. As a project increases in scope, its nonlinearity increases geometrically. PNP's project is a great example. You might think that once we talk to the project administrators, we should be able to develop a roadmap to guide us out of the abyss. I doubt it. We should talk to them, and we will apply project physics to better understand our status and direct our resources, but that won't get us to the Promised Land."

Biff nodded. He was beginning to understand.

"And, if you don't know where you're going anymore, or why a project is being done, it's a good time to think about canceling it."

"Believe me, Jack, I wish it were an option," Biff said, taking a pink pill from a bottle without a label and downing it with a gulp of cafeteria coffee.

See The Critical Path

"Biff, I'm ready to meet with key members of the project team, but let me share some other concepts first," Jack said.

"Go."

"You have a large project underway to connect your systems and processes to Big-Box. This is a big job, and big jobs come in way late and over budget."

"I thought they don't come in at all."

"Right," Jack grinned. "Many fail totally. I challenge you to tell me what percentage of the Broadway project is actually complete. Stanley is using a visually magnificent and expensive piece of project management software to report on and supposedly guide the project's progress. At best, it produces colorful graphs that show you how late you are."

Biff took an ivory colored pill from his drawer. This one was larger than the other. Jack paused, wondering what it was. Biff absently rolled the pill between his left thumb and forefinger, and listened.

Jack continued, "Imagine driving from Chicago to San Francisco. There is a shortest route from here to there. The farther the destination, the easier it is to get lost along the journey. My guess is that PNP is way off the critical path. You may be in Miami and not realize it. That's why you need a qualified but impartial party like Reality Check to tell you exactly where you are. Neither your consultants nor your technology vendors have the incentive to tell you the truth, assuming that they can even get a fix on your position."

"We need Waze to determine the shortest path to our goal," Biff said.

"And to highlight that path on a map," Jack said, smiling. He enjoyed their interplay, the seasoned crime fighter and the corporate doer. "You're a good client. You don't try to rattle me with management prattle."

"What do you mean?" Biff asked.

"Forget it," Jack said.

Beware: The Fully Integrated Enterprise

"But Jack, let's go back to your trip. Are shortcuts possible?"

"Large systems projects are like large weight loss goals," Jack said.

"Another analogy?" Biff responded.

"Sorry," Jack smiled, "I'm playing the game I know."

"Okay, go on."

"Do weight loss goals ever work? What happens? When people start a diet, they set stretch goals. They may start strong, cut back on fattening foods, and even begin exercising. They see results in a week or two and they feel good. It's easy to stay focused on a diet when the scale is reading lower, just like it's easy to invest when markets are going up. Yet, why do 90% of all diets fail? It's the same reason that so many investors lose big money in bad times."

"Why?"

"Because people fall prey to scary information. It weakens, disheartens, and disables them. We fear losing more than we are emboldened by the prospect of winning. The dieter sees the scale stop going down and it may even go up. The investor sees his stock dip and feels weak. What do most people do? They lose their resolve. The dieter gives in to temptation and the investor sells out in a down market. Their goals are postponed for another day."

"Keep going."

"IT projects fail for similar reasons. Organizations set overreaching goals. Projects kick-off with excitement and fanfare. Then, a gully forms in the project, splitting the work into the activities that are going well and those that aren't. The latter eventually sabotages the project because the team focuses on the former."

Biff nodded.

"People focus on what they can control, not what merits their attention. As in the diet and the falling market examples, the parties responsible for reigning in failure often do the opposite and exacerbate the problems. They attend to project tasks that are clearer and easier to define, instead of staying the course on the most challenging and confusing issues. This allows the losing, failing components of the project to invade deeper and deeper, eventually sabotaging the entire effort. Everything slips off the critical path."

"I've seen that," said Biff.

"Once slipping retrogrades to spiraling, you're out of control and free-falling into the IT Black Hole. After that point, you may experience an interesting peculiarity about the way people approach deadlines. When a deadline nears, people often bear down and work harder. Trouble is, the game is usually over by the time they discover and start attacking the real problems."

"How do we deal with it?" Biff asked.

"By setting realistic goals," Jack answered. "Actually, there are two options. The bad option is to dynamite the dam on the project budget and throw massive resources toward the biblical objective of a fully integrated enterprise. Frankly, I hate the notion of the technology-powered, integrated enterprise that the big consulting and software vendors tout. Enterprise and technology should never be used in the same sentence. Companies that strive for such lofty goals rarely achieve them; instead, they spend like crazy in search of a myth."

"Is there a better way?"

"Use Little-Triangles," Jack said.

Little-Triangles

"Little-Triangles?"

"Broadway has too many moving parts preventing you from focusing your analytical microscope. The thicket of problems is too dense."

"And those problems are all interrelated?" Biff asked.

"Yes, and therein lies their complexity, but there is a core, underlying issue at the heart of the other problems, and that is the sheer massiveness of what you, Stanley and PNP have undertaken."

"Go on," Biff urged.

"Ungainly scope creates incredible confusion when you're trying to isolate problems. Most companies suffer from scope creep on large projects. Your scope isn't creeping. It has run amuck. Remember the golden triangle of cost, quality, and time? The triangle is only useful when you have total clarity on what you are trying to accomplish, in other words, the scope or quality. Stanley is so focused on building a massive integrated systems plant to power every point of light in the company…"

"The thousand points of light?" Biff cut in ruefully.

"Yes. Grand plans fail, unless you have either unlimited resources or the only foggiest sense of what you're trying to achieve." Jack said.

"Why? Because at some point you'll stop and declare what you have at that point is what you sought in the first place?" Biff said.

"Exactly. Only military dictators have the unlimited resources and the authority to represent a pitiful failure as a marvelous success. Mortals like us have don't have that luxury."

"Is that another reference to Iraq?" Biff inquired.

"No, it's not. Although to an organization like PNP, your technology undertaking can seem like winning an unwinnable war or completely building a Pharaoh-era pyramid. You're better off breaking a project down to Little-Triangles or bite-sized chunks. Break the big pyramid into little pyramids. Your team can solve problems one at a time, and in rapid succession."

"Okay," Biff responded.

"Think of a pizza pie composed of eight slices, or eight Little-Triangles. It's much harder to eat a whole pizza without cutting it. When you eat a slice at a time, it's the same amount of pizza, but it's much easier to handle."

Jack walked over to the whiteboard in Biff's office. The board was full of next year's budget numbers from PNP's last executive meeting.

"May I show you what I mean?" Jack said, picking up an eraser.

Biff nodded. "Those budget numbers aren't realistic anyway. They're last year's numbers that the sales guys increased by fifteen percent. Last year's budget was fifteen percent more than the group put down a year before," Biff noted with a sigh.

Jack laughed. "Seen that before."

"Anyway, go ahead and erase the numbers."

Jack erased a large swath in the middle of the board and drew two large equilateral triangles. He subdivided the second triangle into nine smaller equilateral triangles.

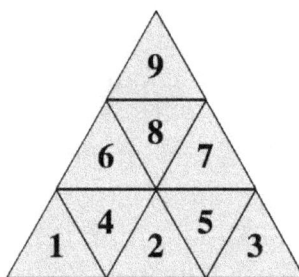

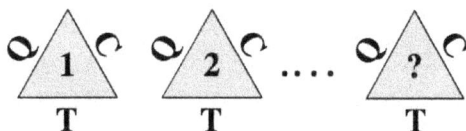

He labeled the legs on the big triangle Cost, Quality, and Time.

"Quality is the same as scope, right?" Biff asked.

"Yes, both assume a certain accomplishment to be achieved—consuming a whole pizza, for example, or bringing a new system online. Also, I use the term Cost instead of Resources because Resources consume Cost."

"Okay," Biff nodded.

"Biff, this is PNP's project right now." Jack pointed to the first large triangle. "It's been going on for eighteen months and is still not done and since no one can accurately tell me what has been accomplished so far, it's impossible to estimate when you will be complete and how much effort will be required."

"Tell me about it," Biff said, frowning.

Jack numbered the smaller triangles one through nine. "Each Little-Triangle represents a little project, with its own budget, scope, and timeline. You may do more than one of these projects simultaneously, but only if you have the bandwidth. When properly scoped, these little projects should require no more than sixty to ninety days to complete."

"Suppose one project depends upon another?" Biff asked.

"Dependencies are inevitable, and that further increases the value of the Little-Triangles approach. By cleaving apart the large triangle you can better see the dependencies. Of course, a traditional approach is to have milestones with major deliverables at set completion dates, but the trouble is that executives tend to be more tolerant of missed milestones than missed projects."

"Okay," Biff said. "I buy that."

"Also, deadlines focus attention and Little-Triangles prevents long stretches of activity without accountability. Another huge advantage of Little-Triangles is that let's say you decide to do the nine little projects in sequential order. Well, by the end of the fifth or sixth little project, your customers may change their requirements, or there may be new competition, or newer, more relevant technology. You may want to recast the seventh triangle completely in order to be more responsive to changing market conditions."

"So we could see when we've mis-guessed a triangle or scoped out the wrong project at the wrong time."

"Exactly, Biff. With Little-Triangles, misplaced assumptions come to light more quickly."

"And to use your language, that can save us cost and time by cutting out scope that we don't need anyway."

"You got it, man. Eat the pizza one slice at a time. You'll eat less that way. By cleaving apart the massive triangle, it's easier to identify and attack risk."

Biff nodded, "So where do I start?"

"Separate the requirements into 'must-haves' and 'nice-to-haves.' The requirements your customers can't live without are the ones your team must focus on first," Jack said.

"Talk to our customers? On a technology project?" Biff asked incredulously.

"Yes! Why companies consider this a novel concept, I'll never understand. The longer you wait for their input, the greater the risk of mis-guessing, to use your expression."

"It seems so obvious when you say it that way."

"People generally know what to do, but they struggle to summon the appropriate wisdom at the right time. It's the same with technology projects. Each individual on the team gets so intense about his or her problem that the sense of teamwork is lost. The angst starts to steamroll into a mass of instability. Ever watch a propeller when one of its blades breaks off? First it vibrates, and then it shakes violently before it flies out of control and self-destructs, and it usually takes the airplane it's attached to down with it. Isn't it amazing that with all of our management science and remarkable technology, the average project is still over budget or over time by a factor of three?"

"Astounding," said Biff.

Jack nodded. "The beauty of Little-Triangles is that when you break apart the big one and refine the cost, quality, and time of the little ones, and you add them all back into the reconstituted big triangle, it will be leaner, make more sense, be cheaper, and take less time to complete the original hulk."

"Ah, so the whole will be less than the sum of its parts?"

"Exactly. And the reconstituted one will be a heckuva lot less risky...."

Strive For Clarity And Forget Multi-Tasking

"All right, doctor, how do we get out of the thick rough, then?" Biff said.

"We have to find the ball and sight the hole we're aiming at," Jack responded, wondering if Biff ever played with Stanley on a vendor-sponsored golf junket.

"Can you be more specific?" Biff said.

"Clarity of direction drives greater productivity and energy. Clarity is also a great antidote to confusion-borne lethargy," Jack said.

Biff was trying to make sense of Jack's comments when Biff's office phone rang. "Yes, Gert? Okay, I'll tell him," he said, into the phone.

"Jack, Annie and Marcus are waiting in the lobby."

"Thanks, I've already filled their schedules today."

"You don't need to see them?" Biff asked Jack, putting down the receiver.

"Not now."

"Who are they meeting?"

"Your CFO and his direct reports," Jack responded.

"Why?"

"To quantify the money you've spent so far and evaluate whether you're likely to receive a return on that investment."

"I'm not optimistic about what they'll find out."

"They'll also meet with the IT staff to review the project plans, risk management documents, and other project tracking tools."

Biff paused. "Let's move on," he said.

"Okay. We can get out of the rough by focusing on the areas of the project that appear to be the most broken. If any of these areas falls outside the scope of what we're trying to do with Big-Box, then it's off the critical path and it should be postponed or eliminated. The areas that are on the critical path must be broken down into little projects that can be managed sequentially."

"Do we have enough time to attack the little projects sequentially?"

"To move effectively you have to single-task," said Jack.

"As opposed to multi-task?"

"Exactly. Multi-tasking is a fallacy. Hold two thoughts simultaneously in your mind for ten seconds. You can't do it. Your attention inevitably jumps back and forth between the two. When you try harder to hold both thoughts, your stress level rises. This happens on projects. If you're lucky, your attention will switch between only those two thoughts, but you'll probably find that your mind wanders away."

"Okay."

"The simple rule is that the more tasks you try to focus on simultaneously, the greater the likelihood of total failure. Effective leaders aren't multi-taskers; rather, they are rapid-fire single-taskers who get things done quickly in sequence. Save parallel processing for computers, not for people and not for projects. Seek small tasks with clear deliverables and recognize that rapidity and linearity imbue a team's members with momentum, energy and clarity."

"You're saying it's better to do one thing right and right now than do a lot of things wrong."

Fail-First

"Right on, Biff. Separate your activities into Little-Triangles, and then use Fail-First on your most challenging triangles."

"Fail-First?"

"Yes, it's a radical but effective approach. Set unrealistic time-frames for those triangles. Why? When you overload the project team, they will be forced to focus solely on the critical issues and avoid the two hour status meetings that everyone else spends two hours preparing for that have no impact on a project's outcome. In the meetings that I plan on attending later today, the team will focus on what they think are the key issues. In reality, they will likely spend the most time on the least important issues, the ones that are easily identified and framed. People naturally shy away from a lack of clarity despite the fact that those unclear and difficult-to-see issues are the ones destroying the project."

"Jack, that's true. We spent two hours discussing the paint schemes for the lobby and about twenty minutes discussing Broadway at last week's executive staff meeting."

"Why?"

"Because Broadway seemed so hopeless. We tabled the Broadway issues because we agreed that they would get fixed by the technology team."

"That's it in a nutshell. You can't do that any longer. People ignore the ticking time bomb because it's easy to focus on what's easy. Hey, it's easier to read *People Magazine* than to muster the concentration to get through *The Economist*."

Biff nodded.

"As executive sponsor, you must make sure the team is tackling the thorniest issues."

"Okay."

"Biff, let's summarize. Use Little-Triangles to break the massive project into little projects. Understand the objectives, risks, and resource requirements for each little project. Remember, the mega-critical path is the sum of the micro-critical paths."

"Why not just say that the whole is the sum of its parts?" Biff asked.

"Because then I couldn't charge the big bucks."

"Wrong, when you're clear, you can charge more. I pay for results, not bullshit," Biff countered firmly, but with a smile.

"I stand corrected," Jack said seriously. "Once you have each triangle identified, you sort them by risk. Do Fail-First on the project that you rate the riskiest."

"Okay, I got it so far."

"By setting a Fail-First project to last a maximum of thirty days, the team will be able to pick up the pieces and complete that triangle in sixty to ninety days the next time."

Biff nodded. "Okay, Jack. By turning up the heat on the team to complete the little projects in highly constrained timeframes, the PNP folks will see where the problems are and quickly move up the learning curve. Then we'll back off a bit, modify each of the remaining small triangles separately, and then apply the right resources. Then we'll add the small triangles together and we should be pleased with the results."

"You got it!" said Jack.

Be Lean & Stay Fit

"This reminds me of Lean, or Lean Manufacturing. We use these principles throughout our operations," Biff said.

"Is that so?" Jack asked, without giving away his dubiousness. Jack knew that Lean referred to the principles of running operations with a minimal amount of inventory, capacity, capital, and people. Jack continued, "Lean pushes an operation to run smoothly; without a lot of fat around, everyone stays more focused on the critical path."

"We ought to apply the same principles to our projects. In other words, use lean thinking to scope, to staff, and to execute our technology projects."

"Right on, Biff," Jack said. "Lean projects are rapid and goal-focused. They're not about computerizing everything. It's equally important to take a Lean Data perspective."

"What's that?"

"Trimming any data that you think is a nice-to-have and setting a high water mark for what you must have."

"But we have to capture and sort through a tremendous amount of data every day."

"That thinking is part of the problem. Too much techno-flotsam and data-jetsam is clogging up everyone's perspective. You're going to have to get rid of it in order to get fit."

"What do you mean?"

"All you need to know is what you need to know to make better decisions."

"But users are constantly proposing changes or new reports that they claim are must-haves."

"Biff, that's part of the problem. You still haven't locked down scope and you're deep into implementation. Can you imagine how much money you would spend on building a house if every day you gave in to another need, another preference, or another requirement?"

"You mean another whim, don't you, Jack? I always hear the same sob story about how a proposed change has life or death implications."

"Require each team member to submit a credit card number when he joins the project team." Jack said.

"Why?" Biff replied.

"Because we'll tell them that we'll charge $200 every time they request a change after the design freeze."

"Then no one will respond."

"Not true, because you'll also offer a $2000 credit to whomever proposes an idea after the freeze that's accepted and results in a positive outcome. Only the most confident people will risk their money to get the big payoff."

"So you're telling them to put their money where their mouths are?"

"Yes, and to share the risk. If you treat people like they're capable, they'll usually act more capably."

"Will that us get on track?"

"It's a start, but it only helps once we understand where you've veered off course."

"How do we do that?"

"Biff, there are three types of errors that you obscure when you are running fat."

"Three types?"

<CONTROL>, <ALT>, And <DELETE> Errors

"Yes. What does the expression <CONTROL><ALT>-<DELETE> mean to you?" Jack asked.

"Are you kidding? I feel like my life is about to be <CONTROL><ALT><DELETE>'d if we don't get this project back on track."

"Ha, don't worry. We'll get there."

"We'd better. I'd like to boot what we have into the trash and reboot with fewer and clearer objectives, a shorter timeframe, tighter cost controls, and a more focused team."

"Great answer, but let's understand how you got here. CONTROL errors occur when you lose control on the time and/or cost dimensions relative to the scope you are completing. You're moving inefficiently, but in the right direction. Your triangles have outgrown your ability to manage them. This is dangerous because once they present themselves, CONTROL errors grow rapidly. Maybe your monthly budget was X and now you are spending 2X on the way to 5X?"

"We're experiencing this now. We're at 3X."

"That's too bad," Jack began, "especially since you may not be getting closer to completing your scope objectives. My sense is that your errors are more ALT than CONTROL. In other words, you're on a path toward alternate goals that are wrong for PNP."

"Like if we're building scope that we don't need?" Biff asked.

"Yes, when you spend time, money, and attention building technical capabilities that your customers don't care about, it's a bridge to an alternate reality."

"A bridge to nowhere?"

Jack nodded.

"So a CONTROL error tells me that I might be aiming toward the right goal, but not making good progress at getting there?" Biff said.

"Yes."

"And an ALT error tells me that I'm going in the wrong direction. In other words, I'm aiming toward the wrong target."

"Exactly," Jack nodded again.

"What about DELETEs?" Biff said.

"DELETEs are the ultimate errors. DELETEs typically result from a toxic buildup of CONTROLs and ALTs. DELETEs cause your organization or business unit to be deleted from existence," Jack explained.

"Like Lehman Brothers during the crash of 2008?" Biff asked.

"Correct, if you apply this way of thinking to their investment portfolios. Lehman deleted itself by assuming massive risks that its decision makers didn't understand. Its triangles grew so large that their managers couldn't move nimbly enough to pull in the sails when the perfect storm began raging in the housing and credit markets."

"What can we learn from their failure?"

"Don't undertake risks when you don't understand potential outcomes. Keep your triangles small. Whenever an organization attempts to re-computerize much of its business simultaneously, DELETE errors are an ever-present risk."

"Jack, theoretically I see what you're saying, but in the real world it's not always possible to measure risk when you're confronted with a decision."

"True, and sometimes you need to send a hundred thousand men into battle on a single day, but your chances of a successful outcome are greatly increased when you can slice up an ungainly pile of risk into discrete, analyzable pieces."

"I guess it's easier to do that when you've fought other battles before and have the experience to make wisdom-based decisions."

"Exactly," Jack said. "The more wisdom you employ, the less likely you'll make a DELETE error and lose the war. That's why you have to correct CONTROL and ALT errors before they become DELETEs."

"So how do we get out of the Black Hole?"

"By mastering the seven keys to escaping DELETE that the keyboard inventor unwisely left out: Project, Customer, Team, Technology, User, Value and Change. They will keep you out of the Black Hole."

Biff nodded.

"As we talk more about Project, you'll see that ALT errors have to be resolved first, because it doesn't make sense to focus on efficiency if you're going in the wrong direction."

Biff pushed his chair back from the conference table. He stretched his arms out and then cracked his knuckles. He looked up at Jack.

"My wife has a Mac," he said wistfully. "I hear they never need to be rebooted."

"Biff, never trust what you hear on TV. Macs have their own reboot sequence!"

"Jack, you keep telling me about all the things that I'm doing wrong. How do we do this right?"

"You gotta Get High!"

"What?" Biff exclaimed.

Jack stood up as Biff motioned for Jack to erase the list of prospective lobby paint colors.

Get High!

Jack drew five stair-stepped boxes on the board, and labeled them. "There are five components of a technology project, corresponding to these five boxes," Jack began. He then added lines and labels to the drawing.

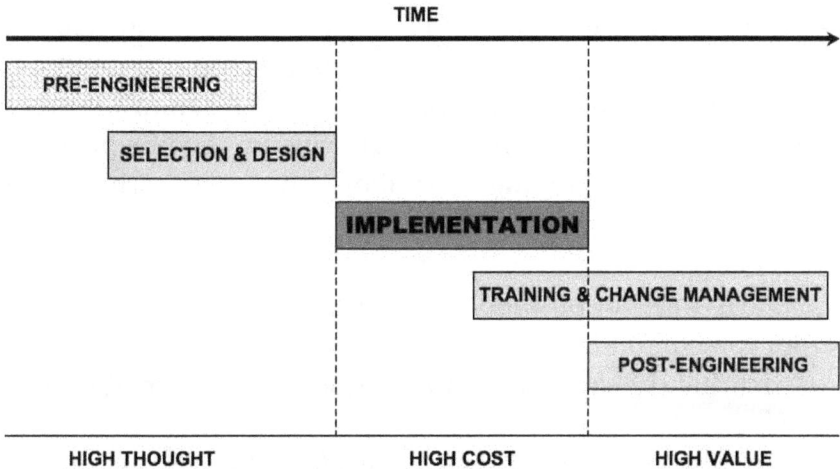

TIME

PRE-ENGINEERING		
SELECTION & DESIGN		
	IMPLEMENTATION	
		TRAINING & CHANGE MANAGEMENT
		POST-ENGINEERING

| HIGH THOUGHT | HIGH COST | HIGH VALUE |

He stepped back from the whiteboard, "Biff, this is a basic technology implementation model. Your consultants probably touted more complex models. Get High! focuses on the technology as a provider of long-term value, versus a consumer of cost. There are three main phases to a project like PNP's: High Thought, High Cost, and High Value."

Biff nodded.

"The right way to leverage technology," Jack started, "is to invest heavily in up-front thinking. When an organization needs a new capability, a team is formed and its members develop a set of requirements. These requirements are used as a shopping list during technology selection. There may be technology already out there that could save you time and money."

"Like ThickWare? I don't feel I saved either time or money."

"Trust me, you have. You don't want to build one of these things from scratch."

"Okay, go on."

"Once the software is selected, the business and technical people produce a design or blueprints for how the new system will operate. These specify what the system will do and how it will look and feel. Many organizations invest an enormous amount of time designing a system without having thought through how that system is supposed to support the organization's business strategy. In other words, they start drawing up the blueprints for the house without thinking more about what neighborhood they want that house to be in."

"What is Pre-Engineering?" Biff asked.

"Clarifying your business objectives and simplifying processes before you computerize."

"Isn't that the same as the Re-Engineering that Pro-Con peddles?"

"No, Re-Engineering uses a clean sheet of paper and encourages a holistic look at everything. It's good in theory but incredibly expensive and time-consuming in practice. Pre-Engineering is all about trimming the fat from what you've already got. It's quicker and much less expensive."

Biff nodded, "Like an integrated steel mill versus a mini mill?"

"I guess, interesting analogy."

"What's the next step?" Biff asked.

"Once the blueprints are complete and the resources are ready, it's time to build. This is the most costly phase because it includes not only the hardware and software costs, but also the people's time needed to make it work."

"I thought the major portion of our costs were the software license fees we paid to ThickWare."

"How much did you pay?"

Biff told him.

"OOOwwwch!" Jack exclaimed dramatically. "I bet you paid more than Big-Box paid for the same technology, and they're a hundred times your size."

"What do you mean?" Biff responded angrily. "Stanley said that we got 70% off the list price."

"Biff, that's like believing you are getting 70% off the gold jewelry price in the mall because the sign says so. Trust me, the salesman from ThickWare who closed PNP is riding with his top down right now somewhere in Cabo."

"Come on, Jack. I feel lousy enough already. Keep going."

"Like building a house, the big money is lost to the change orders. This is why it's critical to Pre-Engineer up front. A leaner Pre-Engineered project minimizes your ALT errors and will get through High Cost quickly. You want a brief High Cost phase because that's where your CONTROL errors eat away at the financial value of your investment.

"Then we experience High Value?"

"Right on, that's where the harvest occurs."

Biff nodded.

"Again, when High Thought is thorough, High Cost is shorter, because you don't spend money until your itinerary is clear," Jack added.

"And then?"

"Then Post-Engineering leverages your new technology platform to deploy new solutions to your changing needs. Like decorating the house and updating the décor as styles change. If the house has good bones, it'll serve as a solid base through generations of styles, like a good technology will adapt to changing requirements."

"Seems idealistic."

"It doesn't have to be. Most companies are so exhausted after finishing the build; they wind up moving their best people off the project team moments before entering High Value. It's akin to spending two years searching for buried treasure and then not opening up the strongbox to take the gold."

"So how do we decorate the house, if not all at once?"

"One room at a time, and don't you dare make your selections without having your wife with you," Jack said with a smile.

Biff didn't respond.

Jack continued, "Look at it in terms of planting years versus harvesting years. A planting year is High Cost and must be paid for with many years of High Value harvest. In most businesses, there are no government subsidies for bad harvests. This ain't like farming corn."

"No, it's not," said Biff.

"The sooner you get out of High Cost and into High Value, the sooner your team's hard work in High Thought pays off. Sometimes you need to push the boat out of dry dock while the cabins are still being painted."

"But how do we deal with new requirements?"

"You may need to modify or upgrade the technology as the world changes, but you can often reuse the Pre-Engineering work you did years ago and grow the new technology from that. Or, you may acquire another company and reuse most of the implementation work you completed in High Cost to integrate the new company into your operations."

Biff nodded.

"Post-Engineering, or continually re-purposing, adapting, and modernizing a well thought-out technology can go on for years, even with a rapidly changing technological landscape."

"Okay."

"If you properly structure your company's information in High Thought, you'll be able to leverage the data in a myriad of ways to adapt to customer changes," Jack responded.

"Can you tell if this was done correctly here?"

"I can't yet, but that's one of the areas we're going to dig into. Surprisingly, an organization's data tends to be stable over time.

For example, you've probably captured customer name, contact info, and order history the same way for years."

"True."

"The way you analyze that data and the decisions that you make based on those analyses change more rapidly. You've heard Big-Box mention their need for Analytics. Once you connect to Broadway they'll analyze data in new ways that you haven't thought of."

"Makes sense but we seem so far away."

"Let's stay with it. We are making headway already."

"I'm sorry Jack, but I have to stop here," Biff said, pausing. "I'm already late for an appointment. Please come back at 11:00. Gertrude has arranged a plant tour for you."

"Great. Thanks," Jack replied.

"Your tour starts in the Frying Pan Room," Biff said.

"The what?" Jack asked.

Biff laughed. "When I became CEO I renamed our conference rooms after our product lines. We also have the Dutch Oven, the Double Broiler, and the Cookie Sheet."

"I see," Jack responded cautiously.

"Jack, you're late too," Biff said, gesturing Jack toward the door.

KEY 2: CUSTOMER – DELIVER A TRANSCENDENTAL EXPERIENCE TO YOUR CUSTOMERS

WEDNESDAY, JULY 13TH 11:00 AM

Jack re-entered Biff's office after the plant tour, hoping Biff would be late. He wasn't.

"Let's get started," said Biff. "You're going to meet with Horace Green. Horace is one of the two merchants we deal with at Big-Box. In our business we use the term 'Merchant' to describe the person who makes buying decisions for the retailer."

"So Horace is the face of Big-Box?"

"For PNP, yes he is. Lucky for us, Horace happens to be here today, doing a site visit. I won't join you because Horace may be more candid if I'm not there."

"When and where should I be?"

"He'll be here in a half hour," Biff said, motioning toward the conference table in his office. "In the meantime, why don't you clue me in on how we can leverage this huge technology investment to get closer to our customers."

"Good," replied Jack. "Customers have come to expect what I call a 'Transcendental Experience', which is an integrated experience that transcends the technology used to deliver that experience."

"Okay. Go on."

"Technology is rarely an end-all other than for geeks like me. Technology's value is in what it can empower, accelerate, or improve the quality of."

"I see that, but be specific. Let's put it in terms of customer commitment," said Biff.

"Good," said Jack. "Commitment to the customer varies by industry. Your service expectations differ when you lunch at the Ritz-Carlton versus when you apply for relief at the welfare office."

"I may be doing that if we don't get this right, so let's get it right."

"A Transcendental Experience makes you feel wholly valued and completely attended to in the business relationship."

"Like staying at the Ritz-Carlton?"

"Right. Although it may not be possible to always deliver the Transcendental Experience to all customers, it is an ideal worth striving for."

"I know when I don't see it," Biff said.

"Yes," Jack paused. "Say you call your credit card issuer from your home phone about a problem on your bill. An electronic voice response system reads your caller ID tag and then asks you to put in the last four digits of your social security number to verify your identity. You do that and you feel good so far. Then a live agent picks up the line and re-asks you for your card number, name, and address. You're a little ticked off, but you figure with all the identity theft they are trying to incorporate an extra measure of security."

"Happens to me all the time," Biff said.

"Then you ask a question about a three-month-old charge that posted to your recent bill. The customer service agent tells you that he can't handle that question and he transfers you to another agent that looks at previous charges. After a two-minute hold, an agent that speaks English very differently than you learned it picks up and asks you to repeat your card number and your address. Then you struggle to remain calm as you and the rep at the other end of world learn to understand each other. Then, the crowning moment, ten or fifteen minutes later, the rep reads off the card taped to his desk, "Thank you Mr. Harper, did I provide you with excellent service today and have your needs been completely met?"

"Now the curse words are coming to mind."

"Exactly, and you may vocalize your frustration as you hang up the phone after the rep asks you if you would like to participate in a brief, five minute survey to improve customer satisfaction."

"Okay, what can they do about this?" Biff asked.

"The bank processing your credit card could have shortened this experience considerably by having the technology to pass your information throughout their internal infrastructure without asking you to re-verify your identity. They should have enabled, with either the right tools or the right information, that first rep to solve the problem," Jack said.

"When you have a problem at the Ritz-Carlton, the first person you tell won't send you to another person who can solve it. That first person may seek out other resources, but generally stays with you as your advocate until the problem is solved," Biff observed.

"Right, why can't a bank do this? They should have shown more respect for your time by not wasting it with their cheesy survey invitation."

"And yet," said Biff, "they get away with it."

"Why do you think that is?"

"Because I have no choice. I could switch to another credit card and get the same experience. I have all three cards anyway," Biff said.

"Right, the issuer doesn't do a better job, because it doesn't have to. Where are you going to go? You can either accept the customer experience, or not use credit cards. Credit card companies, phone carriers, and cable TV providers are oligopolies. I doubt that they collude to purposefully provide bad service, but it seems that way."

"I guess as long as any of the players is not profoundly worse than the others, they can stay in the game. So where do I get the Transcendental Experience?" Biff asked.

"From an organization that needs to provide it in order to keep you shopping. Up the quality ladder from credit card companies, at least a little, are the airlines, mid-market hotel chains, and car rental agencies. They do more to keep your business. How did JetBlue grow from four planes to more than two hundred?"

"How?"

"They offered an integrated customer experience that was nearly transcendental. Their website, phone reservations system, and check-in processes worked together to provide an easy-to-buy, easy-to-travel experience."

"The TVs in your seats didn't hurt."

"Exactly."

"But these are all business to consumer, or B2C, businesses."

"Yes, but the same principles apply for B2B. Even though the buying entity is an organization, you are dealing with people and you need to make their experiences productive and pleasant. These principles apply to the IRS when dealing with taxpayers, a hospital dealing with its patients, or a drive-through restaurant dealing with its customers," Jack said.

"So non-chain restaurants have the greatest burden of providing the Transcendental Experience, because a hungry customer has so many alternatives?" Biff asked.

"Depending on the geography, I agree. When options abound and customers perceive low switching costs, a provider's service burden is high. Now that technology contributes to or intrudes upon practically every life experience, offering your customers close to a Transcendental Experience is a competitive differentiator."

"This is good counsel."

"It's like dating. It's a free market and singles that provide or appear to provide a transcendental-like experience are the most sought after."

"Okay, Jack, enough."

Biff looked across the room. Horace was standing in the doorway. Jack looked up and noticed that Horace was dressed more like a person who sells than one who buys. Horace's golden tie gleamed against his crisp, sky-blue spread collar shirt, set against a well-tailored navy pinstripe suit. His shoes were fine leather, and freshly polished. *This guy is the real deal.*

✶ ✶ ✶

"I hear you're a person who gets technology," Horace began, speaking to Jack as Biff left the office. "I'll get right to the heart of the matter. Four years ago, our business picked up and we were coming apart at the seams. We realized that we had to greatly simplify the way we operated to avoid blowing up."

"I read a story about the founders. They are a couple of super-peddlers, aren't they?"

"Yes, so we hired a guy from General Linoleum who was a process improvement expert."

"Lars something?"

"Yes, Lars Lanugo. He changed everything. Now, four years later, we have four thousand stores and we have standard processes and rigidly adhere to them. Our company is well managed and our processes exemplify this."

"I like shopping in the stores," Jack said. "Did Lars start the 'Big-Box for Your Little Box' ad campaign?"

"Yeah, his ad agency came up with it. Now we sell everything for your home, from gas grilles to garbage cans, and from stereos to sinks," Horace said.

"You guys are the super category killer," Jack replied.

"Our customers think pink," Horace responded, referring to the bold pink signs adorning every Big-Box store.

"Me too," Jack said.

"Now, with three million employees, our company is bigger than half the countries on earth," Horace boasted proudly.

Jack nodded.

"One of our edicts involves electronic ordering," continued Horace. "We no longer phone or fax purchase orders to our suppliers' sales offices or manufacturing facilities. Instead, we send a daily electronic order to each of our suppliers' main offices. The order is based on demand patterns in our stores, inventory levels, available floor space, time of year, weather forecasts, and our vendors' stated manufacturing lead times."

"Weather?" Jack interrupted.

"Sure, we sell more stock pots on cold winter days than any other time of the year. Our customers love their chili."

Jack nodded.

"To enable our suppliers to better manage their own production environments, we give them longer lead-times to deliver their goods. We want our suppliers to be profitable in their dealings with us because it enhances their stability and ours. Payment is triggered when a shipment from a supplier is received complete. There are no payments for partials, so our suppliers are motivated to get their shipments to us on time, every time. We have a system of chargebacks in place to penalize lateness. As a company, we decided to eliminate controllable variability. We accept the burden of ordering earlier by trading away the variability of receiving late," Horace said.

"Wow, Horace, that's brilliant," Jack observed. "To grow big, you have to think big and act big."

Horace continued, "We bought ThickWare three years ago to replace our hodgepodge of older software that was lashed together through a maze of home-built interfaces. We made sure that ThickWare supported all major protocols and standards. Frankly, we were unwilling to devote a lot of time and energy to match any unusual requirements from our suppliers because it would have slowed down our implementation. We felt that it was appropriate to pass the responsibility of modernizing along to suppliers. In most cases this has worked very well. Our suppliers that run ThickWare can connect their systems directly to ours. Suppliers that don't have ThickWare connect to us via our Broadway interface."

"But PNP is implementing ThickWare, so why can't PNP connect directly to your systems without going through Broadway?"

"Ah, that's the stickler. Your client is using Version 3.5 and we've standardized on Version 2.4."

"I thought the versions were compatible," Jack said.

Horace clenched his jaw and shook his head. "We made clear to our suppliers when we started this project that we were standardizing on 2.4. Our support team is trained on 2.4 and we have no plans to go to 3.5. Stanley claims that ThickWare assured him that the versions would be compatible. I don't know whether that conversation took place, but the versions don't work together today, so that's why PNP is having to build its own interface to Broadway."

"So if PNP had implemented 2.4 they would be able to hook up to you in a day, rather than a year?"

"Exactly. PNP started late on its Broadway project and that's why we are struggling to hold our business relationship together. Ninety-five percent of our suppliers are already connected to us."

"How did you guys pull this off so successfully?" Jack asked.

"I know this is your game, but I think most technology projects fail because the people who build the systems often have no contact with the organization's real customers. Projects are too often run by the IT departments and the IT team members spend all their time speaking to internal people."

Jack nodded.

"Internal people have an excellent sense of yesterday. You could build a system around yesterday's order patterns, but that doesn't seem wise. The only people who know what tomorrow's business looks like are the customers planning future orders. They are the people for whom the system should be built," Horace stated.

"What about when you build a technology to connect to your suppliers?"

"The same holds true for our suppliers. If we build a system that enables us to do a better job purchasing, we involve our suppliers."

Jack nodded. "Horace, I am so glad that you said this. The notion of an internal customer is so overplayed. Do you know how to tell who the real customer is?" Jack said.

"How?" Horace asked.

"He's the one who writes the check!" Jack said.

"Exactly," Horace agreed, nodding his head approvingly.

Eliminate The Oxymorons

"In fact," Jack began, "The internal customer is the classic, clarity-clouding oxymoron. So many of Reality Check's clients started out by allowing their manufacturing, accounting, or human resources people to dictate the look and feel of their new systems. When the technology vendors and the consultants interview internal people to spec out a system, the new system will inevitably look and feel like the system being replaced."

Horace nodded.

Jack continued, "Say Delores in cost accounting is used to checking her daily manufacturing reports. Her job is to make sure that the raw material inventory is reduced properly. Delores has been doing this job for twenty years. The consultants interviewing her will come away with a clear look at the old ways of doing things; a blueprint of yesterday."

"Sure," Horace said.

"The devil here is that when you make a new system look like an old system, you greatly impair the potential benefits that are available in the new system that weren't possible with yesterday's technology," Jack noted.

"Right, Jack. By configuring the new system to give Delores the data the way she wants, the consultants may make it more difficult for a new potential customer to see PNP's inventory and pricing," Horace said.

"You've traded away potential benefits that the company could be getting by synchronizing with its business partners in return for the comfort of an internal person."

"Jack," Horace began and then paused. "How big of a problem is this?"

"This may the biggest unrecognized challenge in technology projects. The consultants don't talk about the problem because they love it. It's a cash cow for them."

"So the consultants are diluting the potency of the new system that they are being paid to design and implement?"

"Definitely," Jack said. "The consultants conduct design sessions with all the Delores's in the organization and then speculate for hours about customer needs, rather than asking the real customers. Empowering customer representatives to sit in on your design sessions is an enormous improvement over speculating in the dark. These customers will be your users. Your internal people matter, but they have to adapt to the dynamics of the marketplace and must not be held back by their distaste for change."

"So design is everything?" Horace asked.

"More or less," Jack replied. "But remember, we're speaking about the design of the business processes and the customer experiences."

"But, Jack," Horace cut in, "technical constraints and limitations are inevitable."

"Technology is so robust today," Jack said. "It's rarely the limiting factor in providing that integrated, technology-transcending experience. If you can dream it, you can build it."

Focus On The Business Details, Not On The Technical Details

"Agreed. At our last PNP product line review, I mentioned to Biff that it's wrong to expect business to be the domain of technologists. Instead, technology must become the domain of business people," Horace said.

"Ha! You should come work with me. You're better at this than I am."

"Well, the customer is always right, isn't he," Horace smiled. "It sounds counterintuitive, but business is more varied and complex than technology. Business is the true black box and technology is the energy that allows the mystery machinery inside the box to operate. Some technologists would counter that a million details need to be understood when implementing a system. That's why implementations fail so often. Too much energy is paid to arbitrary technical details and not enough to critical business details."

Rona entered Biff's office and said hello. She met Jack's eyes and with a simple nod she indicated that any energy they both felt from Le Maxwell was to remain outside the office. He understood and accepted her terms with a return nod.

She smiled nervously at Horace. "What are you guys talking about?" she asked.

"Horace was describing how Big-Box does systems," Jack said.

"Makes a lot of sense, doesn't it?" Rona noted. "Now you can see why they have four thousand stores."

"Yes," Jack said, staring for a moment at Rona's yellow skirt and ivory blouse. *Wow, this woman never looks bad,* he said to himself. Jack turned back to Horace. "Was there anything else?"

"Businesspeople turn responsibility over to the technology people way too early in a project. A progressive businessperson needs to understand the features and benefits of the key available technologies in the space and remain involved throughout the build," Horace stated.

"Isn't that too much to ask from a harried, overworked business professional?" Rona countered.

"Not at all," Jack interjected, trying to catch Rona's eyes. "A little knowledge at the right time can go a long way toward improving a business. The real issue is convincing the technophobic executive that she has to learn the new language of business."

Excite Your Customers

"The other reason to speak to customers about their requirements is to get them excited about the project. You want them bought in from day one," Horace said.

"You're preaching to the choir, Horace!" Rona exclaimed.

"It's easy to sell salespeople on this way of thinking. Maybe technology staffers avoid seeking out the customers' input because they generally shy away from any contact in which selling is involved. They're more comfortable buying," Horace said.

"That's been my experience," Jack agreed.

"I don't know if Lars Lanugo has time to visit, but Biff needs to invite him to see what's going on here at PNP. He may not like all of your approaches, but the emotional and political points you will win would help to smooth over any technical rifts that occur when you connect to Broadway," Horace said.

"Good idea," Rona nodded.

"Unless PNP involves Lars, you ought to think about how much money you're spending on this project. The money could be better spent by giving us rebates on our next six months of orders from you guys. That would get Lars excited," Horace said.

"I'm not ready to give up yet," Rona replied.

"Well, getting those backorders shipped to us ASAP would help," Horace countered.

Rona looked down at her feet. "We're trying, Horace. We've got six months' worth of 8s and 10s in the warehouse but all our 12s were shipped out mistakenly and we can't get them back quickly enough. The production guys are running three shifts to build your 12s so we can send you the completed Bridgehampton frying pan sets."

Horace looked at Rona and paused. "Stanley and PNP used our Broadway deadline as an impetus to sell your decision makers on doing a complete systems overhaul," he said, turning to Jack. "Your clients bit off more than they could chew, and now they're choking. I doubt that PNP is on track to go-live by the deadline." Turning back toward Rona, Horace continued, "I don't want to posture, but Pots Unlimited is standing by to supply the extra volume to us. They don't have PNP's brand name, but we need pots on our shelves in order to ring our registers. We also have to complete our media buying and advertising program by early January and we can't be in a situation where one of our important suppliers can't ship products advertised in our circulars."

"Of course. We don't want that either. Horace, how can PNP do better?" Rona asked.

"You need to walk in lock step with your customers. This opus of four implementation projects that you're navigating doesn't help us. It creates unneeded risk and we're not excited by it. I hope, for your sake, that it at least helps address requirements or opportunities with your other customers and suppliers."

"Don't count on it," said Rona. "I feel like Stanley is totally in the dark and I hope we're not screwing up all of our customer relationships."

Tirelessly Measure Satisfaction

Horace continued, "Our guys don't have a clear sense about what is going on with Stanley's projects. We don't need to be involved in every decision, but we want to be consulted on decisions that affect us. We want to know that the risks that we take as a result of your technology investments will benefit us."

Jack looked at Rona. She was leaning in, listening intently.

"How should we do this?" Rona asked.

"By tirelessly measuring customer satisfaction. You need to ask us how you're doing in our eyes for two reasons. First, it makes us feel involved and shows us you care about your commitment to supplying our business. Second, it gives us a chance to keep you informed of our changing requirements. And don't worry about asking too often. If we have nothing to say, we won't be put off by your inquiries."

Rona nodded.

"PNP and Big-Box should work together and develop metrics for measuring the performance of the relationship," Jack added. "That would enable Big-Box to maintain a report card on PNP, and well managed businesses always seem to like numbers."

"I like that," Horace said.

"Horace," Rona responded. "I'll commit to that. I'll put together a survey and send it to the key players on your team that are impacted by PNP's project."

"Great. I can't guarantee that everyone will respond, but I bet you'll get a few surprise answers from certain people who feel left out of the process."

"Like who?" Rona asked.

"You'll find out, Rona," Horace said with a sparkling smile. "We need ambassadors facilitating the exchange of both information and hopeful feelings. These projects are opportunities to create transactional intimacy."

Rona recoiled upon hearing the word intimacy. "But we wouldn't want Pots Unlimited to see what we're doing. We need walls somewhere," she protested.

"Yes, Rona, I understand, but realize that we buy from PNP because you make the best products. From our perspective, we want to track your information in the same way that we track information from Pots Unlimited. Standardizing like this helps everyone. If we try to manage your information differently from theirs, our efficiencies break down."

"But that doesn't address our privacy," Rona pointed out.

"Rona, a portion of your privacy comes through contracts and processes that are formally implemented. We already have agreements that require each of us not to disclose the other's data. Beyond that, there's an element of trust that we must rely upon – it's part of that transactional intimacy."

"Interesting that with the tremendous pace of technology advancement, the need for trust hasn't declined," Jack observed.

"That's correct. Look, we have to work together. Show me a trustless environment that functions effectively and then I'll believe that the paperless office actually exists!" Horace said energetically.

Rona and Jack both smiled.

Horace continued, "Please keep us more involved and up-to-date, and test the heck out of our technology connections prior to roll-out. We had hoped that PNP would've asked us to participate in your recent business continuity planning project, but that hasn't happened yet. Also, our Broadway Project Leader mentioned to me that Stanley is not returning his phone calls."

"I'm sorry Horace," Rona said. "I'll see to it right away. There's no excuse for that."

Be Resilient Or Be Replaced

"Our people want to help Stanley and his team so that your system is as resilient as possible. This is incredibly important to us, and I'm not talking only about technology. I'm talking about the whole delivery model."

"What do you mean?" Rona asked.

"Don't think we've forgiven you guys for Katrina," Horace said.

Rona grimaced.

"What happened?" Jack inquired.

Rona answered first. "A few years ago, we participated in several continuity planning sessions with Big-Box in order to ensure that business would be able to recover from an unforeseen event like a hurricane or a flood, or even a terrorist attack."

Horace added, "That's right. Big-Box hired consultants and they conducted working sessions between Big-Box and our major suppliers. We brainstormed about all that could go wrong and then determined the potential business impact of each undesirable event. We then worked together to figure out how to minimize the disruption to our customers if an event occurred."

"Seems like good forethought," Jack said.

"That's right. PNP agreed to maintain a warehouse space with twenty days of inventory in the southeast, I think outside of Atlanta, so that inventory could be trucked wherever we needed it in case of an event or emergency."

"I was in those meetings," Rona said quietly.

"Well, Katrina happened and our stores in the decimated areas needed cookware so the besieged survivors could cook their food on emergency propane stoves. Our business continuity guys called your inventory people and apparently that inventory never got built. There was no warehouse with the emergency inventory. I guess you felt like the probability of an event was so low that you thought you could avoid following through on your commitment," Horace said, turning both palms up and widening his eyes.

"It was an embarrassing and unforgivable mistake," said Rona, jumping in. "Katrina's victims couldn't eat hot food because we screwed up."

"Yes," Horace said, turning to Jack. "Biff apologized profusely, but at some level an apology is not enough. Big-Box is part of our economy and we have a social responsibility to deliver to our customers when they need us most."

"It's like a power company. You don't want excuses, you just want them to get the power back on," Jack said.

"Horace, on my word, Big-Box will have the inventory if that happens again. Biff has already taken care of it," Rona added.

"We've grown too big to have downtime," Horace said. "Maybe that's a bad thing…"

"Larger organizations need redundancy," Jack began, adding, "The level depends on the organization. It's much more important for a hospital to recover power in its operating room than for a ChumpRoast not to lose a single customer's coffee order."

Rona and Horace nodded in agreement.

"Expect a future government agency to enforce strict policies with respect to recovering from power failures, weather catastrophes, and terrorist events," Jack said.

"Security has become part of our life experience," Rona lamented. "Our company has to be as resilient as Air Force One."

"Maybe next time Harrison Ford won't crash it into the ocean," Jack responded.

Secure Time, Data, And Availability

Horace's expression remained solemn. "At Big-Box, security has become more important to us," he said.

"What's your company's philosophy on this?" Jack asked.

"Like everything else we do, we try to find the right balance of protection and cost. We have one uniformed guard in each of our stores at all times."

"Only one?" Rona asked.

"Yes, our Finance and Loss Control departments estimated that having a second guard wouldn't pay for itself in terms of reduced pilferage."

"And when three masked men come into a store to steal the cash?" Jack asked.

"That's when we wish we had ten guards. We apply business continuity principles to security. It leaves holes in our ability to address all possible events and their contingencies, but I don't know any better way to do it."

"How do you apply these principles to securing technology?" Jack inquired.

"We apply the 80/20 rule when possible," Horace answered.

"Meaning what?" Jack asked.

"We think that a few inexpensive simple practices provide us the most value. We use firewalls, file backups, encryption on our websites, and anti-virus software. We also monitor our employees' use of the Internet and restrict certain sites, although our people have very little time to play on the Internet. Of course, everything is password protected," he explained.

"Horace, all this sounds generic," Jack said.

"It is, but realize that we are as focused on securing employee time as we are on securing information. I'm amazed that so many organizations today provide open Internet usage under the guise of productivity. I challenge you to give me one compelling example of an employee needing to use the public Internet during work hours."

"That seems severe," Rona commented.

"Is it? Why? We give our employees the time to do their jobs properly, to be patient with our customers, and to go the extra mile. Our people don't need extra distractions. We pay our people more than any other major retail chain so that when our employees leave work, they can buy any technology toy they want."

"Makes sense," Rona said.

"We also secure data and focus on providing the highest level of availability."

"How does Big-Box manage this?" Jack asked.

"By using the best practices that have already proven effective at other companies. We're not looking to be innovators. We also ensure the integrity of our backups by regularly testing our restore process. I am amazed at the number of businesses that don't do this."

Jack nodded.

"Also, passwords are renewed at frequent but irregular intervals, and we don't accept weak passwords."

"What happens when you're hacked?"

"When security breaks down, we have a crisis response team armed with a plan ready to address the intrusion. If your technology guys," Horace turned to Rona and continued, "read our plan, then you would know what we both have to do when a breach occurs."

Rona looked down, embarrassed.

"Sorry Rona, it's nothing personal, but bear in mind that when a customer buys a defective pot on our website or in a store and sues us, there's a popcorn trail of information that gets pulled into court. Some of those kernels are yours, so it behooves PNP to do this right."

"As technology becomes more enmeshed with everything we do, security will become a greater concern at all levels, from the enterprise all the way down to the user," Jack said.

"That's right, and potential liabilities skyrocket," Horace replied.

"Sounds like Rona got snared into something that she had no control over," Jack commented.

"That's true," Horace said reassuringly. "Any time Rona can go to bat for us, she will."

Move On From Failure Or Languish In Court

"What's the penalty for not doing this right?" Rona asked.

"You end up in court. I have represented many a tech buyer who felt he was oversold by tech vendors and consulting firms," Jack said.

"I bet there's a lot of that going on," Horace added.

"There always is. When there's a gap in understanding regarding a technology contract, it's wider than in other disputes."

"Why is that?" Rona asked.

"Jack, may I take a stab at that?" Horace cut in.

"Sure," Jack replied.

"Because when technology and business people interact, they speak different languages. When I joined Big-Box, I saw a couple of costly legal battles we had with technology vendors. We lost one and won the other, but I don't think we won because we were in the right. We won because our lawyers did a better job."

"How so?" Rona asked.

"The salesman from the software company claimed we would reap massive benefits and we claimed that was the reason we did the deal. We should have never believed him in the first place," Horace said, pausing. "I hate going to court."

"I can't blame you," Rona replied.

"We then wasted three years standing still while our attorneys gathered every email, piece of paper, and press release. We won a few million dollars in the end, but wasted three years. We should have bitten the bullet, written the thing off, learned our lesson and moved on. The bottom line is that you need clear contracts with every one of your business partners."

"Horace, I appreciate your thoroughness. How do you know so much about technology?" Jack asked.

"I didn't start out that way. I began my career in retail but then took a job at a B2B Internet exchange. Boy, was I rich on wish money. I was about to retire in Milan with my wife Shelley when the exchange self-destructed." He continued, "I still have the Ferrari that I bought three days after my first options lockup expired, though," he said, winking at Jack.

"Cool! I want a ride!" Jack exclaimed. "It's hard to have sensible information flow at an organization unless information flows sensibly inside its people's heads."

"So true," Horace said. "I never planned to be a guru but these days business depends on information. I learned about the new world so I wouldn't get caught in the cemetery of the old one."

"I agree," Rona said. "We have to be on our toes, especially in a crappy economy. Too many debunked myths are lying in that cemetery."

"One myth was that modern technologies would somehow reduce the negative impact of normal economic cycles," Jack said.

"People say those things at the end of a boom when they don't see the crash around the corner," Horace added.

"Horace, dead on," Jack said. "Modern technology increases the heights of the peaks and the depths of the troughs because greed and fear are magnified and multiplied by the instancy and pervasiveness of electronic communications."

"Jack, that's a mouthful…we'll talk more when you're in the Ferrari," Horace responded, grinning.

Jack laughed. "Okay, back to business. Have you been involved in any other Big-Box major systems overhaul projects?" he asked.

"Yes, and I learned a lot about how to tackle big, long-term projects. Avoid them! We have a non-traditional approach to technology at Big-Box, and it has enabled us to achieve a sustainable competitive advantage. We don't have a typical IT organization. We don't have a CIO in the traditional sense, but information management is still perhaps our most important activity."

"Could you please explain that?" Jack requested.

"Key information flows from customers through us to our suppliers. Most other information is noisy and distracting. Each business unit such as kitchen supply, flooring, or electrical has a sales team, a production team, an information team, and a supply team. Centrally, we have a knowledge management unit and a technology infrastructure unit to gain efficiencies in purchasing and deploying technology," said Horace. "But our flooring and our kitchen supply businesses are very different."

"Of course, but you sell everything in one store," Rona challenged.

"Yes, and we use one point-of-sale and customer transaction processing system for our entire business, but we made sure that this system worked in each of our behind-the-scenes business units before we introduced it into our stores."

"When I buy at Big-Box, I barely notice the systems. Everything just works," Jack said.

"You know we use Radio Frequency ID or RFID tags on all our merchandise?" Horace asked.

"Sure, so customers don't even take items out of their carts," Jack said.

Horace nodded.

"But what about privacy?" Jack added.

"It's definitely an issue. We don't want our shoppers to feel uncomfortable. We researched this extensively and found that most people were fine with our methods. There were some vocal dissenters, and we respect their concerns, but determined that it was more economical in the long run to use the RFID tags."

"The erosion of our privacy is the price we pay for increased efficiency," Jack observed.

"I don't like the idea of cameras on traffic lights and Big Brother watching my Internet surfing," Rona countered.

"I generally agree, but in some cases too much privacy interferes with effectiveness," Jack responded.

"Like when?" Rona asked.

"When you call 911 the operator automatically knows the location you're calling from. You may not like their ability to track you, especially if you're witnessing a crime and are afraid of being brought into the justice system, but it helps the police to respond and save lives," Jack said.

"Hmm," Rona said.

"Especially if that caller is about to become a victim in that same crime and doesn't realize it yet," Horace added.

Jack nodded and said, "Horace, let's talk more about how you guys manage technology. What about the benefits that companies supposedly get by moving to a so-called shared services model?"

"Where you have one human resources department and one MIS department that provide services for your entire company?" Horace asked.

"Yes," Jack said.

"Like outsourcing, that concept seems to go in and out of fashion with every business cycle. At Big-Box, we don't believe in shared services. Our business units have different needs and sharing services is like painting all the rooms in your house the same color. Sure, it may seem cheaper because you can buy all the paint at once, but then no room is just right. We needed to tailor our business units to the needs of each market segment's customer."

"Makes sense to me," Jack responded. "Your customers care a lot less about your internal efficiencies than they do about feeling valued."

"So, Horace, how does Big-Box handle big technology decisions?" Rona prompted.

"The infrastructure department sets operating standards for all of our businesses but they don't have final say over the business units. Suppose a newfangled software package becomes available that would help kitchen supply. This package doesn't make sense for the other units. Should we avoid it because it can only help a portion of our customers? Of course not."

Jack nodded.

"So how did you decide on ThickWare? Doesn't it impact all your business units?" Rona asked.

"The heads of the business units got together and decided," Horace said.

"But how were they able to screen out phony salesman's claims from the real features and benefits without having the technology people involved?" Rona asked.

"Look, we pay our people well. Bob Stanley who runs Housewares made sure that he understood the technical implications and risks of what we were doing. One of his right hand people has a PhD in Technology. Bob made his decision independently of the group. Out of our twelve businesses, Bob and nine others opted for ThickWare. Lars helped persuade the other two."

"Persuade or push?" Jack prompted.

"Maybe it was a little of both, but I assure you that each business unit Vice President is thrilled now, based on last year's bonuses."

Jack and Rona nodded.

"I need to run," Horace said, standing up as he glanced at his smartphone. "Is there anything else?"

"Not now, but this has been extraordinarily interesting," said Jack.

"Horace, thank you so much. We won't let you down," Rona added.

"I know you won't," Horace said, looking at Rona.

The group broke up. Rona caught up with Horace to speak about a quality problem with PNP's non-stick skillets. Jack walked into the lobby in order to check his email on his smartphone.

Ten minutes later, he walked back to Biff's office. Gertrude was gone, but Biff looked up from his desk and motioned for Jack to join him at the conference table. Jack settled into the now-familiar chair across from Biff.

WEDNESDAY, JULY 13TH 12:10 PM

"Biff, I'm learning a lot."

"Good," Biff said, thinking about the thousands per day he was paying to school Jack. *It had better come back to us in spades.*

"Here is a key issue," Jack began. "Two types of business processes exist: those that give you a competitive advantage, and the perfunctory processes that support the first type. When implementing a major business system you must understand the difference between the two. If you devote your resources to the second type, then you're distracting yourself from the first. In many cases, the best types of supporting processes are out-of-the-box from the software companies."

"Can you give me an example?" Biff asked.

"Accounts payable. Do you really care how it's handled, so long as your vendors are getting paid and not complaining? Why spend time and money crafting your own process when the software companies have already figured it out by incorporating the best practices of many of their clients?"

"I'm not sure I understand," Biff responded.

"Why write your own newspaper for a million dollars when you can buy someone else's for a quarter? It's the same news. Take advantage of someone else's investment."

"Makes sense. Leverage other people's money and experiences," Biff said. He paused and added, "Tell me what you've concluded so far."

"You've done some things right," Jack began. "First, buying from a top-tier software provider gives you several advantages.

ThickWare has a lot to lose by having a failed customer implementation splashed all over the press. They want to help PNP get this project back on track. Even though your relationship with them is strained right now, recovery is possible. Second, by investing in ThickWare, you made a bold statement to your customers that PNP is committed to aggressive growth. Your customers, those big retailers, get excited when they see you invest millions in technology. They figure you know where consumer demand patterns are going. Third, you appear to have decent talent across the board on this project. Your team, plus the vendors' people and the consultants may have enough domain knowledge to pull this off."

"What do you think of Stanley?" Biff asked.

"I'm not certain yet," Jack responded.

"Really?"

"Yes. If I may be so bold, I think Stanley got so far off track because you didn't rein him in earlier. IT people are responsible for deploying cost-effective technologies that deliver value to the business people. On this project, the business people have been totally reactive, taking a hands-off approach and only getting involved to fight fires."

"I would like to get back to Stanley when we discuss staffing," Biff said.

"Okay," Jack agreed.

"Has Rona been helpful?"

Jack answered without breaking stride, "Rona has provided me with a perspective on how your customers think. We've spent a lot of time talking about Big-Box. It gets me back to the fourth positive point about the project. The business people are now very interested in making it successful, although their effectiveness is weakened by the project team's structure. This is fixable, if you're willing to make hard choices. The fifth and final point is that your largest customer is effectively sponsoring you. Big-Box wants you to be successful. Despite their bravado about dropping PNP after the first failed transaction, they don't want that to happen any more than you do. It would disrupt their brand, which is based on merchandising products from premiere manufacturers like PNP."

"Our relationship with Big-Box is at its lowest point since I started working at PNP."

"That's a major concern," Jack said.

"I'm tempted to spy on Pots Unlimited. Their relationship with Big-Box gets better as ours gets worse."

"Take PU seriously. Remember that old line about staying closer to your enemies than your friends."

"Agreed," said Biff. "Rona mentioned that you like to quote movie lines. I wonder what Pots Unlimited says to their customers about PNP."

"La Rochefoucald said that 'the opinions of our enemies come nearer to the truth about us than our own opinions,'" Jack said, rising confidently from his chair.

"Who?" Biff said.

"He was a seventeenth century French writer. He must have been a project manager at heart when he added, 'it is not enough to have great qualities, we should also have the management of them.'"

"So true," Biff responded, looking at pointedly at Jack. "Technology is worthless unless it works. Yutang said, 'when small men cast big shadows, the sun is about to set.'"

"Point taken, sorry for trying to show off," Jack said, sitting back down.

"Listen Jack, I'm worried about those same privacy issues that Rona is concerned about. How should we address these?"

Balance Carefully On The Privacy Tightrope

"Technology has become more and more pervasive or intrusive, depending on how you look at it," Jack said.

"Do you think Pots Unlimited could spy on us electronically? Are our customer records and product engineering drawings safe?" Biff asked.

"If they're determined enough, they will hack you, but it's probably tougher than you realize. I assume that your proprietary information is well secured behind firewalls. If it's not, then you do have something to worry about."

"All I can do is rely on what Stanley tells me."

"Hire an independent computer security firm to hack into your network. Then you'll know whether it's safe."

"Without telling IT?"

"Yes," Jack said.

"You think we're vulnerable?"

"Maybe, because the firewall between personal devices and corporate IT continues to erode."

"What do you mean?"

"People use their personal smartphones to send work emails and they send personal emails from their employer's computers. Security and privacy are becoming more challenging because wise policies have to reach beyond traditional corporate boundaries."

"We take privacy seriously. We have all employees sign a pledge that they will use their technology for business purposes."

"That's a good start. And I assume that you protect all employees' payroll and personal information, including social security numbers?"

"Again, we have software that does this, and I am assured by the technology group that it works properly, but how do I really know until we get sued by an employee who believes that his information has been compromised?"

"Consider testing for this as well. You don't want to run afoul of privacy laws."

"What about email?" Biff asked.

"Email is actually more private than you think, precisely for the reason that you think it isn't."

"How's that?" Biff said.

"When an email is sent, it's like yelling into an echo chamber. The reverberation goes on forever as dozens or hundreds of copies of that email are routed to servers throughout the world."

"So how does that increase privacy?"

"If you educate your users about the implications of this reverb effect, they'll probably be more judicious with their email usage. Specify in your employees' contracts that they'll be held responsible for sending confidential or inappropriate emails, and they'll pay more attention. Also, so many billions of emails are sent each week that picking nuggets of confidential information out of a mountain of chatter is both expensive and time-consuming."

"Okay, we'll update our policies and practices," Biff said.

"On the other hand, you wouldn't believe the stuff I see. You have to assume that the camera on your desktop is on at all times, even when the light is off. Big Brother is there and he's all around you. How do you know that your smartphone isn't being used as a listening device for Pots Unlimited?"

"Ridiculous. I have it with me at all times."

"So? Maybe they sent you malware that enables them to listen and you downloaded it last time you turned your smartphone."

"Come on, Jack," Biff replied. "That's silly."

"Don't be so certain."

"Okay, enough," Biff exclaimed, pushing back from his desk.

Jack stood up and turned toward the door. He considered asking Biff to have lunch, but figured Biff would initiate the offer.

"Lunch plans, Jack?"

"Not yet."

"Okay, just curious. I am going to stay here and catch up on my reading. DoubleWide's is right down the street from the mall.

Maybe they'll give you that Transcendental Experience that you crave."

Jack nodded his thanks and left, feeling less powerful than a few moments earlier.

Rubbing his stomach as he left the plant, he wondered if DoubleWide's wait staff would sing if Jack told them it was his birthday.

KEY 3: TEAM – USE THE RIGHT TEAM

Jack did Doublewide's quickly, and wolfed down two iceberg salads and two orders of fried biscuits with his chili. He fought to stay awake during the drive back to the office. *Damn, why do I always overeat at lunch? Why can't I remember before I eat how I'll feel afterwards?*

WEDNESDAY, JULY 13ᵀᴴ 2:00 PM

"Welcome back, Jack," Biff said. "Hope you had a good lunch. I've been thinking…how do I know that I have the right team on this project?"

"That's critical. The team is always more important than the technology, but you should answer your own question. Do the employees, consultants, vendors and customers on your team collaborate, compete, or commiserate with each other?"

"Each of the above. Most of our folks work well together, but there are a handful of back-stabbers and whiners in every crowd."

"That's typical," Jack said. "That's why you need a strong leader to keep the players on track."

Assign A Wartime General

"Who?" Biff asked.

"You!" Jack said, smiling broadly.

"I'm already on the team."

"I disagree. You're on the project steering committee, a meaningless distraction that has been kept asleep at the wheel by spurious progress reports. The project is going to crash unless you wake up."

"It's already crashed," said Biff.

"No, but it needs a wartime general to get everyone in line."

"A what?"

"Think wartime. When you amble along in peacetime it's a lot harder to maintain direction and momentum. There's no tiger chasing you with its mouth watering, so there are only weak penalties for not keeping up."

"Okay."

"You do your best work when there's a knife at your throat. A wartime general seeks quick and meaningful results. He'd rather bring twenty men into a short battle with a clear surgical objective than spend three months sending a thousand men up a hill to find out what's on the other side." Jack stood, shook off the Fog of Biscuits, and continued, "Never underestimate the hunger or aggression of your enemy. It's kill or be killed. Show results immediately and keep showing them. Yesterday's victories don't solve today's crises."

Biff listened intently as Jack continued. "In peacetime, when people have the freedom to dream unencumbered by the harsh deadlines of reality, large fantasy projects get pushed by those who are able to politic for the resources. Goals are grandiose and vague and no one's head is on the chopping block. In wartime, the clock is ticking. Objectives and deadlines quickly rise to the fore. Need breeds speed, to quote a crusty old general I met last year at the Army & Navy Club in DC."

"I see. So while the peacetime generals are pontificating on the nightly news, the wartime generals are the ones in the trenches, getting the job done," said Biff.

"Exactly," Jack replied. "A wartime general clarifies objectives and injects a project with the energy that either converts commiserators into collaborators or leaves them in the dust. He publicly crucifies the whiners. That keeps the rest of the team on its toes. There is no room for negativity when people are accomplishing challenging goals. The wartime general admits when he errs and this breeds a culture of acknowledging and addressing mistakes. When uncorrected errors linger because no one accepts blame, the cost and time to get back on track soar."

"Go on," Biff urged.

"Lead this project General Harper. Delegate your other responsibilities to your subordinates. Only you have the unquestioned respect of everyone in this company. You understand PNP's business better than anyone."

Biff nodded.

"The seer who first observed that the devil is in the details was prescient. Nothing could be truer. Recall Vilfredo's famous notion: Eighty percent of a project's activities takes twenty percent of its resources and twenty percent of the activities consumes eighty percent of the resources. When you get started, it's difficult to identify your project's troublesome twenty percent and lead the team toward attacking it. Weakly directed teams always start by tackling easy problems."

"Don't you mean Pareto?" Biff asked.

"His first name was Vilfredo. We're on a first name basis."

"Jack, I had hoped you were going to solve our problems."

"I can't. I can help, but you have to make it happen."

Biff nodded.

"You probably didn't want to hear that and if you would like, we can break off our engagement now and you owe me only for expenses incurred."

"No. I know you're here for the big payoff once we succeed. By the way, Jack, I think the expression was that god is in the details."

"Exactly. Thank you."

"It'll be difficult. We're in the middle of sales budgeting now. Also, I leave for China next month for our new plant's opening, plus I'm helping our manufacturing VP evaluate new production facilities stateside."

"You mean to handle extra anticipated volume."

"Yes."

"Not much point in building new factories if you can't ship from your existing ones," Jack observed.

"You're right," Biff said, rubbing his carved chin. "What about Stanley?" Biff added.

"Take the reins from Stanley."

"He won't cooperate."

"Make him the technical project manager but don't plan on him hanging around."

"Stanley checked out before he ever showed up," Biff lamented.

"Get him re-engaged," Jack urged. "Lead him toward the light of success and opportunity."

Fix Out Of Whack Compensation Systems

"Okay, Jack, enough preaching. The teamwork part I can handle. What are your other recommendations?"

"Should I start with the minor ones or the major ones?"

"The major ones. We need to attack the biggest problems first," Biff said.

"I'm glad you think so. The major problem that your presence will fix is this project's lack of leadership. You have good people on the team, but you need your best people. The natural leaders of the company must be signposts for a happy ending to this melodrama," Jack said.

"We can do that. Senior management, the shop folks, we're all committed."

"Commitment is the first ingredient for success. The second is clarity on where the ship ran aground."

"What do you mean?"

"Stanley's charts show the project shooting ahead like a straight arrow, but when I look more closely, I see a wandering ship, buffeted by different agendas and priorities. An IT guy running the show rarely captures the full attention of business people."

"I should have realized that," Biff said.

"Business people may sit through requirements interviews, go to training sessions, and even dig in with the consultants as they configure the software. But business people won't invest their full energies into a technology project the way they invest their passion and time into their normal jobs. Why? Because technology executives don't evaluate business people. The managers of those business people, who are rarely on the project teams themselves, see only the time their people contribute to a technology project, not how much value they add."

"So you are implying that even though we may have good people working on the project, we're not getting their best level of performance?"

"Correct. Business managers or executives rarely tie their people's compensation to the contributions those employees make on IT projects, so most organizations' incentives are out of whack with their objectives."

"That's the case at PNP. It's hard for us to motivate our business folks to get involved with any IT project. I thought they wanted to avoid Stanley."

"Stanley may be part of it," Jack replied. "Until companies incentivize strong IT contribution, we'll continue to see the 'A Player' business people do their darndest to avoid being sentenced to manning an oar in the IT galley. The A players will gravitate toward more interesting projects and the consultants will have the IT project for themselves. When that happens, failure is all but inevitable."

"How do we manage the twenty-seven consultants?" asked Biff. "They aren't being well directed."

"How effectively have they been performing?"

"How can I tell?" Biff asked.

Jack sighed and shook his head. "You don't know and that's a problem."

"That I know," Biff said, also sighing.

"Get to know the consultants. Some may share issues that you are unaware of. Your presence will show them that you're committed to the project's success and invested in their work. On your shop floor walks, you wouldn't chat with only the supervisors, you talk with the production workers. Use the same approach with your hired guns. Talk to the line level consultants, and you'll get a crisper sense of what's going on."

"I can do that."

"Now let's talk about the other people in what Steven Covey called your Circle of Influence, namely the team members from the IT vendors, the consulting suppliers, and, most importantly, from Big-Box. You need to enroll all of these people in your mission. ThickWare needs to be treated firmly, but give them a role in the fight for victory."

"How?"

"Offer a carrot. Let them know that if they solve these problems, you'll speak their praises."

"Okay."

"Maybe Big-Box can lend you talent, or at least wisdom, to help you tackle the ThickWare problems."

"Jack, I need to pull this team together. We need a small victory with Big-Box now, at least a field goal."

"Agreed. It doesn't matter what it is, as long as it's doable and enables your team to rebuild emotional unity and clarify shared goals."

"Jack, I like your style." Biff paused and waited until Jack's eyes locked on to his. "I'm not used to being spoken to so directly by a consultant."

"I'm glad you're willing to hear me out."

"What's next?"

"Projects rarely fail because of poor technology. IT project outcomes depend on the team members. Failure happens when people don't interact effectively with the technology and with each other."

"You're oversimplifying. We're having real technology challenges."

"Look, software may be buggy and hardware often fails to work out of the box. Most software and hardware companies address quality in the field and after the sale because of competitive pressures to release new versions and upgrades. Their business is not quality driven; it's cost and time driven. Technology vendors know that once you commit to a technology, switching costs can be incredibly high. That's why vendors invest more in selling than in quality."

"So true. I would love to throw ThickWare out of here now, but I can't."

"With respect to the human issues, most everybody wants to do a good job and see the project through to success. The thwarters or evildoers are usually easy to spot."

"And eliminate?" Biff prompted.

"Exactly. The people who operate on the margins of motivation and entropy are the ones you must win over. When the infantry gives you that extra effort, you have a greater chance of winning the war."

"Okay, okay," Biff responded. "You're an orator at heart, Jack, but it's time to move. Who would you like to meet next? Your timing is lucky because all of our senior executives are in town this week."

"Let's meet with your Director of Manufacturing," Jack suggested.

"That would be Dr. Meyer Steadman," Biff raised his voice, calling, "Gert, open Meyer's Outlook and book Jack at 7:45 tomorrow morning."

"Yes, Mr. Harper," Gertrude replied from outside Biff's office.

"Good thinking so far," Biff said. "Okay, Jack. Let me digest what I heard." Biff glanced at his watch. "I'm fifteen minutes late for a meeting," he added.

Jack had a feeling this wasn't true, but he remained silent.

"I'm tied up for the rest of the day," Biff said. "Maybe you can start working on your Reality Check Assessment Letter. I'll need to share it with Roscoe & Lauer to justify the changes we're making."

Jack nodded.

"I'll join you and Meyer tomorrow morning. No word of this to anyone else, please, not even to Rona."

Could Biff know about the kiss at Le Maxwell? Jack thought as he nodded, without meeting Biff's eyes.

WEDNESDAY, JULY 13TH 3:00 PM

Maybe I need to eighty-six this thing with Rona, Jack mused as he wandered toward the Dutch Oven for the CRM project status meeting. Customer Relationship Management was software that enabled a company's sales force to better understand, serve, and profit from its customers. From lead tracking to profitability analysis to call center management, this software was being put in place to automate PNP's customer-related business processes.

Jack arrived at the Dutch Oven. The thirty people present included Stanley, the CRM Project Leader, several PNP salespeople, and a dozen consultants. Three of PNP's most seasoned salespeople were designated as SuperUsers, acting as mentors to guide less experienced users. The Pro-Con consultants were working with the SuperUsers to understand PNP's business processes. Pro-Con would then configure CustHug accordingly. Pro-Con was also responsible for connecting CustHug to ThickWare.

Stanley began the meeting by sending a link to a summary of the project's progress vis-à-vis the timeline. Next, the CRM Project Leader, Mel Quitoast, stood up and read the CRM Open Issues List aloud. The shop floor people had nicknamed the Project Leaders the Brown Nosed Legion. Whenever a technology problem occurred in the plant, there was a cry of either "Lunchmeat" or "BNL."

At Stanley's request, Mel introduced Jack Bluto as a consultant helping with the Big-Box integration project. Hardly anyone looked in Jack's direction, probably because they assumed Jack was pinch-hitting for Manny. Manny was out on disability after injuring his hand while trying to dislodge a stuck Diabetic Cola can from the cafeteria's vending machine.

Stanley rose again, Mel sat down, and Stanley continued, "You can see from the timelines on our web-based project portal that CRM is on track."

Each consultant from Pro-Con and Bajupta was hunched over his PNP-supplied Fujohara tablet computer. Some were following the timeline discussion, some were on Facebook, others were sending emails, and one was Tweeting.

Stanley continued, "Our steady progress is due to the good work of the team, and I thank you for that. However, our continuing hardware problems are interfering with our ability to finish the configuration and test the system. Unless these are resolved by next Thursday, the timetable will slip."

Venkat Chadran, the lead consultant from Bajupta, raised his hand.

"Yes?" Stanley asked.

"Do we have an understanding of what the problems are?"

"We think so, and we're waiting to get a firmware patch from our hardware provider that will allow the new software to recognize the display boards that we're using in the call center."

"When is the patch expected?" Venkat asked.

"It will be here for damn sure by next Monday," Stanley replied firmly.

The meeting continued. There were fourteen items on the CRM Open Issues List when the meeting started. Five were resolved and nine new ones were added. Jack's eyes glazed over until Venkat raised his hand again and told the team that his second in command, Sandeep Mohawney, was leaving to take a job with a different consulting firm and would be replaced shortly with another qualified CRM expert from Bajupta.

"I don't need to know about consulting firm administrative matters," Stanley said, waving his hand. He grunted and adjourned the meeting.

Jack followed Venkat and touched his shoulder as they left the room. Venkat turned around. Jack introduced himself and they shook hands.

"Tell me about Sandeep's role," Jack requested.

Venkat explained that Sandeep had been the coordinator of PNP's SuperUsers for seven months. Sandeep had implemented the CustHug CRM software at four other companies. Venkat minimized Sandeep's critical connection to the project by explaining that Bajupta was Level 5 certified.

Jack thanked Venkat and they shook hands. *No need to argue with this guy*, Jack reasoned. *I may need his help later.*

Don't Send A Consultant To College

Bajupta defended itself by claiming that it had earned the highest level of professional software development certification and therefore its processes were virtually people-independent. *Hogwash*, Jack realized. *I know how costly Sandeep's loss is to the team.* Sandeep walked out the door with critical, expensively acquired knowledge paid for by PNP. Jack decided to use this example to explain his concerns to Biff:

Bajupta billed for Sandeep's time at $100 per hour. On his first day at PNP, Sandeep was worth more than $100 per hour, because he brought a wealth of information and wisdom to PNP that his previous clients had helped fund. Perhaps his initial value was actually $150 per hour. As the project progressed into the requirements gathering stage, Sandeep's value dropped to $70 per hour as he spent his time recording the input of PNP's employees. Why? Because this task could have been adequately performed by a less seasoned consultant, at a lower billing rate. From there, Sandeep's value rose steadily as the design or blueprint of the system was being developed in High Thought. During High Cost, his value increased enormously because he knew the software well and now understood PNP's culture and unique attributes. His accumulated knowledge may have been worth $1000 per hour. By not having him there any longer, the team would now spend dozens of man-hours solving problems that Sandeep could have solved in a few minutes, because Sandeep's experience enabled him to know where to fish to find solutions to problems that surely would confound his successors.

To replace Sandeep's work, Bajupta would have to provide ten new resources at $100 per hour or five senior level resources at $200 per hour. When a consulting firm switched resources, the client squandered its learning curve investment. Maintaining good documentation supported a transition, but it rarely indemnified the client for its loss.

Consulting firms buy their employees' training with their client's dimes. It's all On the Job Training, or OJT. When a new consultant starts a project, he often *works for several weeks before he understands the client's organization, its systems, and its processes. If that consultant bills at $150 per hour, it could cost $50,000 before he becomes productive. That's what the client would pay to send him to college for a year. If that consultant leaves before the job is done, replacing him becomes incredibly costly, both in terms of money and time. Staffing changes cause even the scantiest triangles to bulge, generating large CONTROL errors.*

Clients should require minimum engagement times with severe financial penalties if the consultant gets reassigned or leaves the project. The client has to put the burden of retention back to the consulting firm. The smartest clients (those who have been burned the most) always require free time from a replacement consultant. A battle hardened client incorporates 'Learning Curve Chargebacks' into every contract to ensure that when a consultant who has moved up the learning curve leaves, the client is indemnified for that wasted schooling.

WEDNESDAY, JULY 13TH 5:00 PM

Stanley leaned his head into the open door of the consultants' work area.

"Bolsnevik," Stanley called to one of the independent consultants. "Come here please."

Bolsnevik followed Stanley into the hallway.

"I'm sorry, Bolsnevik. I've got to let you and Anton go. The bean counters in management are telling me to cut back on the number of consulting firms we are using."

"But we're almost done writing the data conversion routines."

"Pro-Con will handle it. I'm sorry."

"But we're half the cost of Pro-Con, and they're going to have to start over," Bolsnevik protested. "I can cut the rate another twenty percent."

"I'm sorry. I think your firm has done excellent work here at PNP and I'm delighted to give you a strong recommendation."

"Maybe you can keep us on retainer, in case you experience more hiccups with the interface configurations?" Bolsnevik suggested.

"That doesn't make sense for us now, but I would like to keep up our relationship. What's your home address? My wife and I would like to have you stop by for the annual pool party that we host for our friends."

Bolsnevik squirmed while forcing a smile. His work visa had expired three months ago and he was working illegally. "Er, may I email my address to you? My wife and I will be moving shortly and I want to make sure the invitation doesn't get lost in the mail."

"My pleasure. Thank you again for that crystal doll set you brought for my wife." Stanley paused for a moment, and then continued confidently, "We'll make sure that PNP pays your bills right away."

WEDNESDAY, JULY 13TH 6:30 PM

Arriving at the BigEight, Jack stopped in the lounge and secured two plastic cups of Old Style beer as the hotel was closing its free happy hour. Spilling beer along the hallway, he made it to his room, ready to review his notes from the day.

He sat down and picked up the television remote. He depressed the channel up button. He held his finger there and scrolled through the channels. The instancy of the remote, like an Internet browser, wasn't good for Jack's attention span. He sat in a trance for six or seven minutes and then tossed the remote on the floor.

He texted Rona and invited her to call the hotel to say good night. An hour later, chomping on the last bite of a Chicken Cordon Bleu room service dinner that tasted like it came out of a can, Jack picked up the ringing phone.

"Hello."

"Hi Jack," replied Rona, in a cheery voice. "How was the status meeting? Sorry I missed it."

"I'm sure. Seriously, based on what I saw today, there are too many consultants at PNP. It's a surefire recipe for an expensive failure. PNP can't properly manage them. Do you know how were they chosen?"

"Who knows," Rona remarked.

"Companies think that they're buying certainty and results when they sign with a big name consulting firm. PNP didn't buy Pro-Con, it bought an assortment of consultants that happen to work at Pro-Con right now."

"What do you mean?" asked Rona.

"Do oranges that you buy at Kroger taste any different than ones you buy at Piggly Wiggly?"

"So consultants are like oranges?"

"No, they're like orange juice. Once you start drinking it, you don't care where the fruit came from."

"I don't understand," Rona said.

"Me neither," Jack laughed.

"Okay."

"Seriously, are PNP's consultants qualified? How many have been properly interviewed and vetted? When I see the offshore guys, I see massive projects with a lot of bodies. That is exactly what you don't need when you are focused on a deadline. The more moving parts, the more likely you'll have a train wreck."

"We are in a train wreck," Rona replied.

Beat The Consultants At Their Own Game

Jack continued, "Consultants can only do so much, because consultants serve multiple masters. They have their own companies to deal with. No consultant is free to focus solely on his client, unless he's a lone-ranger."

"I hate consultants," Rona declared. "Funny though, you don't seem like a leech. Not yet, anyway."

"Thanks, Rona, that's the best compliment I've had in a while."

Rona chuckled.

"Seriously, most consultants are dedicated," Jack continued. "Some have the potential to be great, but please understand the nature of the consultant/client relationship. Consultants are temps with fancy titles. For every queen bee that is a true thought leader, scores of drones are buzzing around."

"So why do we use them?"

"You have no choice. The consultants are presumed experts in the technology that you're implementing. PNP probably didn't have the spare people to staff the project or the time to train them. Also, once a project is completed, consultants go home."

"I don't think they're ever leaving."

"Rona, most consultants are as powerless on a large project as your employees are. You weren't with us earlier when Biff and I talked through why large IT projects fail. Yet, I have to tell you in the same breath that a select few companies do pull off massive projects with remarkable effectiveness."

"That's the kind of consultant double-talk that I'm used to," Rona said impatiently.

"Okay, you're right. I'm sorry."

"I found the article you wrote last year, 'Johnny Can't Read, But He Can Sure Consult.' I didn't realize that consultants love troubled, pre-bankrupt or even bankrupt companies because they get paid ahead of employees and suppliers."

"You found it on the Internet?"

"Yeah," Rona said.

"Consulting is a tough business. Many people have negative views of consultants. We're perceived as skeptically as lawyers are."

"It's justified," Rona said.

"No, it's not. Like with lawyers, a few well-publicized bad apples can spoil the reputation of the bunch."

"Okay, I buy that."

"Rona, let me tell you about a defining incident from early in my career, the first week after I became a consultant. It happened at a major oil client when I was working for Pro-Con. Warren Wiggins, the partner in charge of our consulting practice, took me to call on the Chief Financial Officer of our client. After Warren and I arrived at the CFO's office, we got down to business. The CFO was very distressed and told us, 'this accounts receivable project is incredibly important to our company. According to your people, the Hunkasys 9100 system is supposed to be the best one out there. Well, your guy who helped us select it is now gone, and we are up the creek. Who are you going to send in to finish the job?'"

Jack continued, "I listened and wondered why I had been brought along to this meeting. I assumed that Warren was trying to teach me how to deal with the client relationship side of the business. I was totally unprepared for what happened next," Jack paused and continued, "In response to the CFO's question, Warren looked at me and said to the CFO, 'Jack Bluto is the most qualified person in our office to implement the Hunkasys 9100 Accounts Receivable system. He'll handle the job. He will start on Monday.'"

"Wow!"

"Rona, I thought it was a joke. I barely knew what accounts receivable were. How could Warren be selling the CFO on this? I was squirming like crazy!"

"I bet."

"The CFO then turned to me and asked: 'Jack, how many implementations have you done?' Before I could get a sound out, Warren looked me right in the eye while telling the CFO: 'This has to be done right the first time and that's why Jack's your man.' The CFO responded: 'Okay, you'll get the resources that you need, but I want weekly progress reports. Nothing can get in the way of us getting this technology working.'"

"So what happened?"

"Before I could say anything, Warren responded: 'Of course, we understand. I'll give this project my highest level of attention. Let us go now so we can get started.' Warren ushered me out of the room without allowing me to get a handshake from the CFO. As we walked out the door, Warren handed the CFO an envelope. I was silent during the car ride back. I tried to piece together what had just happened. Warren never lied, but he omitted the truth."

"Unbelievable. What a lightweight!" Rona said.

"The truth was that no one in that Pro-Con office knew anything about the Hunkasys 9100 Accounts Receivable system, so no one was more qualified than me. Also, Warren probably would give this project a higher level of attention than any others, although that still meant next to nothing. I remembered what a Princeton classmate had told me about his experience with a Pro-Con competitor. The partner at that firm told my friend: 'Our goal is not to solve problems, it's to create them so we can bring in a lot of billable bodies.' If a client ever comes to you with a small fire, throw gasoline on it. We fan the flames and then make money by attacking infernos, not by putting out small fires.'"

"That's over the top," Rona exclaimed. "What was in the envelope?"

"Second row tickets to The Final Four. Warren's secretary told me."

Rona shook her head.

"That was my initiation into consulting. I wanted to move up at Pro-Con and get promoted. I wanted the prestige of being a partner someday so I didn't confront Warren. I plowed through the accounts receivable project in eight months. By working eighty-hour weeks, I never let on that I was doing it for the first time. Some months later, at the next client, I implemented the same accounts receivable system in two months for exactly twenty-five percent of the cost that the oil-company had paid. The first oil company had financed my education and the second company benefited. To me, it didn't seem right, but I kept my mouth shut."

Rona jumped in, "We ought to review the resume of everyone who consults on our projects. Also, I would refuse to pay for Flynch's hours. He's on site only to sell more business. I don't want to see a bill for his time unless he's doing real work."

"Makes sense," Jack said, adding, "It's amazing how clients fail to qualify the consultants they hire. The golden rule of buying consulting services is that you are never, never buying a consulting firm; you are renting the individuals who will staff your project. Consulting firms provide little standardized training to their staffs. Team members are never interchangeable. Every firm touts its methodologies, but if you examine their methodologies side by side, you'll see that most are very similar. The next time a consulting firm's honcho crows about his firm's winning methodology, ask him how many of the consultants whom he is proposing for your job have been tested on that methodology and what their test scores were. That'll shut him up."

"Is this true for all the consulting firms?" Rona inquired.

"Sure, for the accounting and outsourcing firms, too," Jack said.

"Hmm," Rona said. "I thought most of consulting arms of the accounting firms went out of business."

"Not true. These guys have been reborn as independent entities. Some are publicly traded, and most renamed their executive positions. Old partners now have more traditional corporate titles, but their business models and practices haven't changed."

"So those firms still exist?"

"Yes. Their consultants are wearing new uniforms, but they're playing the same old games."

"Who else is in this space?"

"Dozens of other management consulting firms, all with varying specializations that may include technology, but do you want to hear about this?"

"Not really."

"What would you like to hear about?"

"Not this stuff. I'm sick of it."

"We could talk about our good-night kiss in Le Maxwell's parking lot."

"We could," Rona said.

"Why don't we talk in person?"

"Interesting…go on…"

"Meet me for a drink?" Jack said, surprised by his boldness.

"Sure," Rona paused. "I'll be there in twenty minutes."

"Okay, see you soon," said Jack. He learned long ago that if you don't ask right away, you never will. Contemplation provides a breeding ground for fear, and strangles action.

WEDNESDAY, JULY 13TH 9:15 PM

Rona arrived, still wearing her work suit. He met her downstairs and they sat in the nearly empty BigEight lounge.

"Jack, let's bag this and go to ChumpRoast. I can't seem to flush that ingredient out of my system that makes me so addicted to their coffee."

"Is there one near here?" Jack asked.

"Three minutes," Rona said.

"Good," Jack replied, as they stood up and walked outside to Jack's car.

"Ah, the Tapir," Rona remarked playfully, "Looks like a pig with a trunk."

Jack returned her smile.

"I'll follow you there," Rona said.

☆ ☆ ☆

The barista handed the Super Chump to Rona, and her lean fingers struggled to hold the cup.

Jack stared at her, wide-eyed. "Gosh, that looks like a fifty-five gallon drum! How can you drink that much coffee?"

"I'm stuck. The more I drink, the more I need. Like your consulting," Rona joked.

"I'll tell you a funny story about Pro-Con."

"Another story?" Rona asked, shaking her head.

"As I was walking by the offshore guys today, it reminded me of when they interviewed me in Atlanta a few years ago."

"Did you get the job?"

"Hold on, let me tell you what happened."

"Sorry."

"My meeting was on Peachtree Street. Can you believe that some people don't know Peachtree is the only street in Atlanta?" he quipped. "I was going to the interview and I came out of MARTA, the local subway system. I was two blocks from the interview when the sky opened up. It was one of those drenching storms in which you're waterlogged within ten seconds. My new wool suit and wing tips were soaked."

"What were you doing in Atlanta? I thought you were in New York."

"I spent my first year in Atlanta and then transferred."

"Hmm."

"Do you want to hear the rest?"

"Sure."

"I ran into the office building, but when I arrived, the water was squishing out through the eyelets of my shoes. I had ten minutes before my interview with the partner in charge."

"What did you do?" Rona asked.

"I went to the men's room and stripped naked in a stall. I wrung out my underwear, my socks, and my suit. It didn't occur to me at the time what my suit would look like after I wrung it out. Well, you can imagine how misshapen it was. It looked like a gorilla put on the suit and then wrestled alligators."

"What did you do?"

"I took out my Bic Pen, one of the clear plastic hexagonal ones. I put the suit on the countertop by the sink and, using the pen as a squeegee, I pushed most of the water out. After putting the suit on, I presented myself to the partner. He was sniffing and kept looking around the room. I smelled like a wet dog, and on top of that, I did a terrible job on the interview."

"So what happened?"

"I got the job!"

"What?"

"He knew he was going to hire me anyway."

"How do you know that?" asked Rona.

"I didn't know it at the time but later realized that it was because consultants are almost always hired and fired in droves and rarely as individuals. When the economy picks up, consulting firms over-hire and when it turns down they overly trim staff."

"So consulting firms lead the economy?"

"Correct. Consulting firms provide the clients with a buffer against economic swings. Clients have policies that enable them to hire consultants more easily than full-time employees."

"So, would it be safe to conclude that you'll get the best consultants during the worst times?"

Jack hadn't expected her to draw this conclusion. *Shame on me,* he thought. "Right on, Rona. When times are getting good, consulting firms open their doors to new hires. A guy I worked with at Pro-Con was previously a night watchman. Pro-Con rebranded him as a security consultant and his billing rate went up fifteen-fold until the economy sputtered and they canned him. When consulting firms trim down, they keep their best people. Those are the times you'll get the best quality of service."

"Makes sense."

"In the old days, clients weren't wise to this, but in the past few years, the sophistication of consulting buyers has increased dramatically."

"How come?"

"Because so many alums of the major consulting firms have gone into careers in industry."

"I see. So what happened to the wet dog?"

"Well, I had a heartbeat and my responses to the interview questions were within three standard deviations of what was expected, so they brought me on board, trained me for a week, and sent me to help clients do things that I never did before."

"I like that story," Rona said.

"Interesting how little my personal qualifications mattered."

"Hmm."

"When an animal is hungry enough, he'll eat anything. When these firms get busy, they'll hire anyone, even a guy who asks about a company's methadone program during the interview," Jack said.

"The consulting firms sound crazy! Biff explained to me what your Little-Triangles concept is. It's the antidote to too much consulting."

"Thanks, Rona. Companies wouldn't have to hire so many consultants if they didn't start mega-projects. And they wouldn't need outsourcing firms."

Rona nodded. "Is outsourcing the same thing as consulting?"

"Once you put your toe in the water of that black murky pool, many false friends will try to lend a hand."

"Sounds like piling on consultants that you don't need."

Evaluate Outsourcing And Offshoring

"Exactly. Rona, consulting is a high-end version of the staffing business. Outsourcing is similar. They're all related. Clients outsource their non-core processes when they decide to focus on bolstering their core, competitive advantages. It can make sense because a client figures that the outsourcer is expert at the business functions that the client doesn't care about."

"Like clients buying a software package versus writing it themselves?"

"Yes! You turn over the keys of the business function or business process to the outsourcer. The outsourcer benefits from aggregating the purchasing of many clients and arguably gets the best discounts from its vendors."

"How long do these things last?" Rona asked.

"Clients sign multi-year outsourcing deals that are renegotiated throughout the deal term. They build in renegotiation clauses because they can't possibly predict their needs even two to three years into the future."

"So who actually does the work?" Rona inquired.

"Sometimes the client will merely transfer all the employment contracts of the department being outsourced to the outsourcer. It's a way for companies to shift costs around on their balance sheets."

"So a guy that worked at PNP one day can be working for Pro-Con the next day doing exactly the same job as he always did?"

"Right, the same person sitting in the same seat doing the same job."

"Sounds like financial foolery."

"Maybe, but companies are moving toward outsourcing offshore, also known as Offshoring, to China, India, Eastern Europe, South America, or the Middle East. Why pay an American programmer $100 an hour while an equally capable programmer working in India may cost $25?"

"Does it work?" Rona asked.

"The overseas outsourcers are more particular about their certifications than the Americans because they have a greater credibility burden to overcome. Despite a broadband infrastructure that enables a programmer in India to interact with the client across the globe at the same speed as he could as if he were in the next room, problems still exist. No matter how well these guys are trained, you can't fully overcome language, cultural, and time of day barriers."

"So why would a client do this?"

"To transfer risk and enable providers that supposedly are experts in the field to do stuff that the client is not so good at."

"This seems so vague. How do you know the outsourcer is doing his job?"

"These arrangements are governed by Service Level Agreements, or SLAs. These specify the performance commitment by the outsourcer. For example, if PNP outsources its smartphone support to Pro-Con, they would put in writing that for, let's say, a fee of $10 per month per device, they agree to fix any problem within four hours."

"So do organizations actually save money by outsourcing?" Rona asked listlessly, starting to lose interest. *Maybe Jack is too wrapped up in his work to focus on anything else*, she thought, sipping her coffee.

"Sometimes," Jack answered. "If a company has ten thousand devices to manage, it may be cheaper to have an outsourcer do it. The outsourcer may have ten clients this size and would be able to spread its fixed costs over a larger customer volume. Even with the outsourcer's profit margin built in, it allows for the client to pay less per device this way versus managing in-house. Also, device support rarely has any bearing on a company's competitive advantage, so by outsourcing you remove one more distraction from focusing on the core business. Companies run into problems when they try to over-outsource business functions that do, in fact, contribute to their brand and market power."

Rona nodded.

"Negotiating the SLAs can be illuminating for the outsourcing buyers because it forces them to think through what they need. For example, the outsourcer may try to sell the client on a two hour response time at twice the cost of a four hour response time, and the client needs to understand whether that marginal benefit is worth the marginal cost. Of course, the best outcome is when the client realizes that much of what's being outsourced is superfluous and can be engineered out of the business."

Rona nodded more weakly. "These arrangements sound wasteful."

"Clients move in and out of these agreements depending upon the management team of the moment. A lot of movement tells you that the client is uncertain about what it's trying to accomplish. Also, outsourcing and consulting help to create a mercenary mentality where individuals looking for the largest wage make it difficult on an organization trying to build a culture. And you're right about waste. Outsourced armies tend to figure out how to sustain themselves at a client long after there's nothing left to fight for," Jack said.

"Like Iraq?" Rona said.

"Let's not even go there," Jack declared. "Biff told me how much you hate war."

"No, Jack, I hate the sniveling men that send our families to war but won't send their own," Rona said explosively, like gasoline had just been poured into her carburetor.

"I didn't mean that..." Jack replied quickly.

"So how is this relevant to us?" Rona demanded.

"Outsourcing is a great opportunity for both the client and the outsourcer, but it can also be risky. All parties need to enter into the relationship with the right expectations. It fails when responsibility for performance and accountability are also outsourced. Also, when you outsource or offshore, you lose control of your best resources. Wouldn't you want to keep tabs on your best people?"

"I guess," Rona said, calming down and looking at her watch.

"But wait, there's another topic we have to discuss that's even more important."

"You've got five more minutes and that's it. I'm tired," Rona said, looking at Jack. *He's so enthusiastic and energetic. I wish he would stop talking about work.*

Don't Slip On The Grease

"Rona, why do you think that consulting firms spend millions to sponsor professional golfers? They want to put faces on their brands."

"So why not use their client's success stories?"

"Because it's nearly impossible for a consulting firm to stand behind a specific dollar benefit it provided to a client on any particular project."

"Is that because there is no benefit?"

"No, but when effectiveness and clarity are difficult to demonstrate, a pro golfer's winning image acts as a good stand-in."

"Hmm," Rona said.

"Why are the galleries of big time golf tournaments full of corporate decision makers charged with the responsibility of selecting technology providers? Are CIOs or the VPs of Purchasing swayed by the opportunity to play golf with big name professional players at corporate events, or to have their pictures taken with the stars? Ask yourself."

Rona nodded.

"You may see managers from the local school board enjoying the pomp and vendor largess at these events. Does this fun and frolic steer those buyers toward decisions that are not as well thought out as they could be?" Jack said, pausing, "I know a CIO at a New York hospital chain that pushed through a fifty million dollar technology purchase after attending the Super Bowl courtesy of the winning vendor."

"That's sickening," Rona said with conviction.

"In reality, the benefits of these technology projects are often so murky and inconsistent that no major technology vendor or consulting firm dares to publicize the return on investment that all of its customers receive. Sure, there will always be a flagship client's success story that gets touted, but what about the other clients that are technology's victims?"

"You think it's that bad?" Rona asked.

"I know it is. The savior here may be the Internet," Jack said, smirking.

"Why?"

"Vendor golf is dying because technology buyers can't bear to spend four consecutive hours away from playing on the Internet."

"Lunchmeat plays golf in his car."

"What?"

"Lunchmeat's Mercedes has a full onboard mobile office. Fujohara, the company that won a big contract for our desktops a month later, supplied it. Meanwhile, every day when I pass by Stanley's car, I see that system in there and it makes me sick. That day he took me to lunch a couple of years ago, we stopped to pick up a part for his Harley-Davidson at the local dealership. We spent an hour there as Stanley got tied up talking with another Harley owner that he met on a vendor-sponsored ride through Sturgis."

"Wow," said Jack.

"You should see the chrome on Stanley's bike. He's screwing around on that bike rather than fixing our damn code. The guy is the classic Loud Harley, Little Shifter."

"You mean big hat, no cattle?" Jack asked.

"I guess."

"Grease is grease, no matter how it's disguised, whether it's a technology conference or a cash bribe," Jack added.

"Biff told me that Stanley attended a boondoggle at The Sebum Springs Resort last month. Apparently, Stanley was awarded Technological Cookware Magazine's Thought Leader of the Year award. PNP paid for Stanley and his wife to attend, but Stacey sprained her ankle getting off the bus during the companions' winery tour. They stayed at Sebum Springs for four extra days while she recuperated," Rona said.

"I bet Biff loved that," Jack said sarcastically. "Rona, I see this all the time, especially with professional sports. Ticket prices have skyrocketed, and yet technology and consulting vendors fight to get the best seats for their customers and prospects."

"But isn't this how business has been done forever?" Rona said.

"Yes, and I like the camaraderie aspect of it, but little else, because when the computer salesman takes the CIO to the Super Bowl because a big deal is on the line, that CIO is motivated to steer business to that salesman. I hate to call these slippery gratuities bribes, but it's hard to come up with any other word for it. The CIO benefits personally and his organization may not be making the best decision for itself, its employees, or its shareholders."

"This goes on in other areas, not just technology."

"You're right, and it's all greasy. Organizations must require reporting of grease receipts and those receipts need to be capped at very low levels. And that goes for everyone on the totem pole."

"That won't go over well."

"Maybe not, but it's a strong step toward a free-market meritocracy where buying decisions are made based upon price and quality, not the munificence of the sales rep nor the personal greed of the buyer."

"Yeah. I can only imagine how much grease the defense contractors sling to win those billion dollar war contracts. At least a few people are living high off the hog while our boys are getting killed, and I think that's disgusting," Rona said.

"Trust me, Rona, it's the way the world doesn't work. Drug companies greasing doctors and lobbyists greasing lawmakers all drains the effectiveness of the meritocracy. Grease should never be a rite of passage."

"That's what happens when we vote for leaders based on our fear and not on their character," Rona said.

"Rona, chill out," Jack said gently. "I was talking about grease in the technology business."

"So what do you call that dinner at Le Maxwell the other night," Rona asked coyly.

"That's what I call romance," Jack responded, winking.

Rona returned the smile as she pushed back from the table at ChumpRoast.

"Enough of this talk. My ear is about to fall off. Tell me something that will make me smile," Rona said.

"I'm staying the weekend."

"That's nice. Want to go apple picking? You'll love our Northern Spy Apples."

The edges on Jack's lips turned down slightly. "Sounds great," he said.

"See you tomorrow?" Rona said.

"Yes…"

With that, Rona popped up like a piece of toast and left before Jack could say another word.

What's going on? Jack wondered. *I figured I would at least get a kiss.* He shook his head.

WEDNESDAY, JULY 13TH 11:00 PM

Jack's smartphone rang. Annie and Marcus, the two Reality Check analysts assigned to PNP, were calling.

"Hi, guys," Jack started. "I'm sorry I couldn't see you for dinner tonight."

"All's fine," Annie replied.

"What did you find out?" Jack asked.

"We'll email you the detailed report tomorrow, but let me give you the highlights," Marcus said.

"Shoot."

"The CFO has no role in any of the projects. He's on the steering committee, but he hasn't attended a single meeting. Except for Rona Sims, none of the senior marketing or sales people has been meaningfully involved in the design of the technology," Marcus said.

"Jack, Marcus and I reviewed the project plans with Stanley's team. They're recording progress against the plans, but we asked several times to examine the design documents and other deliverables, and were promised that the docs would be emailed to us, but we haven't seen them yet," Annie said.

"Do you think the docs exist?" Jack asked.

"I don't know. Can you push for them?" Marcus asked.

"I'll see what I can do, but don't let that hold up tomorrow night's reports."

"Understood," Marcus said. "I'm working on the Reality Check Assessment Letter. I'll send you the first draft by Friday night."

"How does it look?" Jack asked.

"Same mistakes as we always see. The tech guys are throwing money at the problem but aren't getting closer to the solution. Also, PNP's key business executives are totally divorced from the project."

"I'm not surprised. Okay. I'm sure we'll cross paths tomorrow. Annie, we're going to do two three-hour Reality Check seminars for all the PNP staff either next Wednesday or Thursday. We'll have the second shift crew and executive management in the morning seminar and the afternoon seminar will be for the first shift crew. Stick to the basics; these guys are barely evolved past the primordial soup with regard to implementation techniques."

"Great, I'll be ready," Annie said. "I'll assume that they have no effective checks and balances in place."

"I don't see any," Jack answered. "Hey, you guys are going home on Friday night, right?"

"Yes, but I'll be back next week for the seminars," Annie said.

"And I'll be available on phone or video, and I'll come back if you need me here," Marcus added.

"Thanks guys, good work. Good night," Jack said.

✳ ✳ ✳

Meanwhile, Biff was finishing his second scotch in his study. It was the only room where he could avoid the thumping of Amelia's house music. "What am I going to do?" He wondered aloud, as he poured a third. *I can't break off the bottle or the meds. I'm getting more like my father every day.*

✳ ✳ ✳

THURSDAY, JULY 14TH 7:45 AM

Biff led Jack into Dr. Meyer Steadman's office. Meyer, a spry, sixty-year-old Operations Research professor was enjoying his second career at PNP.

Beware Of The Bait & Switch

"If you ask me—and you are—" Meyer said, "The number one problem is the consultants. We have nearly thirty of 'em and I have no idea what they're doing. We're paying them to learn ThickWare 3.5 and they aren't solving our problems. These consultants are not the stars who came out to sell us. The consulting executives promised they wouldn't bait and switch us, but they did and Stanley allowed it. Now we have a group of junior people who don't have the skills to get the job done."

"Go on," Biff said.

"Who manages these people? Can't we do better than this?" Meyer demanded.

"The problem goes deeper," Jack interrupted.

"What do you mean?" Biff asked.

"There's a core flaw in the way that PNP is managing Pro-Con."

"You mean Flynch?" Meyer chimed in.

"Partly. Flynch is actually in the position of hiring consultants for PNP. Stanley signs off on the hires, but he's a rubber stamp. From what my team observed, Flynch calls the shots."

"That's silly," Biff said angrily. "He's just a vendor."

"I'm sorry, Biff, but I don't think so. I heard that last week Flynch ran the project status meetings for two days in a row when Stanley was on a site visit to Fujohara."

"Why the hell was Stanley there anyway?" Biff asked.

"I was told that he met one of Fujohara's chief engineers at the La Costa technology conference and Stanley wanted to see if he could learn anything to use at PNP."

"And I probably paid for his first class ticket," said Biff.

Biff grew angrier, but his anger was directed inward. *I fell asleep at the switch and got suckered into squandering resources on boondoggles.* Biff realized that when Flynch managed the project meetings, he was acting as boss over the Pro-Con consultants, the other consultants, the vendors' teams, and the PNP employees assigned to the project. This was a clear conflict of interests. *How could I have been dumb enough to put a fox in charge of the henhouse?*

Don't Outsource The Success Of Your Project To Outsiders

Jack sensed what Biff was thinking. "You can't relinquish control or accountability like that. Flynch is paid based on the amount of revenue he generates. He has monthly sales bogies to hit, just like a car salesman or a cop writing tickets. By elevating him to buyer, you encourage him to pile on resources and slow down the timeframe."

"We should dump Flynch today," Meyer said.

"You can, but that may set you back even further," Jack said.

"But we can't be so dependent upon the consultants," Biff responded.

"Consultants play a critical role in what you are doing," Jack replied. "it would take too long to train PNP people on Thick-Ware. Plus, they wouldn't have the battle-earned wisdom that your consultants have from their experiences with other clients."

"How much expertise do we need?" said Biff.

"It's pivotal. One A player can be more helpful than five B players because he's able to recognize the critical path. Would you rather have your birthday dinner prepared by five mediocre cooks or one great cook?"

"Jack," said Meyer. "That analogy doesn't hold because there's a certain workload here, and we need extra help to get it done."

"Exactly my point," Jack said. "You need the bodies in here to configure the system, write the reports, handle any custom code and device configurations, and test all of the interfaces. You don't need the A's to do that. Consulting firms can supply the manpower."

"But I should have never expected them to get ThickWare up and running?" Biff asked.

"No way," Jack said, rising from his chair. "I bet you have a few strong consultants here from Pro-Con but making this work is your job. Never, never expect outsiders to finish a project for you. When your meetings have three PNP people and thirty consultants, you will fail."

"What's the right ratio of consultants to internal staff?" asked Meyer.

"There's no magic ratio, but if you have more consultants than PNP employees, then the consultants will be learning and teaching each other about your business and when the project ends, they'll leave with that knowledge. Again, you must own the success of the project. And having the guy who is selling you the consulting services also acting as the de facto hiring manager is absurd."

Biff and Meyer both nodded.

Jack continued, "Look at what's happening from a 10,000 foot level. Biff, you said earlier that PNP is in the second fifth of companies. You were candid and I appreciated that. The managers of companies in the top fifth seem to nail whatever they attempt. They consistently earn impressive profits and have great reputations. They adapt well to change. They excel at the fundamentals and have the discipline to complete major projects.

The bottom fifth is the opposite of the first. It contains companies with the worst processes, full of kinks. These companies lack the leaders to muster the focus to turn these losers around. Their wheels are stuck in the mud and they're on the path to oblivion. They've given in to the dark side.

The fat middle, if you remember your bell curve, comprises the middle three-fifths, the group that PNP falls into. Fat middle companies succeed or fail in each effort, depending on how intelligently they attack it. These companies are made up of good people who can run as a team if properly directed. They are not the stars; they are the plodders. These companies drive our economy."

"You're describing companies using the same terms that I use when I describe our workers," said Meyer.

Use SMEs To Spotlight The A Players

"Agreed," Jack continued. "You have your A players, your B players, and your C players. The A's are the top fifth, the C's are the bottom fifth and your B's are the fat middle. How you ride the B's is everything."

"It's an art form to get the best efforts out of the average players. The A players always give their best and the C's never do," Biff responded and paused. "You're right, Jack. The B's are pivotal."

"Exactly, and having a large complement of consultants on the team doesn't help the morale of your B employees," Jack added. "Imagine asking an employee who earns $65,000 a year to do the same work as a consultant who is making $150,000," said Jack.

"It's a big de-motivator," said Biff.

"What have you seen with your other clients, Jack?" Meyer asked.

"It's always a people problem. Companies rarely assign their best people to big projects. Executive management is too protective of its best people. Instead, the A players tend to stay in their normal jobs while large projects are handed off to the B's. The A's interface with the project team but not for long enough to have an impact. Then a subtle but interesting dynamic occurs. The A's get frustrated with the way the B's run a project. This becomes pronounced when the project begins to slip deadlines. The B's, rather than respond to the A's, become more insular and less interested in tackling the project's most challenging or controversial issues. The A's lose interest, stop contributing and then you're in the Black Hole."

"So what you're saying, Jack," Meyer noted, "is that we shouldn't castigate the consulting companies when we bait and switch our own people?"

"Meyer, that's right on. An effective CEO understands his organization's priorities and apportions talent accordingly. Talent is always an organization's most important asset and when it's mismanaged, sub-optimization results. I don't know enough about the talent landscape at PNP but whenever you have a large project with many moving parts organized into a few hulking triangles, it becomes harder to load a project with the right talent. Maybe Stanley is using A players to lead the projects, but I don't see that yet. The problem is that their leader is a B player at best. I hate the cliché about a chain being only as strong as its weakest link, but you know it applies," Jack said passionately.

Jack knew that Biff understood these theories, but was Biff the type of leader, that A player, who could bring the right technique to bear at the exact moment it was called for? *Could Biff grasp not only the technical complexity of the project, but also the emotional landscape, with its eddies and currents of individual motivations, insights, and confusions?*

Jack looked at Biff and continued, "The A leader knows how to size up the situation and correct course. He must be resilient."

"Look, Jack, you talk a lot about leveraging A players, but how do you know who knows what when it comes to the consultants? Everyone over-sells," Meyer said.

"True," Jack responded, "especially when a new consultant joins the project team. You need to quickly size up whether a consultant has the knowledge to solve your problems. Interview and background check them with the same level of scrutiny that you apply to your full-time employment candidates. Make certain that each consultant has both the experience and the skills that the consulting firm represents. If not, he may be a smart consultant, but a smart consultant without subject matter expertise is worthless. What good is a neurosurgeon if you need to fix a leaky toilet?" Jack said firmly, and paused. "Always use an SME to qualify consultants."

"A what?" Meyer asked.

"A Subject Matter Expert. Never start a project until you have the SMEs available to do those evaluations. Even if you overpay for the SME, the savings you will reap by making better hiring decisions will be enormous. The SME can design or obtain competency tests for the consultants and ensure that they are the right people for the job. He knows what questions to ask."

"Interesting, tests for incoming consultants," said Meyer.

At that moment, Biff realized that Stanley would have to be moved aside and quickly. *I must take control but I don't understand enough yet.*

C.R.A.P. On The Time Toilets

"Have you walked through the consultant work areas?" Meyer continued. "Why is there even a work area for consultants? Shouldn't they be interspersed among the PNP project team members? Most of the day, they sit in their cubicles in front of the Internet. How many hours of email and other forms of time-robbing e-waste are we paying for? Do you realize that most of my field people share a single broadband line while the consulting team is using three? That doesn't seem fair. How many more times can I tell my people to work harder when the consultants are reading personal emails on the dual 30" monitors that we bought for them? Come on now, did we really need to buy them subwoofer speaker systems? Do they need to hear 'You've Got Mail' in baritone stereo?"

"Meyer, you're dating yourself. I don't think AOL says that anymore," Jack quipped, adding, "The project team is probably watching reality-show clips on YouTube."

Biff sat stone-faced.

Jack continued, "I've seen this before. Give people a chance to waste time, and they will. We're all time squanderers, but some waste more than others, especially when there's no supervision. A couple of years ago I helped a potato chip company get their CustHug project back on track. They had about fifty consultants in a dedicated, cubicled area. They all had telephones, Internet, and email access. The consultants came from five different firms and despite being in close physical proximity to each other, they weren't communicating effectively. They stayed in their cubes and in their cliques. After spending a day working with a couple of these consultants and walking through cubicle row, I couldn't believe how many people were using the Internet. They were watching it like it was a TV, surfing the URLs as you might change channels when you sit at home with a cold one after a hard day."

"I feel that way too," Biff responded. "Surfing the Internet is no different than playing video games. My stockbroker says that the Internet was introduced into our country by terrorists looking to destroy our economy from the inside out. After the stock market got killed at the turn of the millennium, Al Gore shut up. It's a good thing he found something else to crow about."

Jack looked up, surprised. *These words sounded like they were coming out of my own mouth.*

"Sorry Jack, continue with your story," Biff said, acknowledging his tangent.

"Anyway," Jack began. "My client blocked inappropriate websites, but the consultants were still accessing information that had nothing to do with solving their client's problems. They also were spending time on telephone calls that were unrelated to the project. I thought about the locks that they used to put on the finger holes of old style rotary dial phones, to prevent outgoing calls. We needed a solution like that for their smartphones."

Meyer nodded.

"Each team member was moving the ball forward on their project a mere two to three hours per day," Jack said.

"How'd you handle it?" Biff asked.

"I sat down with the CEO and we drew up the C.R.A.P. plan."

"Crap?" Meyer said, looking puzzled.

"Yes, we crapped all over the time toilets," Jack exclaimed proudly. "C.R.A.P. stood for Consultant Redeployment Action Plan. We came in one night after the consultants had left, pulled out the cubicle walls, and disconnected Internet access. We installed a cell phone reception blocker. We called the executives of the consulting firms the next morning to brief them on the new procedures. Guess what happened. Productivity tripled."

"I bet they were pretty angry," Meyer guffawed.

"C.R.A.P. wasn't intended to humiliate the consultants, it was designed to enable them to concentrate on their work, while stimulating teamwork. Consultants don't need an oasis, they need openness," Jack said.

Meyer's head bobbed up and down in agreement.

"Have you ever been to a Wall Street firm's trading department?" Jack asked.

"No," Biff said.

Meyer shook his head no.

"Wall Street traders are among the most highly compensated employees in the world. The more successful the trader is, the less likely he is to have a private office. In fact, firms jam their best employees into small spaces to enable collaborative brainstorming and decisioning."

"That's so different than the traditional office setup," Biff said.

"Cubicles are the silver medal winners in the international time toilet competition," Jack exclaimed. Turning to Meyer, he continued, "The gold medal goes to the Internet, the greatest unproductivity tool of all time! Now we have smartphones and tablets that allow us to waste time more efficiently than ever before and from wherever we want."

"Jack, I know you're kidding, but there's more than an element of truth to what you're saying," Meyer said.

"Maybe your smartphone enhances your productivity. For most people, though, it's a time toilet full of inane electronic chatter."

"Jack, let's get the conversation back on track," Biff requested.

"Biff, one more point please regarding unproductivity," Jack added, "Why do technology people go to industry conferences? They go to find better jobs. These trade shows and the organizations that sponsor them create a de facto collective or labor union for CIOs and other technology executives. The shows rarely result in new revenues or decreased costs for the company that pays to send its people there."

"I've been to trade shows that customers have attended," Biff asserted.

"Those make sense. It's the grease-pit shows that I object to; the mutual adulation societies, where inbred ideas become even more inbred. By the way, I hear Stanley shot an eighty-nine at Sebum Springs," Jack deadpanned.

"Okay, wise guy," Biff chuckled. "I know you're playing me now."

"In every tease or sarcasm, a hidden truth exists," Jack said.

"Seriously, you're right. I'm the sucker who approved that Sebum Springs bill. It's amazing. If our guy who buys lawn care services took free sod for his house, he'd get fired," Biff said.

"How many of our tech guys bought their own personal copies of Microsoft Office?" Meyer asked.

Biff remained silent. Last week he had upgraded Amelia's PC with the latest version of Office using PNP's corporate licensing code.

"Okay, enough. Let's move on," Biff said. "I need to take over. For now, Stanley will be my eyes and my ears on the technical issues, and he'll manage the consultants with my oversight. I thought about assigning that responsibility to Meyer or someone who better understands our business processes, but I don't want to add another layer of decision-making. Meyer, you can be the SME on the project. Make sure that we have the right consultants and best people in the company on this."

"Will do," Meyer said.

Biff didn't know how vindictive Stanley might get and hated the idea of having to build a case against him. This was not like the Old West when disputes were settled man to man, with guns and clarity. This was business and there were lawsuits, Equal Employment Opportunity Commission requirements, career-limiting moves, and burning bridges. Biff decided he would rather risk the wrath of Roscoe & Lauer than moderate his position regarding Stanley.

"Jack," Biff began, "I'll speak with Stanley this afternoon and reassign him to his new role. I want his Project Leaders reporting to me from now on. Also, I'll hold off on going to China. We need to fix our problems here first."

"Good, I like it," Jack answered.

"What else?" Biff asked.

Treat The Consultants Well

"Once you have the team in place, you have to treat all your people as if they're A players, including the consultants."

"You mean consultants are people too?" Meyer asked sarcastically, his nose turning up slightly.

"Yes," Jack laughed. "Their firms have little ability to support them in the field. Don't isolate or marginalize the consultants; let them feel like full-fledged team members. Give them t-shirts and invite them to the company picnics. I can't tell you how many projects I've seen where the consultants were spiritually isolated by the client."

"That probably fuels employee resentment of their presence," Biff observed.

"Of course," Jack said. "It's a lose-lose. Make each consultant into a team member because you want him to feel accountable to your Project Leaders, not the consulting firm overseer who occasionally drops in. You'll get more mileage out of your consultants and reduce the poisonous, value-erasing resentment by your full-time employees. It's a great opportunity to turn a lose-lose situation into a win-win."

"But how do you deal with resentment stemming from the disparity in pay when the consultant earns much more money than the employee does for the same job?" Meyer asked.

"Emphasize that the entire team is working toward the same goal. Also, that consultant billing at two hundred dollars per hour probably takes home less than a third of his billable rate. His firm keeps the rest, so the disparity isn't so big."

Biff motioned for Jack and Meyer to continue their conversation as he resolutely stood up and left the room.

THURSDAY, JULY 14TH 10:45 AM

Biff crossed the threshold into Stanley's office.

"Yes, Biff?" Stanley said. His meaty hands were clasped together on a clean desk.

Biff paused. *He seems to have been expecting me*, Biff observed silently.

"Hello, Stanley," Biff finally said. "We need to make changes to the project team."

"Is it because that Jack Pluto or whatever his name is told you to?"

"No, these are my decisions. I've given you plenty of opportunities to get our Big-Box situation back on track. I know you've been working hard to make that happen, but I don't see results."

"What are you saying?"

"I'm not satisfied, and I want to relieve the pressure from you by taking the reins."

"So you're going to lead an IT project? You must be smoking something."

Biff ignored the provocation. "Stanley, I need you, and the rest of our team needs you. I want you entirely focused on connecting to Broadway. Your technical staff and the technical consultants will continue to report to you and you'll report to me."

"And if I say no?"

"That's your decision, and how you make it will demonstrate your interest in remaining a member of this company. Speak with Buck Roscoe if you want to, but I think you know what he'll say."

"We have three other projects going on, you know that. We can't slow those down. We have contracts in place."

"I'm considering how to handle all that."

"But we've sunk millions into this so far."

"Exactly," Biff said. He stood up, eyed Stanley's walls of golf pictures and vendor awards, and strode out.

Stanley face turned ashen. This demotion was an ice pick in his eye. As a career-climbing professional, his track record was based on well-promoted successes and well-hidden failures. Stanley's eyes drifted to his wall of fame, adorned with plaques from CompuSquat, CustHug, Pro-Con, *Tektanic* and others, lauding Stanley's contributions to the Information Technology field.

Biff turned the corner and approached his office. For a moment, he pitied his CIO. *Stanley's not that stupid*, Biff mused. *How could he get so caught up in this game?*

KEY 4: TECHNOLOGY – LEVERAGE TECHNOLOGY TO ENABLE BUSINESS, NOT DISABLE IT

THURSDAY, JULY 14TH 10:55 AM

Biff approached his office door and did an about face. He walked into the plant and continued straight down the main production aisle. *This is my plant,* he thought. *My plant.* He liked that expression. He saw Earl adjusting the controls on the slitter. Two men pushed a buggy of 8" non-sticks toward Quality Control. The workers were busy and focused, and Biff felt pride in PNP. For a moment, Biff relaxed. *I make the best cookware in the world,* he said to himself. *I started from nothing. Now I run this place.*

How do I keep it going? By using common sense, he told himself. *It doesn't take long for tomorrow's technology to be piled on top of yesterday's trash heap. Customers are what matter. Customer relationships will outlast the technology being used to maintain and manage them, despite what technology vendors say. Business is built the same way as always: by earning trust, pricing right, and delivering on time with acceptable quality. Jack is right.*

Biff turned and walked to within earshot of his office. Jack was still talking to Meyer.

"…the software vendor can be enormously helpful. Good vendors already know the best practices in the field. For your non-core processes, that is, those that don't give you a competitive advantage, you want to adopt whatever is easiest or most efficient. Use whatever works, don't burn your people out analyzing yesterday. Build a system as quickly as possible to leverage tomorrow now."

Biff moved closer to the doorway. Meyer looked exhausted as Jack continued, "To move forward, we need to meet with each of the project's executives and I don't care whether they come from PNP, Big-Box, Pro-Con, ThickWare, or wherever."

"That'll take time," said Meyer.

"Do it by video. You guys are burning nearly $100K a day and not getting anywhere."

"I know," said Biff, as he strode in.

"Recognize that each person you speak with is playing the game with his own agenda. You have to tease out the truth, clarify your objectives, and bring everyone on board. Getting the technology to work will be challenging enough without divisiveness among the vendors," Jack said.

"Okay, so we'll bring everyone back on board and move forward," said Meyer.

"Maybe everyone will get on board, maybe not. We may have to make a couple of these guys walk the plank to show the others that we're serious. The bottom line is that we need to be objective and not be weighed down by the gravity of sunk costs and lost time," Jack added.

Don't Be A Petri Dish

"But we spent three months figuring out which technology to use," Biff eased his way back in. "You don't want us to waste that."

"It was wasted," Jack replied. "Why did you do it that way?"

"You've got to be kidding. How would we choose the best technology without evaluating the choices?" Biff looked over at Meyer and continued, "We always do a requirements definition and then go through a formal selection process for any major piece of technology that we buy."

Meyer nodded in agreement.

"Consulting firms oversell selection. It's easy money for them. Reputable software companies make good systems, and when you choose among mature products, any of them will usually do," Jack asserted.

"Really?" Meyer asked incredulously. "But different vendors offer different features."

"Really," Jack smiled, trying not to sound condescending. "There's a ninety-five percent overlap of what they offer and a vendor's unique features that don't overlap you don't want anyway."

"What should we have done?" Biff inquired.

"Spend an hour writing down your must-haves and then whittle that list to a half-page. For standard-type functionality like you guys are seeking, you'll likely find that all the vendors will satisfy your requirements."

"And if they don't?" said Meyer.

"Then you need to whittle the list down further," Jack responded.

"So unless we are buying a system that will give us a competitive advantage, we want to stay really simple," Biff said.

"Precisely. You can buy the weakest system out there but if you implement it well, you'll be a hero. I'm not talking about emerging technologies in which the competitive products may be vastly different. In your case, you're buying what is basically an accounting system. You could have bought the software from any of the major vendors."

"We thought we were saving money with ThickWare by using a pre-production or beta version of their next release," Biff explained. "Their sales team claimed that they would focus the software around PNP's unique business processes, and Stanley negotiated a better price because of it."

"You mean 3.5? And you believed them?" Jack asked.

"What, I shouldn't have?" Biff countered.

"Companies using a beta version are destined to go the way of the Betamax," Jack said irritably. "Look, software companies often release pre-quality products to get a jump on their competition—"

"Pre-quality?" Biff said, cutting him off.

"It's the sucker's tax. When you are the first kid on the block with a new technology or a piece of software, figure that a smarter kid will get a better and cheaper version a day later."

"Sounds like we're scrutinizing our pennies while our dollars are flying out the door," said Biff.

"Exactamundo, as the Fonz used to say. ThickWare probably made it seem like you were getting a once-in-a-lifetime deal. Let's hope it's not a life-ending deal for PNP. If you had bought 2.4 instead of 3.5, you wouldn't even need to do Broadway."

Biff sighed heavily.

"You have to evaluate your technology purchases using expected cost—the planned costs adjusted for risk."

"Like expected value?" Meyer asked.

"Yes, measure what your CFO calls Total Cost of Ownership, or TCO. That takes into account all the extra costs that weren't quoted to you by the vendor who offered you this flimsy Betamax deal. Like you said, Biff, don't worry about the pennies spent to acquire the technology. That's the ante to get in the game. The big money is spent on the implementation, and the really big money comes back to you in spades if you play your cards right and are able to reap that bountiful High Value harvest. The returns will build that ski house in Aspen."

Biff felt far removed from that dream. "So what can we do now?" Biff asked uneasily.

"Implement change in manageable chunks, to control its risk. You can buy a lot of technology at once, but you can't make it all work in one fell swoop. It's impossible."

Jack sensed Meyer was tuning him out. Jack compensated by raising his voice, as a foreign tourist does when he is asked to repeat his request for directions to the bathroom.

"Jack, take five," Biff requested. Jack stopped, acknowledging his overzealousness.

"Okay," Jack responded. He went inside Biff's bathroom and splashed cold water on his face.

Biff briefed Meyer on what had happened with Stanley. Meyer nodded understandingly at Biff, who felt relieved to have someone so competent and understanding by his side. They had a strong mutual respect: Meyer knew how hard Biff worked, and Biff knew Meyer truly understood production.

✵ ✵ ✵

Jack took a few deep breaths and returned, refreshed and relaxed.

Meyer turned to Jack, "We've put a lot of energy into this already and now you tell us that we're way off track. How do we know that you're not scaring us into buying more Reality Check services?"

"No way. I've already been hired and I am trying to help. Every dollar PNP spends on Reality Check will come back to you ten to a hundred fold," Jack said confidently. "The only person I am focused on serving is the CEO because his interests are best aligned with the owners and shareholders. In fact, I'll piss a lot of people off as I cut through some of the crap that has been retarding your IT projects." Jack kept his eyes on Biff. Biff didn't waver. Meyer backed down, seemingly satisfied.

Right at that moment, Jack felt a vibration from his hip. His smartphone buzzed and he instinctively whipped it out. There was an email from Rona. He looked up at his clients and then, unable to control himself, he clicked the thumbscrew to read the message. 'Jack thanks for a fun time last night. See you soon.'

I'm in. You da' man! Jack thought to himself. Then he looked up into stares from Meyer and Biff. *That could have been a career-limiting move,* Jack realized, vowing not to compromise his professionalism like that again.

If Biff or Meyer were vexed by Jack's indiscretion, they let it pass. Meyer rose, nodded in a friendly manner, and walked out.

"Let's grab a cup of coffee in the cafeteria," Biff said, turning to Jack.

They stood up and left Biff's office.

As they reached the swinging doors, Biff stopped. "I forgot, but I'm ten minutes late for a birthday party in the human resources department. Find Rona and have lunch with her – she understands the problems we're having with Big-Box and maybe she could give you insight into how to deal with the situation."

Jack tried to suppress a smile.

"Come back and see me after lunch," Biff requested.

THURSDAY, JULY 14TH 11:20 AM

Jack walked toward Rona's office. He stopped in the doorway when he heard she was on the phone. Rona's desk faced the doorway but she was turned around, looking out her window. She was crouched over in her chair with the phone clutched tightly to her head. "I told you a thousand times not to call me anymore. It's over, over, over!" she yelled. With the last 'over,' Rona hung up and sat in silence for a few moments before she turned and noticed Jack. "How long have you been standing there?" she asked angrily.

Jack was stymied. *What could I say?* He finally said, "I'm sorry. I just got here. I really didn't know you were on the phone. I heard the last two lines of your phone conversation and that was it. I didn't intend to eavesdrop."

"Okay, I'm sorry, I'm sure you didn't. Now you know why my arms are always tired. It's all this baggage I'm carrying around."

"Maybe I could help you carry some," Jack quipped, "but I ain't no bellman."

"So, why are you here?"

"Hopefully to take you to lunch."

"Okay, but give me a few minutes, I need to call one of Horace's junior merchants at Big-Box."

Rona and the merchant were negotiating a chargeback that Big-Box had sent to PNP because of a late and incomplete shipment. Rona held the phone away from her ear as the merchant complained. It was not that she didn't care what he was saying; rather, she had heard it all before. At the end of the conversation, Rona accepted the chargeback, thanked Big-Box for the business, and expressed hope, albeit with little confidence, that the technology problems would be resolved soon.

Resplendent in her red Chanel suit, Rona looked sexy but professional. Few if any at PNP recognized the designer or realized how expensive this suit was. Jack gulped.

"How about we go to DoubleWide's for chili and a salad?" Rona suggested.

"If that's cool with you, that's great for me," Jack replied. *Wow,* he thought, Rona *would be the only customer at DoubleWide's wearing Chanel, and definitely the only one wearing a Chanel suit that color-matched DoubleWide's signage.*

✵ ✵ ✵

Barry White crooned from the satellite radio as Rona drove them to lunch.

"I heard a rumor today that Biff's job is on the line," Jack said.

"Where did you hear it?" Rona responded.

"Walking the plant." Jack paused. "How do you think he'll react? He seems to be at the mercy of the private equity firm," he added.

"He is, but they trust him. The ladies are not foolish."

"Ladies?"

"Yes, I thought you would've heard by now. Roscoe & Lauer is a front for a silent quartet of female partners. It's a great story. They have the best returns of any Lower Wacker private equity firm. They beat the pants off the blue bloods from the old boys network!"

"Wow, that's kinda wild," Jack said.

"It gets better. Each one is completely devoted to the other three. Barb Roscoe used to be part of the love quartet, but she split off from the pack to marry Buck so they could have a male Wall Street figurehead," Rona explained.

"So the women control the purse strings?" Jack said.

"Definitely. Other than having a big mouth, Buck's brain-dead."

"Awesome. Now that's a new one for me," Jack said.

"With respect to PNP, the ladies felt that having a state of the art IT infrastructure would allow the company to fetch a higher multiple when it comes time to sell," Rona said.

"I'm surprised they think that way," Jack responded. "That's the zaniness that led to the telecom debacle. Companies spent billions on capacity, but no one needed it. You can't build supply and hope that demand will follow."

"Sounds like another *Field of Dreams*," Rona said as they pulled into the DoubleWide's parking lot.

THURSDAY, JULY 14TH 12:40 PM

After a speedy lunch, the pair returned to the plant. Jack left Rona and walked by the project area on his way back to Biff's office. He passed two large rooms full of programmers. One room had Russian signs and the other room had Hindi signs. Jack recognized the logos of the offshore programming firms.

Why are all these people here? Jack wondered. In his Pro-Con days, these firms were known pejoratively as body shops. Was any portion of this computer programming helping to propel PNP along its critical path toward saving the Big-Box relationship? Jack recalled a picture of the pyramid-shaped House of Worship of Niles he noticed on Stanley's wall. Was Stanley building himself this massive pyramid of systems, only to be entombed within it like a modern day Cheops?

Each block of that pyramid represented dozens of hours of work and thousands of dollars of cost. Did PNP's customers value this? It was almost like this pyramid was being dropped, top pointed downward, from outer space. It was about to obliterate PNP, piercing its brand and pushing its assets out in four directions. *How many organizations did these massive technology cancers destroy?* Jack knew the list was long.

THURSDAY, JULY 14ᵀᴴ 1:00 PM

Jack found his way back to Biff's office. Biff was waiting. "What did you learn from Rona?" he asked.

Jack couldn't respond with stories of Rona's polo prowess. He stumbled, answering, "She gave me her version of Big-Box's value proposition underlying this new technology."

"Yeah, Rona does speak like a consultant, doesn't she?"

"Perhaps, but she is very passionate about—about her job," Jack stammered, trying to focus.

"Jack, I am sorry, but my schedule's changed again. Can you come back in the morning?"

Jack was used to this. *The world never stopped for a consultant.* He nodded politely and left.

Jack walked to his Tapir. *I have two hours to kill before the ERP status meeting and I don't care if I'm late. Annie and Marcus will be there anyway. I could stop by the golf range. No, I better visit Gary while I'm in town since I'm already close to the Cook County Jail.*

Gary Gibson was an ex-COO of a software company. He was serving two to five years in federal prison for fraud. Because of executive overcrowding in the federal pen, Gary had been transferred to the Cook County Jail to finish the last months of his sentence. Jack had been to this prison before and knew how to get there from Naperville. He found his way to the visiting area. The guard brought Gary out and sat him down in front of the thick Plexiglas barrier. Gary motioned for Jack to lift the receiver.

"Hey man, great of you to show up. I don't get too many visitors. Most of our old crew is still sore about the last pump and dump deal."

Jack looked at Gary for an extra moment. He appeared much older. Jail was not sitting well with him. "No sweat, Gary. I have a few questions."

"You always do," Gary said.

"Be straight with me," Jack said.

"Did you bring it?" Gary said.

"Yes."

"Give it here."

Jack looked around furtively. The guard turned his head away. Jack quickly took a plastic flash drive shank from his pocket and pushed it under the speaking panel with his thumb. The plastic eight-gigabyte shank had no USB plug. That would have set off the metal detector. Gary would have to snap on the male plug that he hid inside his cell's sink drain. The shank contained a full feature porn movie. The Cook County Jail had PCs, but no Internet. Porn became hotter than cigarettes and nearly as hot as painkillers as a tradable commodity.

Gary took the shank and slipped it into his shoe. "So what do you want to know?" he asked, seemingly satisfied.

Never Blindly Trust Vendors, Analysts, Pundits, Or References

"I want your perspective on what works with technology vendors and what doesn't work," Jack said.

"It's amazing how people make the same mistakes over and over again. The oldest trick in the vendors' book is to sell half-baked, untested software to clients under the guise of it being the latest and greatest version, and then the dumb schmucks think that we're doing them a favor by giving them 15% off the list price. They save cash up front but we screw them on the back end, no pun intended. Beta version bullshit! Never trust vendors, analysts, pundits, or references. Everyone has a motive."

"Even references, that's interesting," Jack said.

"Come on, Jack, don't be naive. Half the CIOs I speak with are willing to sell us their good references as long as we give them a big credit back on their bill or grease them in other ways. The most amazing thing about these guys is that even though they are giving bogus references, they still feel as if they need references from other customers before they can make a purchase. Is that the most laughably hypocritical thing you ever heard? It's insane."

"It's like passing a common needle around while doing drugs. It doesn't take long before everyone gets infected," Jack observed.

"Is it ever good to put blind faith in anyone? You know the cliché about the fool and his money. What do you expect? These companies are in business to sell to you. There is no moral arbiter of truth in the technology game. You know those technology magazines and analyst companies that write reports, do surveys, and consult with you about industry developments and trends?"

"Of course. I read the rags, and I'm barraged by emails to attend their conferences," Jack said.

"Enthusiast magazines exist because of advertising dollars from manufacturers, just like in the auto industry. How many bad reviews are the manufacturers going to tolerate without pulling their ads? There is no *Consumer Reports* in the IT space. There is no unbiased technology analog to the National Highway Traffic Safety Administration that publishes crash-test results. Instead, technology analysts are the same as Wall Street analysts that work for brokerage firms."

"I think I see where you're going."

"The Wall Street analyst's goal is never to squelch demand for stock. How many Sell ratings do you see in their research?"

"Almost none."

"They never want the amount that people invest to decline. They may tell you to shift your money around, but never to pull it out. That's the asset allocation scam that no one's picked up on yet."

"I know what you mean."

"Every major technology analyst firm that I can think of has the consulting and software vendors as its customers. There is no Chinese Wall in this industry, and don't think for a second there is."

"By the way Gary, how's your case going?"

"I dropped the appeal."

"Why?"

"It wasn't going to fly. Instead, I'll be out in another fourteen months for turning over additional evidence against our CFO."

"I thought he got off."

"He did, but the district attorney is pressing new charges."

"What about you?"

"Jack, you know I was a big shareholder in Four Z Software. When I joined them out of Harvard, I received a ton of stock. I was employee number seven and at the height of the boom we had 2000 people in 26 offices."

Jack nodded. He had heard Gary's tale at least a half dozen times.

"We were riding on a soap bubble to nowhere, but we were getting a lot of attention from Wall Street. Whitehouse Nixon had plans to take us public. We were on course but they told us that we needed to get to fifty million in sales. Southern TechEx wrote a favorable report on us after the CFO, the Southern analyst, and I went on this amazing trip to Vegas. We did the whole deal— the Bunny Ranch, Shadow Creek, you know what it's like. Then, the economy slowed and our customers started canceling orders. My crime was that I never cancelled those orders on our books; instead, I doubled them. The CEO offered me more options, with no lockup."

"Was that legal...I mean getting the options without a minimum holding period?"

"You're naïve, Jack. Of course not."

"We were three weeks from going public when the marshals came in and put the cuffs on me. I was three weeks short of having thirty million."

"Wow. Pretty tempting."

"Yeah. Now I'm rotting in prison, my wife has filed for divorce, and my wages are going to be garnished for years to help pay off the shareholder settlement. I have a fat chance of ever working again."

"Maybe I'll hire you. You can tell Reality Check's clients the truth about the way the world works."

"We'll talk about it."

"Any other thoughts?"

"Yes. I've learned through the years that technology is wonderful when it's bought a little at a time, like food. If you buy too much food at once, you have to figure out how to store what you can't consume right away. The other cost of overbuying is more insidious. You look at that food on the shelf and you try to consume it at a faster rate than your body can handle."

"Right," Jack said, "no one needs shelfware. Remember what I once told you about Little-Triangles. Don't stock up on big triangles, because tomorrow you may want something different. The best triangles are plug and play and ready today."

"Exactly. You know what happens when you pre-buy and inventory technology. You get fat and slow down. Rather than an enabler, technology becomes a great disabler," Gary said.

"I can't tell you how many times I've seen companies run away from running lean. Technology should be bought at the time it's needed, never before. Big, ill-conceived projects ought to be starved before they leave the starting gate."

The Panicked Pocketbook

"Ah, but vendors love the big projects. That's where they clean up," Gary said.

"Go on," Jack encouraged.

"Customers beat up the vendors on price up front, but the vendors have the last laugh on every big project I've seen," Gary said.

"So true," Jack responded.

"Big projects are rife with big problems," Gary said. "The vendors' salespeople know that whatever they give up on the front end, they'll make back in spades before the game's over."

"Because customers become desperate?"

"Yes, of course. Once companies realize that their projects are dragging down their core businesses, they panic and throw more resources at their problem in a futile effort to make it go away sooner. Then the pocketbook opens wide. The vendors know when the panic hits, the guy whose job is on the line will open up the floodgates to finish the project. The panicked pocketbook is why all the machinations organizations go through to build business cases and financial models are stupid. Managers rarely consider the real cost of the contingencies."

"I see it all the time, Gary."

"The big tech firms love it. It's the Big Con. Billings on the project run amuck and the client's executives feel so vulnerable that they respond by hiring more consultants. And you know that once a project team grows past a certain size, there's no chance of victory."

"So how do you prevent this?"

Beware Of People Ready To Jump Into A Vendor's Warm Bed

"Don't go to bed with a vendor without protection. Consider two prophylactic measures: first, engage an impartial auditor to monitor the relationship. Second, watch out for your people who are too eager to please the vendor. Maybe they're tired of working at the big ole' manufacturing company. They may be seduced by the consulting company or become addicted to the grease. Where did you get that term from anyway, Jack?"

"Atlanta," Jack said. "I was a junior consultant watching my partner sell a client at DoubleWide's during a mega-greasy hamburger lunch."

"That's great," Gary laughed. "The clients get addicted to the Big Con like you get addicted to the taste of the grease in fast food. You know it's bad for you, but you can't stop stuffing your face."

"Is there a way out?" Jack asked.

"Come on, Jack, you know the answer. Strong leaders find the greased pigs in their organizations and turn them into human sacrifices, and invite the whole company to watch. Tell your client that when he hires a consulting firm, the contract must have a two-way, no-poach clause. Consulting firms love to dangle job prospects in front of a client's employees. It's another trick the consulting firms use to secure their long-term revenue streams."

A loud buzzer sounded, signaling the end of the visit. A guard tapped Gary on the shoulder. After a nod goodbye, Gary was whisked back to his cell. That night, Gary traded the porn shank for three cans of Spam.

THURSDAY, JULY 14TH 2:55 PM

Jack beat the rush-hour traffic back to the plant in order to catch the last half of the ERP status meeting in the Double Boiler. He stood in the back of the room and as Mel Quitoast began reading through the ERP Open Issues List. Jack looked at his watch and tiptoed out.

He wanted to better understand PNP's business processes. *What better way than to learn from the people who worked in the plant?*

Jack had always felt comfortable with the factory workers. They were straightforward and wouldn't take bull. *The beauty of doing the same thing every day is that there is little likelihood that you'll become confused about priorities,* Jack mused. He liked the factory workers' banter about beer, cars, and guns, and even though he was a city boy, Jack usually added a credible comment to the conversation.

He found Earl McCweeg at his station. Jack figured that he and Earl were about the same age. Earl was wearing an outfit that Jack would have worn back in high school, a black Led Zeppelin concert t-shirt and jeans, except Jack never had a pair of steel-toed safety shoes like the ones Earl was wearing.

Earl was changing a roll of thick corrugated paper on the slitter. The corrugated paper was slit into strips corresponding to the depth of a pot, then wrapped outside the pot during packing. The slitter had a safety guard shielding the operator from the blade, but Earl was operating the slitter without the guard in position. The sharp blade glistened menacingly.

Earl adjusted the slitter's speed as Jack recognized Eunice from the cafeteria. Eunice was stacking the cut corrugated into neat piles. *Eunice must be about seventy. I bet she's in the fifty-year club here.* Eunice's back was to Jack; she was wearing gray sweatpants, safety shoes and a pink T-shirt with a large grinning kitten on the back.

"What a sweet lady," Jack murmured to himself. Eunice turned around and he shot her a smile, which she warmly returned. He read the words on the front of Eunice's T-shirt: 'You can pet my Kitty, but don't you touch my Putty.' Jack looked up, mouth agape. *Maybe I should stop assuming I know how people think.* He looked away, glad that it was so noisy in the plant.

Jack tapped Earl on the shoulder. Earl turned and smiled. "I guess you're ready to see what the impo'tent folks are doing here," he drawled. Jack knew that Earl had meant important, and Jack smiled inwardly at the slip.

"That's right! Can you take a coffee break with me?" Jack asked.

"I'll do better. It's time for second-shift lunch. My wife always makes me an extra sammich. You can have it."

"Great, let's go," Jack gulped, expecting either baloney or headcheese.

Earl opened his Dale Earnhardt lunchbox and pulled out a thermos with a large '3'. He then took out two cellophane wrapped items and said, "pâté or lobster roll?"

"Pâté, I'd hate to take your lobster roll," Jack replied in a surprised tone.

"No sweat, let's each have a half."

Jack took a cup from the condiments area and Earl poured Jack spiced green tea from his thermos.

"My wife and I appreciate good food. She's a sommelier at Le Maxwell. Ever been there?"

"Yes, I was just there – it's really delicious."

"Thank you," Earl smiled merrily, feeling worthy of a portion of his wife's praise.

"Tell me about PNP."

"You want the straight dope or the politically correct version?" Earl asked, grinning.

"The dope."

"Okay. PNP was a great company. The founder, Marv Schwartz, hired me fifteen years ago. Marv was a ball-buster but a great guy, and he loved this place more than anything. We developed a reputation for making the best products. Our brand was great and we made money. The employees were treated well. Then, things fell apart. Marv had two sons. The smart one became a doctor and the other one was a screw-up who bumbled around the plant in a golf cart. Irwin, the second son, bought a ton of new production equipment that we didn't need in the name of efficiency. I'm no accountant but I know the old equipment was fine. It was fully deprecated, or something like that."

"I understand," Jack said.

"The new equipment caused our costs to skyrocket and the Chinese, who had just entered the market, buried us. Marv had to declare Chapter 11 bankruptcy when he couldn't meet a debt payment. We were bought out of bankruptcy by Consolidated and after six months, the Schwartz family was gone. Consolidated never did anything to improve the business. They took over and wiped out the debt by getting the lenders to take thirty cents on the dollar. Consolidated then sold the business to Unified. Probably no one made more money than the people from Consolidated because I heard that Unified paid three times what Consolidated paid. Unified couldn't make things happen and after we failed trying to do an LBO, we were picked up on the cheap by Roscoe & Lauer."

"Sounds like an ugly baby that no one wanted."

"Yeah," Earl nodded. "Jack, I know you're interested in the systems. We had an ingrown system."

"You mean a homegrown system?"

"No, I mean an ingrown system. Like an ingrown toenail, it got more painful while becoming harder to remove. Finally, Unified replaced the system with CompuSquat. It sucked, so Unified took some old ThickWare software from one of their other companies and tried to make it work here. When Roscoe & Lauer took us over a couple of years ago, they brought in Lunchmeat to redo all our systems. The guy has never met a proposal he didn't like and never gets tired of spending other people's money. Remember those games where you had to spend a thousand bucks in the grocery store in ninety seconds? Now we have more consultants working on the project team than we have second shift workers on the plant floor. If that is not a recipe for chaos, then I don't know what is. I hear that Big-Box is going to drop us if we can't get the problem solved by the end of the year."

"That's true," Jack replied.

"And that's after Lunchmeat made Biff cancel our Easter break."

"What? Why?"

"That dickhead made us work four extra shifts to stress-test the software, so we sat around pounding keys rather than taking vacation. And the damn thing still doesn't work!"

"Any suggestions on what to do about it?" Jack asked.

"Yes, and it's pretty damn simple. When customers are having a problem with what we're manufacturing, we invite them to the plant so they can tell us what they need. Our people get with their people to solve the problem. On the technology side, things are different. When our customers claim to have a technology problem with us, we tell them not to worry, and that we'll solve it. Then we hire more consultants. This never works. The more consultants we hire, the worse our problems get. We need to bring the Big-Box people here and have them join our project team," Earl declared.

"Shared effort and shared resolution," Jack said. "Nice!"

"We can't build something and hope they'll like it. We have to be in this together."

Maybe Earl should be calling the shots, Jack thought. "Go on," he prompted.

Earl spoke for a few more minutes about the history of the company and complained about Roscoe & Lauer's indifference to the way PNP was managed. Then he noticed the clock on the wall, "Sorry, Jack, I have to hop. I'm finishing a split shift today and I've got three more rolls to run before I clock out."

"Earl, this was great. Thank you!"

"Stop by Dante's tonight. Some of the guys will be havin' beers."

"If I can."

"Cool."

THURSDAY, JULY 14TH 4:30 PM

Jack walked to Biff's office. Biff was reading his email, and looked up as Jack approached.

"How's it going Jack?"

"Good, I'm getting ready to attend another status meeting. You going?"

"No, but sit down for a minute. I want to talk with you about something."

"Great. What's up?"

"I've been going through the project budgets and reviewing the invoices from the technology companies and the consulting firms. It seems that we're paying a lot more than I thought for the technology."

"How do you figure?"

"Best I can tell Jack, we've rewritten most of the software that we bought."

Don't Customize

Jack grimaced. "I hope not. Why you would pay employees or consultants to customize technology that has been designed to be state of the art? When ThickWare creates a software program, they plan to sell it hundreds or thousands of times. Why would you take what they have spent millions of dollars developing and attempt to improve upon it?"

"I approved a lot of these expenses because I was under the impression that the software didn't support all of our business processes."

Jack's grimace became more pronounced. "Biff, that's the oldest scam in the software business. It would almost be laughable if it weren't a lose-lose-lose for all parties. The software vendors lose because the customizations often prevent their technology from functioning properly. The consultants lose, but they lose the least. They get to bill for a lot of extra hours, and their customizations rarely add the business value that they were supposed to. They may lose a few points of reputation, but they make up for it with lots of your cash. You lose because even if everything works on the day you turn it on, what happens when the software vendor upgrades their systems? Your customizations may be hardwired around the old version and new customizations have to be redeveloped for the upgraded version."

"Speaking of weak links, it seems like we took a forged steel chain and replaced some links with plastic ones. When we try to pull our company along, it's pretty obvious what's going to break," Biff said.

"Exactly. In my years doing this work, I have learned this pivotal little rule. It goes like this: Don't Customize! Let me say it again: DON'T CUSTOMIZE!!!"

"Okay, Jack, I heard you."

"Unless you absolutely cannot avoid it, use the out of the box business processes supplied by the software vendor," Jack said.

"But suppose the vendor's processes don't match our business requirements?"

"Ask yourself whether you understand your requirements and know the difference between your must-haves and nice-to-haves. Ask your customers for help. They'll be more open to a stream-lined procedure or process than your internal people. Never force your customers to change and don't allow your employees to force you to remain stagnant. When in doubt, change the business to fit the software, rather than the other way around."

"Jack, I need to get more into the details. I don't know how much our team is trying to customize."

"It may be a lot more than you realize, Biff."

Partner With Vendors Who Will Sell You Little-Triangles

"These customizations could be creating a lot of risk for us," Biff replied.

"Of course. That's why you need to partner with vendors who will sell you Little-Triangles. The best software companies allow you to do things in logical chunks."

"Jack, you're stressing me out."

"Biff, it's a gut feeling at this point, and the Reality Check team is still gathering data, but you may want to think about cutting off the oxygen to everything but Broadway."

"Jack, the pain in my gut tells me the same thing, but I need to account for the millions we already spent with ThickWare, CustHug, and Pro-Con."

"You know it's sunk."

"Believe me, Jack, I know. Roscoe may not be so forgiving."

Jack nodded. "Biff, I understand. Look, I'll get out of your hair for now," Jack said, anxiously rubbing the plugs atop his crown. "I'm off to a Supply Chain meeting."

THURSDAY, JULY 14TH   5:30 PM

Biff pushed back from his desk. He needed air. He walked slowly outside and got into his cherry-red Cadillac. Biff swung by his usual spot. Maxie's Dance Parlor was located across the street from the United Airlines cargo storage facility behind O'Hare Airport. Nikki, his usual, noticed his glum mood.

"What's the matter, sweetie?" she asked, running her long, bright red and glittered fingernails on his neck, behind his ear.

"We're trying to put in this new computer system at work, and we're having a tough time."

Nikki settled comfortably into Biff's lap. She wrapped her arms around his neck. "Does progress ever improve anything? It doesn't make people happy."

"What do you mean?"

"Has any of the fancy toys you've bought make your life better? You have a smaller phone and a faster PC. So what."

"You're right, Nikki," Biff said, downing his first double.

"I know I'm right, sweetie. The things that felt good generations ago are still the things that feel the best today. Smaller and faster don't make for better lovin'," Nikki said, slowly grinding into Biff's lap while gently massaging his earlobe.

Biff's lap didn't respond, but he smiled anyway and took out his wallet.

"Put that away," Nikki said seductively. "This dance is on me."

✮ ✮ ✮

Jack walked to a large dry-erase board mounted on the wall near the cafeteria. Today's production schedule, by manufacturing line, was shown in large, multi-colored writing. Once operational, PNP's new ERP system would automate the process. There would still be a schedule, but rather than that schedule being a quilt of manufacturing constraints, expedited orders, and executive edicts, the new computer driven schedule would strive to optimize PNP's manufacturing assets while increasing on-time delivery performance. *That's the slick talk the ThickWare salesman used,* Jack concluded.

Jack passed the loud hydraulic press department. The operators knew, by sight, which pots, pans, or accessories were being run. If a machine churned out the wrong part, whistles would sound, warning lights would flash, and people would move quickly to address the problem.

The clanging of the presses motivated Jack to duck into an unfamiliar hallway leading away from the shop floor. Fifty feet down the hall, Jack passed a large window. He looked into the data center, the room housing PNP's computer servers, software, and network equipment. This was the locus of the spider's web of cables that spread throughout PNP's operation in Naperville. The room also contained the electronic routers, switches, and hubs that enabled Naperville to connect via the Internet with PNP's other manufacturing plants, its customers, and the outside world.

Jack took two more steps, stopped at the formidable steel door with its biometric locking system, and peered through the thick security glass. The operator must be on break, Jack realized, because there was a half-eaten sandwich sitting on an open piece of plastic wrap atop a keyboard. Jack saw a yellow Post-It note clinging to the operator's monitor. Jack put his face up to the glass and squinted. He could just make out the list of all the systems administrator's security passwords. "Wow," he muttered softly and stepped back. He looked around the room and saw at least seventy servers stuffed into six large racks. A half-filled bucket of water was on the floor next to one of the racks. Jack observed the slow drip from a rag-wrapped pipe above the server array. *Hmm,* he thought, absently touching the plugs atop his head. *If that pipe bursts, it'll be a DELETE error in the making. I must warn Biff.*

Jack looked back at the servers. *On the shop floor, if you watch the machines long enough, you can figure out what they do and how they worked, whereas in the data center, the more you stare, the less you understand.* Ironically, the computer operator had no idea whether the massive flow of data moving through the servers was right for the business. On the shop floor, products were built to satisfy specific customer orders or in anticipation of future customer orders. In the data center, information about what was happening on the manufacturing floor, the customer's order department, the supplier's shipping department, and PNP's banks was flung around electronically at the speed of light. The data certainly existed, but it had no definable form; it couldn't be viewed or touched in the same way that physical inventory could. *Maybe it was data's inherent intangibility and invisibility that made it so insidiously difficult to manage,* he theorized.

Why do companies load up on data that they don't need? Didn't executives realize that while it didn't consume physical space, except nominally in the extra storage drives needed to house it, that extra data created confusing noise that further obscured important business signals? Lean Data makes good sense, and reducing distraction was more important than playing out "what-if" scenarios. Oh well, he mused. *Maybe CEOs will eventually realize that mass and speed are usually opposites.*

Jack remembered that he owed a call to Karen O'Toole, a *Wall Street Telegram* reporter who was writing a feature story on data excess. He punched a button on his smartphone and said, "Dial Karen." Jack had dated Karen during his Rocco-Link days.

Avoid Steaming Piles Of Big Data

"Hello," Karen answered immediately.

"Karen, how are you, darling? How's the story on Big Data coming along?"

"Not good. Taking flack from my editor. Thoughts? I only have a few minutes."

"Yes. Companies need to treat bytes of data like units of physical inventory. More is not better."

"Does the obsession with Big Data create even more chaos?" Karen asked.

"Yes. Companies expend enormous resources consolidating their data into data farms that require expensive software and staff to manage and the cloud just makes it cloudier. There's always a two-fold race going on. Companies add more data capacity and fill it with more noise. It's a bad symphony. No wonder so many IT projects seem like pure confusion."

"How does that tie in to my story?"

"Seamlessly. Rather than trying to figure out how to manage all that data, that fat organization needs to 80/20 its data and determine which twenty percent is helping the organization function and separate it from the eighty percent that is consuming cost."

"So companies have too much data?"

"Ridiculously too much. The big winners are the capacity vendors, whether on-premise or in the cloud. Vendors love anything that sells more hardware. Many organizations don't understand the real cost of data. You have to consider not only the equipment costs like servers, but the backup and recovery systems to retrieve that data that you'll never need anyway. Most of all, there is the opportunity cost of spending your time managing these steaming piles when you ought to be figuring out how to get value out of the twenty percent that matters."

"Good stuff, Jack, anything else?"

"I can't stress enough that companies need better analysis of data, or Analytics. Also, Lean Data organizations tend to be nimble in other ways while Fat Data organizations are glued to the ground."

"Suppose there are regulatory or compliance requirements?"

"Different story. You need to prudently meet those needs and archive intelligently, but still keep your decision-making data light and portable."

"Great. I gotta hop, Jack. Please call me the next time you're in L.A."

"You know me."

"That's right, you louse. If you don't call me next time, don't expect to have your name on the technology page any more. Goodbye, sweetie." Karen hung up.

Jack grinned, while still staring at the servers.

☆ ☆ ☆

THURSDAY, JULY 14TH 8:30 PM

Jack walked into Dante's. Earl and Myron were seated at a long table. Several nearly empty beer pitchers sat on the table.

"There he is," Earl exclaimed loudly. "The guy who unfucks IT projects!"

Jack smiled appreciatively.

"Hey buddy," Earl said to Jack. "We're finishing up. Most of the crew already split."

"Sorry guys. Couldn't make it any earlier."

"Did you see Rona in that red suit?" Earl asked, turning to Myron. "I'd jump that thaang in a second if I could," Earl said quietly, nodding his head up and down.

Jack listened intently.

"Myron, you da' man!" Earl added.

"What? Why do you say that?" Jack asked cautiously, sitting down.

"Myron is the one man at PNP who got the job done with that girl," Earl chirped as Myron grinned with large, white gleaming teeth. Jack looked at Myron and wondered why he wasn't named Moose.

"They say Ole' Biff had a chance with her but blew it," Earl said. "They say Biff dined her in Acapulco and tried to romance her and win her over. They say that Rona wanted it right away and Biff wanted to go slow. They say that by the time Biff made his move, Rona checked out and he got squat."

Who were They? Jack wondered.

"Two weeks after Rona dumped Biff, we had our Christmas party," Earl continued, turning to Jack. "This was a couple of years ago. Everyone went to Pluto on the eggnog and before the night was over, sexy Ms. Rona grabbed Myron, took him into her office, and danced around his Maypole!" Earl exclaimed, savoring every second of the conversation. "And Myron, I bet you had just as much to say then as you do now when you were showing her how to operate the upside-down punch press!"

Myron smiled, acknowledging Earl's words without a hint of smugness.

Jack could not stop looking at Myron. *How can I compete with this Zeus? I'm a shrimp with a bad hair transplant. Did Rona require a Zeus to please her?* If so, Le Maxwell would become a mere Schedule C deduction on this year's tax return.

☆ ☆ ☆

FRIDAY, JULY 15TH 11:45 AM

After a long morning of meetings, Jack's stomach was rumbling and he chose DoubleWide's for a chili and a salad. As he got into the Tapir to leave PNP's parking lot, Rona pulled into the space next to him and waved.

Jack, trying to disguise his uneasiness, waved back. Rona got out of her car. Jack studied her skirt. *It must be two inches shorter than the legal limit,* Jack thought.

"So, what are we doing this weekend?" Rona asked, leaning into Jack's open window.

"I have to work all day tomorrow, but I hope to see you tonight and maybe tomorrow night," Jack replied stiffly.

"Loosen up, kimosabe. It must have been a hard week for you."

"Yes, it has, but we're making a lot of progress." *Two days ago, I would have devoured this level of interest from Rona,* he thought. *Now I'm not so sure.* "How about dinner tonight? I heard about another great place."

"How 'bout dinner at my place," Rona said, leaning in farther. In fact, why don't you check out of the hotel and save us the money. We're paying for your expenses, right?"

Jack nodded.

"Well, I want to be a good corporate citizen, so why not stay in my spare room for the weekend?" Rona said, leaning back out of the Tapir's window.

"Wow, are you sure?" Jack asked nervously.

"I wouldn't ask if I weren't sure. It'll be easier for us to hang out."

"I can't argue with that logic," Jack smiled. "6:30?" he asked.

"Yeah, I'll email you the directions. Don't bring anything – I'm all set." With that, Rona whipped around and strode into the plant.

When it was safe, Jack turned around and watched the last part of her catwalk. *What a sexy outfit,* he thought. *She looks great in chartreuse.*

As he lunched solo at DoubleWide's, Jack couldn't stop squirming in the hard plastic seat.

FRIDAY, JULY 15ᵀᴴ 1:55 PM

Jack returned to the plant, called the president of ThickWare, and was put on hold by his secretary. She returned for the second time. "I'm sorry, Mr. Bluto. He was supposed to be in the Red Carpet Club at La Guardia, but I can't find him. I see the meeting on his calendar. Our system syncs our executives' calendars with the real-time flight departure and arrival data feeds from the major airlines. When a plane is late, the calendars are automatically updated and emails are generated to meeting participants to inform them of revised schedules."

"I see."

"You didn't get an email?"

"No."

"Maybe he left his smartphone on top of the toilet paper holder in the men's room. He did that twice last month."

"I see."

"I'll call you as soon as we locate him."

"Thank you," Jack said, and hung up. *What a lame excuse, especially after I conned him into a meeting by using Biff's name.*

Jack wanted to see Stanley. Jack knew the Reality Check Assessment Letter could be used to justify firing Stanley, but he felt Stanley deserved the benefit of the doubt. Jack went by Stanley's office and learned that he was working from home that afternoon because his pool was being filled. *He's managing a major project that's in crisis. His on-site presence is essential, a sign of commitment. How could he inspire if he refused to act inspired?* Jack wondered.

✵ ✵ ✵

Jack spent the afternoon scribing for Annie and Marcus as they interviewed several of the accounting staffers at PNP. Jack then led an impromptu discussion with the sales department on how they could leverage the future Broadway connection to Big-Box to take market share from Pots Unlimited. After dropping off Annie and Marcus at O'Hare for their flight back to New York, Jack drove to the BigEight and checked out. The desk clerk waved as Jack looked up at the familiar green BigEight sign. *I can't believe I'm doing this,* Jack said to himself. *The Reality Check Assessment Letter is due next week and now I'm sleeping at one of their senior executive's houses. Can I maintain my objectivity?* He put his bag into the Tapir's trunk. *Do I hope she sleeps with me?*

"Yes!" Jack yelled aloud, slamming the trunk closed.

FRIDAY, JULY 15TH 6:15 PM

Jack stopped at the Jewell-Osco supermarket a mile from the BigEight to pick up flowers and wine. Even though Rona had told him not to bring anything, Jack knew that he should. The flowers were a decent selection for a grocery store and Jack found a ten-dollar "greatest hits" bouquet. It had a calla lily, a rose, two carnations, a dandelion, a Gerber daisy, and several other flowers Jack recognized but couldn't name. He also picked up a bottle of Syrah.

He fixed his hair in the men's room at Jewell-Osco. As he wondered what Rona thought of the plugs still visible from his recent procedure, an email came in on Jack's smartphone with the directions to Rona's townhouse. Jack looked again at his hair, distraught at having succumbed to vanity.

FRIDAY, JULY 15TH 6:30 PM

Jack pulled into her driveway. After seeing the skirt that Rona wore earlier, he half expected to see her open the door in a negligee with a Martini in hand. Rona wore baggy black sweatpants and an oversized white T-shirt, with a large black dog printed on the front.

"Hi Jack. Oh no, you shouldn't have," Rona exclaimed, noticing the flowers.

"My pleasure," responded Jack. He stepped into the entry area and saw two dozen, long-stemmed red roses in a beautiful crystal vase, seated atop a pedestal. Rona saw Jack's eye's lock in on the roses.

"Oh, I love *your* flowers," Rona said, noticing Jack's gaze. "Sorry about the frump. I want to get messy in the kitchen."

"I like that," Jack responded disingenuously.

Rona went into the kitchen, and returned carrying a pitcher of margaritas. "It's Mexican night. We're having seafood burritos. I hope you like them."

"Olé."

"You sit down. I'll take care of everything."

Rona led Jack to the screened-in porch of her inviting townhouse. It was a cool night, perfect for alfresco dining. Rona had a new teak porch set and was cooking off a charcoal grill embedded into the back of her fireplace's chimney. She brought out the raw seafood – jumbo shrimp, sea scallops, crab, and swordfish. *A bit fishy for the Syrah,* Jack thought, *but a perfect match for the margaritas.*

"How was your day?" she asked.

"Good. I had an interesting talk with the sales guys about Broadway. They're excited about what it'll do for them."

"I know, but we have to get there first."

"Now is the hardest part of the Reality Check process because it's time to distill down all I've heard during the week, try to make sense of what's going on, and help your company get this wayward project back on track."

"Think you can do it?"

"I think so, but managing the politics will be tough."

"I bet it usually is. How's your drink?"

"Great," Jack replied, handing Rona the nearly empty glass. She tossed the backwash into the sink, re-salted the rim, and refilled the glass from the pitcher. She handed it to him saying, "I've got Coronas on ice, too."

"Thank you," Jack said as he took the glass. Myron's biceps kept popping into his mind.

"Tell me what you've concluded so far," she requested.

"Are you sure that's what you want to talk about?"

"Sure, we have plenty of time to get to the fun stuff."

"Okay, well, PNP needs a defibrillator. Broadway is salvageable, but only with clear and decisive action. In these projects, success should be measured by the long-term impact the new technology will have on the business. All too often, success is defined as getting the technology operational. The original project team disbands, leaving the leverage of the value from the system to a future team. It's incredibly inefficient."

"Is that so?" Rona asked, lightly circling the rim of her glass with her index finger.

"Yes, there's a great loss of knowledge in the transfer," Jack said, observing the motion of her slender finger.

"Hmmm," Rona paused and stood up. "Time to start cooking. Dinner will be ready in a few minutes, if you have to make any phone calls," she said.

"No, I'm just chillin'." Jack responded.

As the burritos were getting closer to becoming a tasty reality, Jack retreated to the washroom. He took the liberty of walking around Rona's townhouse. It was elegant, modern, and stylish –a manifestation of Rona. The red walls in the washroom contrasted nicely with the dark wood in the den. The plush, leather living room sofas were deep rouge, the same color as Rona's lips.

Dinner was delightful. When the margaritas ran out, the Coronas kicked in. The night was cool and the conversation easy. Rona brought in a chocolate soufflé for dessert and as they savored the last bites, they both edged toward a food coma. Jack rose from the table, feeling groggy and foggy.

"Want to help me clean up?" Rona asked.

"My pleasure," Jack lied gracefully.

They did the dishes and settled down in the living room. Rona put on Madonna's *Immaculate Collection*.

"Do you mind if I don't change?" she asked. "I am so tired, I just want to hang out."

"No, of course not," Jack lied again. He missed the skirt she wore earlier.

They sank into a sofa and within moments, Rona and Jack were kissing. Jack opened his eyes every so often to check the wall clock behind Rona. After twenty minutes, Jack gently eased Rona's hand toward his knee, but his efforts were rebuffed. Nevertheless, they continued for almost an hour. Finally, Jack pulled back. "I need to take a break," he gasped. "Between the kissing and the salt from the margaritas, my lips are about to fall off."

Rona smiled, "Okay, but I really dig kissing you. It's time for bed anyway. Let me show you to your room."

Jack got up smugly. He thought he spotted a slight wink. Jack had checked out the upstairs earlier. There was Rona's bedroom and her office. The office had no bed or couch in it. Rona was moving toward the stairs. At the bottom of the staircase, she stopped suddenly and threw open a hidden door, revealing a large utility room with a low ceiling. She switched on a twirled, energy-wise fluorescent light.

"Here we are!" Rona exclaimed.

Jack looked up blankly. He obediently followed Rona into the room furnished with items that didn't fit into any other room. She moved two file boxes and revealed an itchy-looking wool couch. Rona started pulling off the cushions and then she unfolded the sleeper sofa.

"I hope that the bar in the middle doesn't bother your back," Rona said tentatively.

"It'll be great. Thank you so much," he said, gently biting his swelling lips.

"Good night, then," she said, giving him a quick kiss before heading purposefully toward the door.

"Night," he replied.

Rona was upstairs within moments and Jack heard her footsteps above his head. Jack refocused on PNP's challenges. *The next few days will be hard. Things would get acrimonious, especially with Stanley.* Jack was prepared for the onslaught, his skin hardened after having done this many times. He drifted off to sleep.

SATURDAY, JULY 16TH 8:00 AM

The aroma of coffee wafted into the utility room, waking Jack. Rona was leaving for the gym. *She looks delicious in her skin-tight black workout pants and pink top. What a heart stopper. I hope that she wears that tonight,* Jack thought.

"I have fruit, bagels, eggs...what would you like?" Rona said.

"A kiss, coffee, a bagel, and then more kisses," Jack said.

"The first three are on the menu. The dessert will have to wait 'til later. I have a class in twenty minutes."

"Any men in the class?" Jack asked.

"I guess so," Rona said. "Make yourself at home. You can work here if you like. There's an extra key hanging on the refrigerator. After the gym, I need to do errands, visit a friend and then I'll be back here late in the afternoon. Will you be up for going out to dinner tonight?"

"Absolutely," he replied, twisting his back to work out the kinks.

SATURDAY, JULY 16TH 10:20 AM

Jack had driven to PNP, frustrated that he couldn't focus at Rona's. Marcus had emailed Jack the first draft of the Reality

Check Assessment Letter. Jack sat in the consultants' work area at PNP and read through it. *Marcus is right,* Jack realized. Like many Reality Check clients, PNP was tripping over the same avoidable obstacles. *Oh well,* Jack mused. *At least they keep us in business.* Jack mentally reviewed the process:

> *The Reality Check Assessment Letter started with a* **Recap** *of the client's stated objectives and business case (if one existed) for its IT endeavor. Next,* **Observations** *detailed what the Reality Check consulting team had learned during its client interviews and surveys, including the observed symptoms of the underlying problems.* **Risks & Problems** *uncovered the core problems that generated the observed symptoms and project risks.* **Project Analysis** *measured the CONTROL, ALT, and DELETE errors. Finally,* **Recommendations** *offered solutions to the core problems and described how to put the project back on its original course or redirect it for greater business value.*

Jack sat in front of the screen and thought about Stanley, ThickWare, and Biff's low level of prior involvement. Every large project was different, but they had similar characteristics. The best projects had the strongest executive sponsorship and the best project controls. The worst projects were Pass The Keys or PTK projects, as in the children's storytelling game. Stewardship of a PTK project was passed through a series of unlucky managers over the project's life. Requirements changed so many times that any final results bore little relation to the original objectives that had seemed so compelling when the project was conceived. It was as if you put a live chicken in the oven and three years later a lounge chair popped out.

Jack began to edit the draft. He referred to his notes, but mostly relied on his memory of the past week's conversations. There were two battlegrounds to be analyzed: the technical and the political. Technical problems were often overstated, while political problems were understated. With focus and the right knowledge, technical problems could be resolved. It was a matter of finding the solutions and implementing them, but too often, implementation was stymied by political blockades. Smashing through the blockades was never fun, but it was the specialty of wartime generals.

The more complex the project, the harder it was to recognize the core problems and separate them from the easy-to-see symptoms. As a bad project's duration increases, so did this confusion. *A smoking gun is hard to find except after the moment it's been fired,* Jack realized.

SATURDAY, JULY 16TH 11:45 AM

Jack stood up. He walked outside and saw Stanley smoking in the parking lot, near the production workers' entrance.

"Good morning," Stanley said disarmingly.

"Good morning," Jack replied, wary of Stanley's friendly countenance.

"I hope you're finding what you're looking for," Stanley said.

"I think I am."

"My team hit a home run last night. Ahmed and Park figured out what was causing ThickWare to kick out so many of those inventory transactions. They worked all night and ThickWare's technical team is flying in today. That was the last hurdle on the way toward hooking up to Broadway."

"That's excellent. Great job."

"Thank the team. Our management and control processes worked, as usual. Maybe next time executive management will be more confident in my department's ability to deliver."

Stanley flicked his butt to the ground and walked to his Mercedes. Jack cleared his throat and watched the butt bounce off the payment and roll into a puddle, snuffing out its red embers. As Stanley drove off, Jack noticed the STANSTAC2 vanity plate on the Mercedes. He chuckled and went inside.

For the next few hours, Jack pounded away on the keyboard. It was a brain dump; he was wringing out all of the facts from his head that he had mopped up during the week. At 3:30 PM, Jack hit his limit. He pushed back the keyboard after saving the updated Reality Check Assessment Letter in the cloud.

He was tired. *What should I do about Rona? The trouble with clarity is that it enables you to be confused about new things that weren't on the horizon before. Was Rona being prudent or prudish last night?*

✳ ✳ ✳

Biff began his day at the Naperville ChumpRoast. He ordered a Light Super Chump with room and waited in the queue for the new barista to ask and re-ask the orders of the three people ahead of Biff. *Why can't she handle one order at a time from start to finish?* Biff wondered. *She seems pleasant, but I don't like repeating myself.*

The store manager walked through with espresso samples. Biff took one in each hand and quickly downed them both. He felt terrible and needed the caffeine. A dinner party at a friend's house ended in another fight with Constance about Amelia.

Biff would be at the office from 8 AM until his regular Saturday 1 PM game at Hollow Hills. He played most Sundays too, but promised Constance that he would take her to Big-Box tomorrow to choose paint colors for their soon-to-be-remodeled living room.

Finally the barista called out, "Boff, Dark Super Chump!" Biff didn't care anymore. He took a hearty sip and recoiled, grimacing as the burnt-tasting black roast singed his lips. "C'mon," he barked, "I said room!"

✶ ✶ ✶

Rona taught her yoga class at the Naperville YMCA, and then visited Gladys at the hospital. Gladys was recovering from a breakdown after discovering that a guy that she had met online and dated for six months was already married.

On her way home, Rona sat in traffic. *Where is my life going?* Rona wondered. *I'm too committed to PNP. I shouldn't be so loyal. If I keep up this pace, PNP will consume all of me. If I want to have a family, I have to get serious. I can't wait until I'm forty-three to get married again.*

"I can't let Jack get away," she said to herself softly. *We have chemistry, don't we? I wish I knew more about him. He's going to have a tough time convincing PNP to change its direction, especially if the ladies from the private equity firm are in on that decision. Why did he get that weird hair transplant? Do guys actually think it makes them look better? He seems so secure but those plugs probably guard a typical fragile male ego. I don't care,* Rona decided, *I'm going to wear those new five-inch stilettos that just arrived from Milan and we are going to have a good time tonight.* The traffic let up and Rona's mind returned to the road.

✶ ✶ ✶

SATURDAY, JULY 16TH   4:15 PM

Jack arrived at the house before Rona and let himself in. He turned on the television, went to the refrigerator, helped himself to a Corona and lay back to watch the Yankees against the Cubs. *Only one beer for now,* Jack promised himself. *I don't want to get caught doing my Wrigley Walk.*

Jack's Wrigley Walk followed summertime Cubs home games when a few fans staggered out of Wrigley Field, usually sweeping wide angles from the critical path line that they were trying to follow. Despite the variability of their paths, they usually made it home, but if they drifted too much, they wound up in the holding pen of the Cook County Jail, across the courtyard from Gary Gibson.

Jack fell asleep on the couch and was awakened by Rona two hours later, who was peering down from the top of the stairs in a big maroon bathrobe. "I'll be ready in a half hour," she said.

"Okay," Jack replied groggily, as he pulled himself up.

KEY 5: USER – EMPOWER USERS TO CREATE VALUE, NOT WASTE TIME

SATURDAY, JULY 16TH   7:00 PM

Jack showered in the downstairs bathroom. He put on a clean white shirt with his black suit. *Good enough,* he thought. *Maybe Rona will put on something sexy? Naaah, her home life is about comfort. Her stylish, racy look is strictly for the office.*

Jack's thoughts were <CONTROL> <ALT> <DELETE>'d when Rona appeared at the top of the stairs. Her black leather pencil skirt was slit up the side on one leg to reveal the lacy top of her thigh-high stockings. Her emerald silk top hugged her tightly, and plunged in the front, revealing her cleavage. She adorned her contoured neckline with a delicate gold chain, a single diamond dotting its center. Her ears were bare and her hair cascaded in loose, shiny curls.

"You look delicious, better than a pepperoni pizza," Jack murmured. *Wow, could I say anything more stupid?*

Rona smiled provocatively.

They got into Jack's Tapir and Rona gave directions. They wound up at Ahoy, a seafood restaurant deep in the south side of Chicago, adjacent to the quaint jazz clubs long since forgotten by the mainstream. This was no chain restaurant with a menu designed to appeal to everyone while satisfying no one. Ahoy was a neighborhood seafood place featuring fresh lobster and a fun yet atmospheric vibe. It was owned by Jimenez Gonzales, a college friend of Rona's, who looked up with a welcoming smile when they entered.

"Ah, Señorita, don't you look ravishing tonight," Jimenez said.

"Thank you, Jimmy."

"Ahh, and the mister, welcome, you must be special hombre." Jack beamed.

Jimmy ushered them to a corner table topped with mallets, paper towels and a roll of butcher paper fastened to the table's end. He brought a pitcher of Old Style beer.

No menus. I like this, Jack thought. This evening, Rona was in charge. Looking around, he thought, *we are the best looking couple in the joint, though mostly because of Rona.*

A burly waiter came in. His size reminded Jack instantly of Myron. Jack shrank down in his chair.

"What's wrong?" she asked, noticing the shrinkage.

"Rona, the problem with this project is the same as the problems occurring on almost any project that goes bad," Jack said.

"What's that?" Rona said cautiously.

"Forget it, let's focus on us," Jack said, straightening up in the chair.

"I like that consulting advice," Rona replied, smiling.

The lobster came. Bright red claws shimmered on the tray as the waiter unloaded the dual two and a half pound crustaceans. Another waiter brought over a centerpiece of a half-dozen Blue Point oysters mixed in with a half-dozen Malpeques. Jimmy followed the second waiter and leaned his head down to Rona and Jack's level.

"For romance," Jimmy said, smiling as he walked away.

"Maine lobsters are the most succulent," Jack said, gazing at Rona.

"Like lobsters?" she asked coquettishly.

"I love lobster and Maryland blue crab too. Ever try it?"

"Are you kidding?" Rona said, as she began to dissect her prey, pausing to wash down bites of lobster with Old Style. "Tell me Jack, you must have a million girlfriends."

"What are you really asking?" Jack replied, his mouth full of claw.

"Are you dating anybody?" Rona asked, pausing to wipe the lobster juice leaking from the corner of her mouth.

Jack paused. For a moment, he had the upper hand. "Now and then. What about you?"

"I have a lot of first dates," Rona said.

"Where do you meet people?" Jack prompted.

"I'm always working, so it's hard to meet anyone. Recently I went online," Rona answered.

"How's it going?"

"It's amazing how many people use these websites. Since I posted my picture, I get twenty emails a day. I barely have time to respond to the inquiries."

Jack nodded.

"The guys I've met look and act differently from their pictures," Rona added.

"What do you mean?"

"I went out with a guy last month who sounded really nice on our audio chat. He posted a great picture of himself on the beach with a football, in a quarterback pose."

"Just your type," Jack replied evenly.

Rona rolled her eyes slightly and smiled, "Maybe, but I should have done the video chat."

"Why didn't you?" Jack asked.

"The guy said his camera was broken."

"That's a good one. How was he in person?"

"The guy looked nothing like he did in the picture! It must have been old or seriously doctored."

"Is the guy a computer geek?"

"No, a lawyer."

"Rona, it's amazing how the world is changing. Do you realize that the last generation of Americans that haven't made the computer part of their lifestyles is sunsetting?"

"You mean dying?"

Jack nodded, "There's an amazing dynamic taking place. Older people email every day. They're staying connected to stay young. Every kid has a computer and most teenagers have smartphones. Millennials know more about technology than we could ever teach them in a stodgy corporate training class."

"You're right. Times have changed," Rona answered.

Jack nodded, pouring Old Style down his gullet.

Free Your Users To Work Everywhere

"And people aren't tied to their desks anymore," Rona said, ripping apart a large claw.

"You're right. This is the new world. Telecommuting is a major advancement for mankind. I love that I can videoconference from home and connect to anyone around the world."

Rona nodded.

"I travel a third as often as I used to," Jack continued. "Sure, I fly to client sites at the beginning of a project and sometimes when we wrap up, but now most of my meetings take place electronically. It's great."

"So you can call around the world in your boxer shorts as long as you have a shirt and tie on?" Rona said.

"Exactly," Jack smiled, "But I wear briefs, just like a Supreme Court judge," Jack paused to allow his joke to sink in.

"Could you be cornier?" Rona said, noisily sucking lobster meat out of a pincer.

"Did you say hornier?" Jack asked.

"Touché," Rona said.

"Seriously, we're witnessing a historical convergence of home and office. Workers now have the tools to add value from everywhere. Why would anyone want to travel?" Jack asked.

"I know what you mean," said Rona. "I spend hours online at night dealing with our European and West Coast customers. PNP pays me for an eight-hour day but I work twice as many hours. I never go anywhere without my smartphone."

"Ah, the employer's American Dream. Getting you to work more hours for no more pay!"

"I'd rather work more hours at home than travel," Rona countered.

"I agree. It not flying that I hate. It's dealing with the airports, the parking, going through security, and the endless delays. Business trips are going the way of the fax machine," Jack declared.

"My ex used to say that the only people who like business travel are either having affairs or are planning to."

"That fits," Jack said, picking up his lobster by the tail.

User Community Extends Traditional Boundaries

Jack continued. "Technology's pervasiveness changes not only physical boundaries, but also organizational boundaries."

"Because I can use my laptop on a client's network when I'm doing a site visit?" Rona asked.

"Yes, but that's not what I meant. The Internet allows organizations to see their trading partners' information. For example, a Big-Box store manager can look at his Chinese bathtub supplier's shipping schedule via Broadway and know when to expect the next shipment. Extending this scenario, Big-Box's advertising firm may look at this data to better synchronize offers in their next advertising circular, all in real time."

"But we do that now over the telephone," Rona said.

"Yes, but the phone is so linear. Big-Box would need to make thousands of calls to do this for all their stores, and by the time they finished, the world would pass them by."

"And I can view the data on my smartphone in my new office at ChumpRoast?" Rona asked.

"Ha, it's the new office for many businesspeople, isn't it?" Jack replied.

"I make a half-dozen calls a day from there waiting for my latte."

"ChumpRoast is not my cup of tea," Jack said, smiling slyly.

"Very funny," Rona said sarcastically.

"Seriously, it's what I call the monotizing of America. It de-flavors us and I don't like it but it makes life easier to navigate. You remember when you first rode on the interstate highways and noticed that the exits looked the same?" Jack asked.

"You mean that they all had a McDonald's, a Wendy's, and now a DoubleWide's and a ChumpRoast?"

"Exactly, now extend that to the rest of our economic infra-structure. Homogeneity is becoming more pronounced as mega box stores crowd out smaller players. I was in Fort Lauderdale a few weeks ago and the first ten restaurants I passed were the same ten that I saw in Kansas City the night before, and none were the low-cost fast-foodies."

"What does that mean for business?"

"Old barriers are breaking down. Chain restaurants have been giving us beepers for years to tell us that our tables are ready. Now they text you. I was in a place in Phoenix recently where you could use a smartphone app to order your lunch before you got there. It tied into the same order system that their servers used. And, by the way, that restaurant's suppliers were seeing the real-time food flow through the restaurant so that they could accu-rately meet any fluctuation in demand. Technology is eroding both physical and organizational barriers at an incredible rate."

"That's wild," Rona responded. "But why the homogeneity?"

"Because big companies spread their fixed technology costs over more locations."

"So what's wrong with that?" Rona asked.

"When all the systems are interconnected, it's more dire when we have a September 11th or a Hurricane Sandy that shuts everything down," Jack replied.

"So what's the remedy?"

"You never allow technology to grow more powerful than your ability to disengage from it. You have to be able to turn it off," Jack stated firmly.

"Is that practical?"

"In many cases, it's not because we've tied ourselves too tightly to a globally driven supply chain. Technology is the new oil. We've grown like wildfire because of it, but we're inextricably dependent on it." Jack said.

"We're already so addicted to technology – I know I would be lost without my smartphone," Rona replied, adding, "We've lost the oil war – can we still win this one?"

"It's complex. I would classify technologies into two large buckets, the infrastructure and the extrastructures. In the future, there will probably be a handful of global infrastructure providers. They will control the power, bandwidth, reliability, mass data storage, and the recoverability of our connectivity. They'll be the new OPEC. The extrastructures will be everything connected to this infrastructure, from your corporate network to your smartphone. Extrastructures will be sold in more competitive and less risky markets."

"The infrastructure worries me. We can't allow anyone to choke off or hijack our access."

"Exactly. We can't allow ourselves to become caught in a tangle that we can't untangle."

"But it's hard to resist getting sucked deeper into the game, given the incredible new devices that come out every few months," Rona added.

Expect To Be Amazed By New Technology

"The extrastructures are amazing. The computers, phones, and entertainment devices can tempt the devil. Like this lobster," Jack said.

"My brother's eight-year-old got a new video game center and now plays all his sports inside the family's playroom. The kid sweats playing interactive tennis."

"I can't tell you how many of my friends—and I'm talking about guys in their forties and fifties—buy these things. Why join a country club when you can play golf without ever getting off your butt?"

"How fat will that butt get when you never get off it?"

"Not that you have to worry about that issue," Jack said, leaning over the table and overtly admiring Rona's figure.

"Hey babe, that's the product of hard work," Rona responded.

"I dig," Jack responded, slurping up the last oyster. "Ever recognize that technology's power growth is directly correlated with America's fatness?"

"Maybe so," Rona said, gliding her index finger through Jack's discarded oyster shell and then licking the last bit of Jack's cocktail sauce from her finger.

Jack paused and stared, transfixed. He wiped the sweat from his forehead.

"I guess you are right about users being smarter than they used to be," Rona said steadily.

"Maybe, but don't think that we're peaking in terms of what these devices can do. I'm still waiting for Woody Allen's sex machine from *Sleeper*," Jack said.

Rona laughed. "Jack, the devices are almost too personal now. I could swear that this woman was taking videos with her smartphone inside the ladies locker room last week."

"Did you confront her?"

"No, I was mostly dressed and I wasn't sure anyway. Even in the locker rooms you can't avoid the paparazzi," Rona lamented with a wink.

Don't Allow Personal Technology To Get Too Personal

"There is no privacy," said Jack. "Anything ever sent electronically is still echoing on Internet."

"I just saw a news story about that," said Rona.

"There's a fuzzy line between leveraging the Internet to make your life better and putting yourself in a position where your life can be ruined. My friend's teenager posted pictures of himself playing drinking games at a high school party. An Ivy had accepted this kid early admissions and then revoked the offer," Jack said.

"Wow," said Rona.

"Happens all the time. Putting stuff on the web is like getting a tattoo. As long as you never need to change your mind, it's fine." Jack said.

"But how do you know if you are ever going to change your mind?"

"Exactly."

Rona paused. "Do you worry about losing your smartphone?"

"Sure, and I lost it on that MidPoint flight."

"Hmm," Rona said.

"Foolishly, I used to keep my password information for my various accounts stored on my smartphone. I stopped doing this after another buddy lost his smartphone and wallet at a Knicks game."

"Anything happen?"

"You can guess. Someone ran up expenses on Bill's credit cards. He dealt with that easily, but the crook used the information in the smartphone to access his bank accounts. The bank froze Bill's transactions and stopped his automatic payments to his car leasing company and his mortgage company. He's still fighting with the credit reporting agencies to clean up his credit score."

"Sounds miserable. And I bet most people still use PASS-WORD as their password," Rona said.

"Not most, but enough to encourage predators to purloin personal devices. Once a personal device moves beyond its owner's person, privacy may be forever compromised. If I were you, I wouldn't keep more than a couple weeks of emails or records on your smartphone. Real portability means that you can replace it quickly with minimal loss, but the bottom line is that security must be a forethought."

"Come on…everyone does their banking online these days," Rona countered.

"Yes, but you need to look over your shoulder when you go to the cash machine, and the advice applies when doing your online business. Make sure you're on a secure screen and if you are not certain, assume you're not. Never send proprietary information via email. Miscreants are sniffing online for any fifteen or sixteen digit number that comes across on social media sites to use as a credit card."

"But if someone wants to hack into my account and get my info, can't they do it?"

"Probably, but at least wear your seatbelt and drive carefully. Again, if you can't disengage from your technology, then you're too deeply beholden to it."

"Hmm," Rona nodded.

"Speaking of disengaging, what are those pink pills that Biff seems hooked on?" Jack asked.

"You mean the oxycodone?"

"That's it."

"He started taking them for his shoulder, but now he takes them for stress."

"To relieve it or create it?" Jack prompted.

"I'd rather not talk about it. I feel bad for him," Rona said.

Avoid The Email Unproductivity Trap

"Okay," Jack said, admiring her loyalty. "Look, Rona, the Internet is awesomely powerful, but for many it's an all-consuming time toilet. The electronic gateway that PNP is building to Broadway is a great example of how to use technology, but that's an exception to the time toilet rule. Most back and forth on the Internet is equivalent to inane teenage texting."

"Maybe you're right, but when people text, you don't have to be burdened with hearing their conversations," Rona said.

"Too many at-work employees use the net as a peep show. The employee doesn't pay a quarter when he steps into the cube, but the shareholders pay a tremendous price for the wasted time. The Internet should be used to transact business, quicken communications, share ideas, exchange key documents, and perform research. It should be the central nervous system connecting customers, suppliers, employees, and shareholders."

Rona nodded.

"Those squandered hours are lost forever. Have you ever spent four hours on a dating site looking at men? Tell me," Jack said.

"Me, never at work, but I see people doing this at PNP. I can't believe how many hours some people waste," Rona said, adding, "And if they're not on their PC's, they're on their smartphones."

"Doesn't PNP have a policy that restricts Internet usage?"

"Yes, but it's not well enforced. We used to restrict access to certain sites that were obviously inappropriate, but the sales group complained and we restored full access. Most of our users are pretty judicious, but to use your style of thinking, it's probably twenty percent of the workers that waste eighty percent of the time. Most of us are just too busy to waste time like that."

"I bet there's a lot more time wasted than you think, especially with email."

"What do you mean?"

"How many emails do you get a day? Fifty? A hundred? How many of these emails are intended for other people that you are cc'd on?

"I need to know what's going on," Rona said.

"Do you? You operate in a noisy environment. You have to be more attuned to what's going on to pick out the signal. It's akin to an elderly person in a crowded restaurant who is desperately trying to understand what his dining partner is saying."

"I see that," Rona said, using her red pinky nail to scratch out the last piece of lobster meat from the claw. "When I have an issue with a customer and I send an email rather than calling or visiting, it's never as effective."

"That's because email is a great way to hide from the other person's reaction. Sometimes things have to be hashed out face to face or at least voice to voice."

"Agreed," Rona said.

"Eighty percent of emails could be cut out immediately. I wish someone would charge us a quarter for each email sent, so people would think twice about selling me male enhancement, loan refinancing, or that precious opportunity to act as the American custodian of a wealthy Nigerian's bank account."

"I guess the growth of texting and smartphones makes it worse."

"Bingo, people get addicted to the instancy of the experience rather than its quality."

"Jack, did you concoct that word too?" Rona asked.

Jack smiled. "Go anywhere and see all the people chattering on their devices."

Rona nodded.

"Rona, I started describing to Biff the five waves in the history of business computing. I can summarize to you in one sentence where we are today: The Internet, combined with fabulous business software, cheap hardware, and intelligent users, has enabled massive leaps forward in productivity."

"So what's the problem?"

"There's a fourth wave paradox that threatens to undo all of the progress and it's the sum of the time we squander blathering on our computers, smartphones, and other extrastructures.

Slim That Computer-Ass!

"How do you deal with this?" Rona asked.

"Limit these wonderful tools in the workplace to necessary activities. Come on, how many people really need access to social media at work? Organizations mistakenly enable their users to squander whole days at a time."

"True."

"The Internet is like putting televisions on your employees' desks. Also, people who sit all day in front of their computers would be better off moving around, burning calories and getting their heart rates up. Rona," Jack added, raising the volume of his voice, "the true, unspoken cause of our obesity epidemic is Computer-Ass."

"Wow, I bet you're right," Rona said, looking down to see if she had been afflicted. She shook her head indicating that she had not been.

"Like I said Rona, you're the opposite!"

Rona smiled.

"It's challenging to stay mentally and physically fit when all the information in the world comes to you. We've forgotten how to hunt and hunting keeps us fit," Jack said.

"But you can't limit people's information if you want them to be creative," Rona said.

"Rona, maybe I'm naive, but sometimes there's too much creativity and too much information. You need doers, not only thinkers, and when an organization gives its users too many tools or too much rope, users will hang themselves."

"So you encourage your clients to limit access to the Internet to a need-to-use basis?" Rona asked.

"Yes, and here's why. At PNP, when your network crashes, you may lose access to your data for a while and you may even have to shut down your production lines if the problem doesn't get solved quickly. In a more critical environment, things mushroom. When we have a shutdown of the power grid or an airplane crashes, it happens for the same reasons that PNP fails to get its order shipped to Big-Box: randomness, too high of a controllable probability of failure, not enough safeguards, failure to audit, and failure to use Little-Triangles."

"So how do you cut the risk of a negative event and reduce its potential impact?"

"By cutting the din. Lower the noise level so that you're less likely to miss a critical signal when it comes through."

"So how do you cure Computer-Ass? It must cost employers billions in healthcare dollars."

"By getting users back on their feet and solving problems. And if they don't want to get up, take away their chairs. Better yet, make 'em check their smartphones when they clock in."

Rona nodded.

Users Will Only Use What's Usable

Jack knew he was on a roll. "On the other hand, you can't shove a system down users' throats. Users will only use what's usable. They'll find ways around what is too cumbersome. This weakens the system's integrity."

"So?"

"When the male airport screener decides not to look through a foxy young lady's bag after she flashes him a smile, then this weak link jeopardizes the entire multi-zillion dollar screening system."

"How do you avoid this?"

"At some level, you can't engineer all of the risk out of a situation, but in this case, I would build redundancy into the system."

"And use a female screener to back up a male?" Rona asked.

Jack smiled, "You got it, baby. I'll screen your baggage any time."

"I might let you, even though you're a cheese ball," Rona said with a laugh, adding, "Want to dance? There's a great club across the street. Let's see how you move."

"Not yet, I need a few more cups of this fine cheap brew that you're hooking me on."

Two more pitchers and an hour later they ambled out of the restaurant and into a seventies dance club. The scene was from the disco days, with platform shoes, super tight Sassoon jeans, back pocket pick combs, and big hair. Jack saw a couple of white suited discoids right out of *Saturday Night Fever*. The club had the seventies version of the Internet chat room, CB radios, available for the patrons to use. The DJ cut in, "Breaker one nine. Breaker one nine. You got your ears on? This is brown sugar looking for love! Come on baby, what's your handle?"

Jack and Rona danced electrically, especially during "Shake Your Booty" and "More, More, More". Jack put his arms around Rona during "Feelings", clasping his hands behind her back. Rona did the same with her arms around Jack's neck. They were kissing on the dance floor and Jack sensed it was time to go back to her place. He led Rona to the maroon Tapir and they sped to her townhouse. Rona licked the oyster taste off the fingers on

Jack's right hand while he drove. He was psyched; *the caveman's Viagra,* he thought.

When they opened the door to her townhouse, Rona excused herself and went upstairs. Jack was concerned that she would come down in pajamas and that awful bathrobe, but she returned wearing her same sexy outfit. She came over to the couch and nestled in Jack's arms. Both had roaming hands.

Rona whispered, "Oh Jack, you are so what I need right now… it's been so long…" Jack was purposefully silent. *Never, never talk past the close,* he reminded himself. The kissing and touching continued. Just when Jack felt that the moment was right, he reached toward Rona's skirt. Her hand clamped down on Jack's arm, her nails digging into his flesh for emphasis. "No, just kiss me."

"Okay," said Jack.

"Maybe when Broadway is up and running, I'll feel differently," she said.

Jack was 95% sure that she was joking. *I can't ask. I'll have to play out my cards.* He went back to kissing her. Rona's hands relaxed and she began to pant. Jack joined in the harmony. He purposefully yet subtly increased the pace of his panting, trying to induce a sympathetic response from Rona. It worked. A pheromone fan's delight ensued as Rona's natural body chemistry reacted with the Italian leather in her skirt and the Argentinean leather in her couch.

Oh my god. This is overpowering. The natives are going to break down the door. He persisted. As his fingertip inched toward the elastic of Rona's minimal panty, she jumped up and bleated, "Oh god, I have to stop!" She bolted up the stairs into her room, locking the door behind her.

Jack sat for five minutes, unable to think clearly. Finally, he followed Rona upstairs. Her door was closed.

"May I come in?" Jack asked.

No reply.

Jack knocked. Rona unlocked the door and opened it slightly.

"I'm sorry, I'm just not sure what to do," Rona said.

"What do you mean?"

"Part of me wants to be with you, but my mind tells me I shouldn't."

"It's okay…we can take it slow," he said, moving towards her cautiously. She stood her ground. Unsure of how to proceed, he stopped and added, "Rona, sex is like a technology project."

"You would bring up technology at a time like this!" She paused and looked into Jack's eyes. "What do you mean?"

"I can't tell you, I have to show you," Jack said, winking.

"That's the weakest line I've ever heard," Rona replied, smiling cautiously.

"I know. It has to do with something called High Value."

"Biff mentioned your Get High! paradigm. How does it relate?" Rona said.

"Soon enough, my dear. You'll know," Jack said.

"Hmm," Rona said, amused.

The Path To Tomorrow Does Not Go Through Yesterday

"You remember what we were talking about regarding the progressiveness of the users? It's not all that way," Jack said, sitting down on the floor outside Rona's bedroom door.

Rona opened the door three more inches but remained in her room, looking at Jack.

"How, Jack? I can't believe that you want to talk about this now!"

"One of the major problems I see is that organizations upgrade their systems and involve their users heavily in the design of the new technology."

"Why is that a problem? Don't you want input from the people who will be using the systems?" Rona said softly. She opened her door, crossed its threshold, and sat down next to Jack in the hallway. She reached up and pulled the door mostly closed, obscuring the view of her bed. She took his hand in hers.

"Of course, you need some user input," Jack said. "The challenge comes in breaking free from the old way of doing things. I see users squandering the value of better software by trying to configure it for yesterday's business processes—you know, the ones that they are the most comfortable with. The consultants are happy to listen and a tremendous amount of meeting time is spent trying to find a common ground between yesterday and tomorrow."

"How do you avoid this?"

"By not involving the users too heavily in the design and configuration of the new system. Better to involve them in Pre-Engineering and reward them for making process improvements before those processes are computerized. Remind them that the path to tomorrow does not go through yesterday."

"Most people won't get on board with that."

"When an innovative manager designs a hot new product, do you think he asks everyone what it ought to look like? You know opinions are like noses, everyone has 'em."

"I don't think that's the expression," Rona said, smiling.

"It's close enough. Fast movers can't get bogged down. Rather than trying to please everyone, an organization is better off pushing out a trial version of the system sooner."

"You mean something that's not quite ready for primetime? That sounds like a good way to lose longstanding customers, especially if the new technology is flimsy."

"Dead right. It's a balancing act. You want something lean but reliable. Let your market tell you what they want in Version 2.0. If you over-engineer Version 1.0, you'll make less than fact-based assumptions about what's really important and squander time in the process."

"Can't you use market research to hone your offering?"

"Yes, but it's no substitute for the real thing in the users' hands," Jack responded.

"Jack, I think I need the real thing," Rona said, pausing. "What did you say about technology and lovemaking?"

"I said sex is like a technology project!"

"Why, because men are like technology vendors? Over-promising and under-delivering?"

"Yes, sort of," Jack chortled. "Think about what you need for good sex: aligned desires, passion, and timing. If two people get to know each other's requirements, the sex is usually better. When you rush or push too hard, you get dissatisfaction. Maybe the man peaks too quickly or the woman doesn't get going. Things have to follow a critical path in order to work properly."

"What happens when you men can't get it up?"

"Infrastructure dysfunction should be teased out from the experience and addressed by an SME-approved specialist," Jack said stiffly.

"You're crazy!" Rona said playfully. "Tell me more."

"Think of sex like Get High! Romance and foreplay is High Thought. More effort invested here translates into better outcomes."

"So when do we do it?" Rona asked. "In High Cost?"

"Yes, once we take our clothes off and get ready to romp, we enter High Cost. This is where our energy is expended."

"High Cost usually lasts two minutes," Rona protested. "If you're like most guys, you finish and fall asleep. Then I'm in the Black Hole."

"No, no, no. Think about the beginning of a project. Low hurdles are easily vaulted and then expectations about quick results get out of whack."

"Okay, go on."

"Think about the woman's go-live as a hurdle for success," Jack said.

"I'm all for that. If TWERP never gets live then what's the point?"

"You have about the same chance of experiencing success. When a woman tells me 'I'm almost there, don't stop, I'm so close,' I think about that project manager who told me that the project was 98% complete! That's a laugh! At best, I'm only 50% done by this time. I've still got a lot of work to do. That's when my staying power is tested. A project team has to be ready for the hard times. If I can't maintain my focus in one of those "cold slap of reality" moments, the project will fall limp before the job is done."

Rona nodded thoughtfully, "once that happens, it's awfully hard to restart it. The momentum is gone. I get so frustrated when that happens! Some guys even think they've finished the job and they haven't even gotten close."

"Like the CEO who walks away with a massive compensation package after his company's stock is down by a third," Jack said. "And he actually thinks he did a good job!" Jack continued, "If we can keep our focus on the task at hand, we experience your go-live moment. It punctuates and completes High Cost."

"So that's my moment of ecstasy?"

"Ahh, be patient. First I have to hit my hurdle and get live too!" Jack said.

"That should be easy," Rona said. "You're a guy."

"Not so. My hurdle is sequenced immediately after yours on the critical path. It takes a lot of control and endurance for me to hold on."

"Like I said, most guys go dead after they hit their hurdle."

"Right, once I hit it, I'm exhausted. Like men, technology projects have natural refractory periods following go-live. That's when everyone needs to take a short break, cool down, rest up and recover."

"And smoke a cigarette? So when's High Value?"

"That comes next. Companies that engage in post-implementation after-play are the ones that reap ongoing value from their projects. They are the coddlers of value."

"You mean they are the cuddlers after High Cost?" Rona asked.

"Yes, that's the difference between the blessed shareholders at great companies and other shareholders who just get screwed."

"You mean fucked. What about protection?" Rona asked.

"You mean security?" Jack responded.

"No, I meant venereal diseases," she countered.

"You mean viruses?"

"Jack, you scoundrel!"

"Me?"

"Yes!" Rona laughed. "Deep down, I've always wanted a man who is totally unconstrained by other people's standards and paradigms."

"You know what they say about pioneers?" Jack asked smugly.

"Face down? Arrows in their backs?"

"Exactly. That's me."

Rona stood up and yanked Jack's hand. He started to get up from the floor as Rona pushed open the bedroom door. "Come on, get off your Computer-Ass and get me live! I want High Value!"

"You got it, foxy mama!" Jack exclaimed as he bounded over the threshold and closed the bedroom door from the inside.

SUNDAY, JULY 17TH 8:15 AM

Jack tried to slip out of bed without disturbing Rona. She opened her eyes groggily. "Shhh, I have to go. Go back to sleep," he said, and she did. He got dressed and drove to PNP.

Jack knew Stanley had to be removed, but he didn't want to focus the Reality Check Assessment Letter around that point.

Instead, it would be more helpful to lay out the appropriate steps for bringing Broadway back on track. Jack sat at the computer and began to edit Marcus' draft, but stopped after ten minutes.

He walked to Biff's office, where Gertrude had left several boxes of project documents. The boxes contained vendor presentations, budgets, cost-benefit analyses, schedules, Pro-Con meeting notes, and copies of the pages from the ThickWare Requirements Document that he had seen earlier in Stanley's office. Jack read zealously. He found his zone, forgot about lunch, and barely broke stride for hours. The details coalesced in his mind. The answers to PNP's future were here as well. There were rich details about PNP's business processes that must have required hundreds of hours of effort to articulate.

Jack began to cross-reference each Pro-Con consultant's time and expense report against the deliverables produced. There were fewer deliverables produced than normal, given the level of spending, Jack realized. *Wait,* he said to himself, *there must be more here.* He looked up at Biff's desk clock and quickly stood up. He realized that he had been here nearly all day without thinking about Rona.

"Gosh," he said aloud. "What kind of man am I? I didn't even call her."

✻ ✻ ✻

Rona had stopped at the hospital to see Gladys, who was concerned that Jack sounded too slick, another well-schooled player. Rona listened carefully but didn't agree. Rona gave her a hug good-bye, went to her gym for an extended workout class, and arrived at the townhouse a few minutes before Jack.

SUNDAY, JULY 17TH 6:45 PM

Jack knocked on the front door and Rona opened it.

"Hi, I hope I didn't disappoint you last night," Rona said probingly.

"Not at all, I had an amazing time, but I hope you didn't feel pressured."

"Thank you."

"It's just that you dressed and acted so sexy. I loved it. But I also hope you realize I am really interested in you."

"Me too," Rona said softly.

They both smiled in silence for a moment, and Jack was tempted to kiss her, but didn't.

"I think I'll stay in the hotel tonight, if you don't mind. I need to fully focus my energies now on your company."

"I understand. Will I see you after work? I have to visit a customer in Cleveland tomorrow, but I'll be back at night."

"Most definitely."

"I'll make you sandwiches for tonight so you don't have to eat hotel food."

"Awesome, thanks."

"By the way Jack, let's keep a low profile at the office. What we do in private is our business."

"Good thinking."

Fifteen minutes later Jack was out the door and on his way to the BigEight. *Rona's remarkable. I didn't expect to sleep with her so quickly, but I'm glad it happened. I hope it wasn't a one-night thing in her mind. Naaah, it couldn't be, could it?*

SUNDAY, JULY 17TH 10:15 PM

Some of life's best moments are all serendipity, Jack realized as he finished Rona's homemade turkey and Swiss sandwiches while watching the Chicago Cubs game. As he began drifting off to sleep, his smartphone buzzed. He read the text from Annie:

"Just checked into my room here. Hope the weekend at the BigEight wasn't too boring. See you at PNP tomorrow. Annie."

Jack was in the happy zone as he fell asleep.

✵ ✵ ✵

MONDAY, JULY 18TH 8:00 AM

Jack went directly to Biff's office.

"Good morning, Mr. Bluto," Gertrude said.

"Good morning," Jack said.

"Mr. Harper will be at a customer's today, and he said you could continue to work in his office. I heard you were here all weekend."

"Not all weekend," Jack said, trying to remain expressionless.

Jack pored through the boxes of meeting notes. The notes were all printed versions of Pro-Con's electronic files. In most cases, Jack was able to examine a deliverable, such as a process flowchart for paying invoices, and then relate that deliverable to the meeting and interview notes taken by the Pro-Con consultants. The ERP deliverables didn't tie back to the meeting notes, at least not the ones that Jack could find. Nevertheless, the ERP deliverables were among the cleanest, highest-quality work products that Jack had ever seen. He was puzzled.

Gertrude was still at her desk.

"Gertrude," Jack said. "I have a question."

"Yes, Mr. Bluto."

"You wouldn't happen to have these ERP deliverables on your computer, would you?"

"No, but I can pull them up on the network."

"Can you pull up the ERP Process Flows file?"

"Sure, let me try." Gertrude found the PowerPoint document and opened it. PNP's logo appeared boldly on the cover slide. She looked up at Jack, "Here it is."

"That's it."

Gertrude pushed back from her desk. "Go ahead and sit down. I'm going on break anyway. If you get locked out, my password is 'gert.' You can also logon to Biff's computer using my password."

"Thanks," Jack said and sat down.

Jack switched to Slide Show and paged through the slides. *Very professional looking,* he thought. He recognized several names of PNP's employees that were listed on the various process flow slides. Each slide had PNP's logo at the bottom, along with a confidentiality warning and Pro-Con's watermark. *All's good,* Jack thought and he began to push Gertrude's chair back. *Let me check one more thing. Jack switched to Slide Sorter View.* All twenty-four slides came on the screen in a reduced view. *These graphics are just too good and too far along to believe,* Jack thought, shaking his head.

Jack clicked on the File tab and then on Properties. The Summary window displayed. It took Jack a moment to realize that he was looking into the barrel of a smoking gun. The fifth line of the display window read We Love Ewe Condoms.

The smoke cleared. *ERP meant Enterprise Rape & Pillage. Flynch and Stanley were pirating the deliverables from Stanley's former employer,* Jack realized. *Flynch was rebranding King-Con's work with Pro-Con's watermark, assuming no one would ever scrutinize the documents.*

Stanley's sheepskins from UVA slipped off. His barrier was breached. The same was true for Flynch, Jack concluded, rubbing his chin.

Jack pushed back from the table, and then leaned back in. He walked into Biff's office sat there for hours, examining every piece of paper and every file that Gertrude had provided him access to. Finally, his grumbling stomach led him to the parking lot and then to DoubleWide's.

MONDAY, JULY 18TH 7:10 PM

Jack sat at a table in the back. He twice texted Rona, but she failed to respond. Next, he dialed Marcus's smartphone number. Jack explained what he had found.

"That's why you're the boss, boss," Marcus said.

"No, I wouldn't have thought of it, but those docs looked too good."

"Have you told Biff that he's been paying for phantom consulting time?"

"Ha, you mean ghosts on the payroll. Not yet, let's put it in the Reality Check Assessment Letter. It'll give us a couple of days to vet our facts and double check that Pro-Con billed PNP for work that it didn't do," Jack said.

"Very good, boss. I guess that's an old trick: Use the last client's deliverables and change the names. Amazing that PNP's execs never checked that the fancy documents were showing the details of another company's business processes. I bet the CEO at We Love Ewe will be pissed off!" Marcus said.

"I bet. Good night Marcus," Jack said.

"You too, boss, enjoy the fried biscuits. You didn't tell them it was your birthday again, did you?"

Jack laughed and returned to his chili.

✵ ✵ ✵

TUESDAY, JULY 19TH 8:40 AM

Roosevelt Van Buren walked toward Jack in the hallway, wearing a worn pair of denim overalls.

"Good morning, Roosevelt."

"Hi, it's Jack, isn't it?" Roosevelt said.

"Yes."

"Call me Rosie. So, what have you figured out?"

"Do you have a few minutes?" Jack asked, hoping to answer Rosie with the same level of attention he would give to Biff or any other member of the client's organization.

"Sure, shoot."

"Rosie, the problem at PNP is one of imbalance. It's a common problem that results when a project contains too many independent variables. The other type of variable is a dependent variable. Its value is a function of one or several of the independent variables."

"Can you give me an example?" Rosie said.

"Sure. Think about the operations on your production line. You build pot handles, don't you?"

Rosie nodded.

"There are inputs and outputs," Jack explained. "The inputs are the raw rubber stock that you cut into the handles and the labor you use to do the cutting. The output is the handles. The inputs are the independent variables and the output is dependent upon them. It's like the old saying, 'you reap what you sow.'"

"Okay," Rosie smiled.

Jack continued, "This was a simple example in which we didn't consider scrap, the tools consumed in the production, or several other factors. If we did, we would see that adding all of the other inputs or independent variables complexifies the dependencies."

"Jack, is that true? Isn't there a connection between the raw material used and the labor used?" Rosie countered.

"Great point, Rosie. The variables that I initially identified as independent are really dependent on the production order, which is dependent on customer demand, finished goods in stock and many other factors. In fact, almost every value that you measure on the plant floor is in some way dependent upon some other value."

"That makes sense. How does this relate to our project?"

"It's all about balance. A balanced production line produces the optimal level of output, given a series of inputs. In a technology project, the output is a secure and reliable system that successfully processes transactions, and the inputs include the hardware, the software, the interfaces and their integration points, the work that the consultants do, the work your coworkers do, etc. The more inputs, the harder it is to balance the output. When you have a chronically unbalanced situation, the best course of action is to start removing nonessential variables and inputs. When a problem is too complicated to solve, you have to reduce it to a solvable problem."

"So you would encourage us to cut out unnecessary portions of our project so that we can focus on the critical problems, maybe the stuff we don't understand too well."

"Precisely. Focus on the locus. The only way to travel the critical path from end to end is to either vault over or remove the roadblocks."

"Shouldn't we try to pull out the roadblocks before we start our trip?" Rosie asked.

"Want a job?" Jack said.

"Oh, be serious," Rosie said.

"I am serious, but I couldn't poach you away. PNP needs people like you."

Rosie wasn't used to being complimented on his intellect. "I gotta go, the boss is coming," Rosie said, embarrassed.

Biff walked toward them as Rosie walked away. Biff gestured for Jack to follow him back into his office. Jack replayed the conversation with Rosie, adding additional comments regarding the various team members, their agendas, and their personalities. Biff agreed with Jack's analysis.

"Biff, as the new leader of this project, you must be positioned for a big win. That's why we have to limit scope to our most critical objective, getting PNP connected to Broadway. Let's take a machete to the original plan and shelve the other projects for now."

"I know. I know you're right, but if we shut down the other projects now, it'll cost more millions to restart them."

"Let them sit until your team nails Broadway."

"Our folks have invested a lot of blood and sweat. They won't like it."

"They will in the long run. Once you lead the Broadway charge successfully, step out of your project quarterback role and delegate the revival of the other projects to someone else. Let your team see you win and they'll follow your example."

"Good, Jack. Thanks," Biff said stoically, motioning Jack toward the door.

TUESDAY, JULY 19TH 11:40 AM

As Jack left, his thoughts turned to Rona. It had been nearly two days since they were together. He had intended to write her a short poem, but was unable to concentrate on it. He walked by her office and looked in from outside the door.

She was speaking on the phone, and looking out the window. Jack stepped back from the door and listened. He immediately got angry with himself for doing so, but didn't budge.

"Yeah, Saturday night the thirtieth," Rona said energetically. "Right, eight o'clock. I'm so excited to see you."

Jack took another step away from the door. *I can't believe this,* Jack said to himself. *She acts like such a guy.*

"We're going to have a great time," Rona said. She paused for a moment, listened, and then laughed uproariously.

Rona said okay a few times to the caller and then started to hang up when she pulled the phone back to her mouth and said,

"Don't forget to wear those tight little white briefs. I love you in them Myron." She hung up.

Jack heard her chair squeak as she began to get up. He scurried down the hall as quickly and quietly as he could.

☆ ☆ ☆

Twenty minutes later Jack returned to Rona's office. Rona looked up.

"Hi there, Jack," she said.

"Howdy," Jack replied. He allowed his face to lie with a smile. Rona smiled too. They stood in silence for a moment.

"How was Cleveland?" Jack asked.

"Good. I ran into my ex-husband at the airport."

Jack's ersatz smile collapsed.

"I hadn't seen him or spoken with him in over two years," Rona said. "He has a girlfriend who is separated from her husband. And now, can you believe, she's pregnant with my ex! He never could control himself."

"Whatever it turns into, I hope it's right for all the persons involved," Jack said.

"Me too."

Rona pushed away from her desk and stood up. She wore an angular beige suit with no jewelry. She walked over to the door of her sizable office, closed it, and locked the handle. She turned to Jack and said, "I missed you."

Ah, the devil in Prada, Jack thought. Before he could drop the line, Rona grabbed him.

She pressed her lips into his, kissing him passionately. She ran her hand on Jack's chest, sliding her fingers under his quickly rumpling tie and through the openings between his shirt buttons.

Jack wondered what was going to happen next. "I thought this was an outside the office thing?" he said.

"I want you so badly…so badly," she murmured.

Jack was silent as they continued to kiss. A moment later, Rona walked to her office door, turned the lock in the other direction, adjusted her skirt and swung the door open. She walked back over to Jack, maintaining a professional distance and softly said, "Jack, I don't mean to tease you. I really want this to work out."

"I agree," Jack replied, not certain as to what he was signing on for.

"Okay, honey, I'll see you later. Let's grab a bite at Dante's tonight."

"Ciao," Jack responded quietly. Bewildered, he walked toward the cafeteria, trying to fit the pieces together.

Myron occupied Jack's mind as he sat in the cafeteria with a cup of coffee. *Have I been played by Rona? Is she a soulless tiger prancing around for whatever meal suits her at the moment? God, she is so hot. Maybe I should stay in just for the sex. Naaah, I like her too damn much and I want her for the long-term, but I can't deal with not being in control. I've gotta cool it,* he decided.

TUESDAY, JULY 19TH 4:55 PM

The phone rang. Gertrude saw it was Lars and put him right through to Biff.

"Harper, this is a circle jerk. Our customers are getting squeezed by your fucking inability to deliver," said the CEO of Big-Box, his voice rising.

"I know, I know," Biff said.

"No Biff, you don't fucking know. We ran promotions this week in central and northern Michigan for your 8 – 10 –12s and we have no inventory. What the fuck do you want me to do? I'm sitting here in Macon with my thumb up my ass!" Lars yelled through the speakerphone.

"We'll fly some in tonight. We've been building them all morning."

"Your people are going to have to stock the shelves. I'm sick of this. It's your last fuckin' chance. I'm losing share in these markets and I don't need more of my customers pissed off. I just spent six hundred thousand fucking dollars running ads in *Gassy Vegans*. If you people don't unfuck this and get all the backorders shipped out to us by this Friday, we're done. And next time, take me off the fucking speakerphone."

Lars hung up. Biff listened to the dead line. *When the supply chain backs up,* he thought, *it's like when the sewer backs up. Everything begins to reek.*

Biff closed his office door and pushed the latch on the inside, locking himself in. He lowered the blinds, chasing out the daylight. Gertrude knew what was about to happen. The last time Gertrude saw Biff in this mood was the first time Amelia was sent to the principal's office for cutting class. Biff reached into his bottom drawer and pulled out a bottle of twelve-year-old Cragganmore Scotch whiskey. He took a shot glass out of the drawer, spit into it and wiped it out with the top part of the tube sock he kept in that drawer. Biff topped the glass and then took a hearty swig from the bottle before closing his eyes and downing the shot. He started to relax, drowning out the echoes of his doctor's pleas not to drink liquor until his blood pressure went below 140/100. Ten minutes and two more shots later, his thoughts centered on the moment. Biff knew all too well how alcohol excised the past and future from consciousness. The past few weeks had been ultra-stressful, and despite Biff's collected exterior, he was terrified by his downward spiral. There was so much to accomplish and so many unknowns.

Biff downed two more shots, deadening those unknowns. For the next half hour, he cruised golfing websites from his Fujohara

20" laptop. He found a site that showcased the world's top ten golf courses. As he looked down the eighteenth hole at a course in Monterrey, he saw girls in bikinis at the edge of the virtual gallery. Biff thought about typing in the URL of a porn site that he occasionally looked at from home, but he knew PNP screened for and logged this type of activity. It would have generated an exception report listing his terminal identifier and would be sent to Stanley. Biff wasn't drunk enough to forget that he was the one who had authorized PNP's Internet usage policies. PNP had already fired one person for selling homemade china dolls online during working hours.

A few minutes later, Biff went to a lingerie website. He looked at beautiful, scantily clad girls, but no nudity. *Let Stanley try to challenge me on this.* Biff stood up and walked quietly to his office door and listened. It was after 5 PM. *Gertrude must have left by now.* He turned off his office light and returned to his computer. Scowling, he clicked on dozens of bikini pictures. *Damn it, I need the real thing.* The real thing meant withdrawing the large male Ethernet plug from the Fujohara's female adaptor. This disconnected him from PNP's corporate network.

Next, he reached back into his bottom drawer and slipped a male-to-male telephone extension cord out of the tube sock. He stared at the smaller male plugs on the phone cord. He then inserted one plug into his laptop's modem port and the other into an analog line wall jack that had been installed next to his desk last year, ostensibly for a fax machine. Biff then checked the lower right hand corner of the monitor and confirmed that his Wi-Fi and Bluetooth were switched off.

Alone, at last, Biff realized as he pulled a scrap of paper from the tube sock. He glanced at the paper, dialed into his ISP and within a few moments, reopened his browser. The websites loaded more slowly, but his access was unmonitored. He swallowed a single oxycodone as he waited.

His thoughts turned to Martin, and he searched for Manhole NYC, the bar where Martin used to work. There would be little chance of finding Martin; it had been too long. Biff then typed gaydateil.com. He didn't have a profile but was able to view the profiles of other registered members. After looking for Martin with no promising results, he clicked on Harry654. The picture was bland, but Biff couldn't resist clicking on his father's namesake. Harry654 looked nothing like Biff's father. Biff cringed when he thought how his father would react if he knew that his son was cruising gay websites. Biff closed Harry's profile, took another shot of Cragganmore, and clicked on WilburFine69. Wilbur was a college professor who was into kayaking and mountain biking, but Biff wasn't interested. He discovered a search option and requested all men with photos within five miles of Naperville and who were over 6'2". He scrolled down, and his breath quickened. Biff's eyes grew large when they fell upon 'SuperMyron8.' Myron's avatar was a short stocky cowboy with a tall, lavender cowboy hat.

Myron had been the object of Biff's fantasies for a long time, whether he was with Constance or at Maxie's. He clicked on a thumbnail, enlarging a beach photo of Myron. Biff had always believed the rumors of Myron's studsmanship with women. *Could I approach him? No. No way, no way, no way.* Biff rechecked the windows and doors. He settled into his chair and began to fantasize.

As he clicked on a thumbnail of Myron at Navy Pier, Biff's smartphone rang loudly. He fumbled to turn off the phone but in his haze he pressed the wrong button, accidentally accepting the call. It was the pastor of Biff's church, confirming that Biff would run the annual fundraiser. When Biff had done it last year, the church had raised enough money to modernize two schoolrooms. He never flinched during the conversation with the pastor. After he hung up, he glanced at his watch and realized that he would have to hurry to have enough time to see Nikki on his way home. Biff disconnected the modem line, erased his browser's history file and cleared his cookies. He then reconnected his Ethernet cable, enabling PNP's infrastructure to again recognize his presence on the network.

Biff had barely sobered up by the time he drove his Cadillac out of PNP's parking lot. Thoughts flashed across his mind. *PNP. Constance. Broadway. Lars. My blood pressure. Amelia. Myron. I am so confused. I'm drowning.*

Biff slammed on the brakes. A kitten had jumped from a child's arms and Biff barely missed turning the cat into treadfiller. That shook off any remaining effect from the Cragganmore. He realized that he was running late, and he drove directly home. Twenty minutes later, he walked through his front door and was confronted by his prim wife, one hand on her hip and her other clutching the binding ring of a large upholstery swatch.

"You're late," Constance huffed crossly. "We were supposed to pick out the new fabric for the sofa tonight."

Biff sighed, wishing his life was different.

✲ ✲ ✲

TUESDAY, JULY 19TH 7:30 PM

Jack walked into Dante's and spotted Rona, already seated in a booth. She was aggressively chewing a wad of gum.

"Hi, Rona," Jack said.

"Hi, Hun," Rona replied.

"Hun. I like that."

"I bet. Listen, I want to ask you something."

"What's on your mind?"

"Jack, I've been having a great time with you. You're different than most of the guys that I meet."

"Okay, and?"

"So what's going on? Are you going back to New York this Friday and that's it?"

Jack wasn't expecting this. He paused a second too long before he answered, but Rona kept up her smile.

"Umm, the feeling is mutual. You're very cool. I'm not sure what you're looking for—"

Rona stopped smiling and she cut Jack off, "Don't equivocate, Jack. Don't ask me what I want. You're the man here, aren't you? What do you want?"

The waiter came over.

"A Heineken, no glass," Jack pleaded.

The waiter looked at Rona. She shook her head without looking up.

"Want some spinach artichoke dip?" Jack asked meekly.

"Are you kidding? Don't grease me," she said.

The waiter went to get Jack's beer.

"Rona, you're unique. We have a great time, don't we? I love the way you shook your booty at the club..."

Rona started to speak but stopped.

"I expect Biff will want me to come here and help keep things on track. Maybe you could come to New York sometimes – I'd love to show you around."

"So what are you saying?" Rona said.

"Exactly what I just said. What else are you looking for?"

"Something more than that. I'm thirty-nine years old. I told you that I want a family. I'm not here to waste time."

"I'm still getting to know you," Jack said, confused.

"Jack," she said curtly, her voice growing louder, "you don't know what you want. Why are all you men so weak? I know what I want and I go after it. All that talk outside my bedroom door. You want the milk and not the cow. I thought you were a real man!"

Jack gulped helplessly.

"You are nothing other than a massive, steaming heap of confused data, a typical spinach artichoke dipshit!" Rona concluded loudly.

The waiter brought Jack's Heineken and placed it between them as Rona stood up. She took a step away from the booth and then turned back toward Jack. As he reached for the beer, Rona reached into her mouth, took out the gum wad, and used her thumb to shove it down the beer bottle's neck. Half of the beer foamed out of the bottle, onto the table. "There's your High Value, Jack!" Rona said as she turned and walked toward the door.

Jack stood up to follow, but his thighs hit the underside of the booth table and he fell back into the bench seat, dumbfounded. The spilled beer ran over the edge of the table, dripping on Jack's pants. He saw that half the Heineken was left in the bottle. *My glass is half-full,* he mused. He picked up the Heineken bottle and tried to chug the beer but the gum fell into his throat and he coughed it out hard. "Shit," he said loudly. He took a crinkled ten-dollar bill out of his pocket and left it on the wet table. He got up from the booth, and a dozen pairs of eyes watched him slink toward the front door.

As Jack passed the bar, the bartender called out, "Hey man, wanna Mudslide on the house?"

Jack shook his head, his eyes on the ground, and kept walking.

KEY 6: VALUE - HARVEST VALUE FROM IT INVESTMENTS

TUESDAY, JULY 19TH 8:15 PM

Jack sat in his Tapir. *What the hell just happened? We've just met! I should be angry, but now I like her even more. How can I woo her away from Myron, Biff, and all her other men? I just don't know.*

Jack began driving back to the BigEight. *I cannot let this derail me. The client is counting on me. I must deliver. Even though Rona just hit me with this pile of crap, I must focus on the problems the client is paying me to solve.* "I'm no dipshit," he muttered.

Jack knew he had a busy night ahead and his mind was spinning in several directions. He recalled snippets he had written for a business magazine a few years earlier:

> *Engineer variability out of what you do....get rid of time toilets....don't engage in multiple tasks simultaneously.....do things sequentially.....don't jump around.....stay on the path to your goals.*

It sounded so logical, but he was so confused. *Why is business theory so woefully inadequate at solving real problems in real time? Why is it so hard to draw on logic in moments of crisis? Why do diet book readers get fat? Why does the bookstore's Addiction & Recovery section attract the same group of readers year after year? Surely they have the knowledge by now. Why can't they use it to solve their problems?*

Rona intruded into his mind like a persistent pop-up window. *I will focus,* he promised himself halfheartedly. *Why can't I figure out what to do?* His mind drifted again. *Why does a company that has the right plans and knows how to execute still fail? People and variability. People issues drive variability beyond the bounds of business theory. With people, there is often no relationship between their effectiveness and their raw intelligence or education. The ability to "make it happen" is more important than anything, and it depends on drive, passion, clarity, and integrity more than it does upon brainpower. How can I "make it happen" with Rona?* Jack wondered. His stress level rose to the point where only two gum-free beers would cool it off.

TUESDAY, JULY 19TH 8:40 PM

Jack arrived at the BigEight and went up to his room. With a grumbling stomach and some misgivings, he called the number on the menu that he had found in the parking lot. "I'll have the Philadelphia-style cheese steak and two Bud Lights," he said, knowing any menu item containing the word 'style' usually sucked; it meant the restaurant had no idea how to make it, like the Kosher-style ham sandwich that Jack had choked down one night in Birmingham.

The food and the beer came with the standard 22.5% service charge attached to it. Jack sat down to eat, overcome by thoughts of Rona. He dialed her smartphone, but she didn't answer. He didn't want to leave a message. *Should I call her again,* he wondered. *At thirty-six, maybe it's time to settle down. This is a smart, beautiful woman. How many more chances will I have? I'm not getting any younger and this hair thing doesn't help.*

How many more short stories do I want to be a part of? What did I do to screw this up? Jack wondered helplessly. *I really like this girl.*

Jack's smartphone rang, startling him. It was Dirk, a good friend and a senior VP at King-Con.

"Bluto, what's up?" Dirk said. "What city are you in?" he added, when Jack didn't answer right away.

"Chicago. How 'bout you?" Jack replied, his heart still heavy.

"Dallas. I'm between flights."

"How'd you hit 'em at Pebble?" Jack asked, knowing that King-Con hosted one of their largest clients at Pebble Beach last week. The client's IT executives were paired with touring professionals from the seniors' golf tour. King-Con paid the tab for the event and termed it a 'Learning Outing'.

"Great. Pebble rocks!"

"What's on your mind?" Jack asked.

"We're trying to get into Interpharm to pitch a new service offering. We met their second-level guys and they like what we have. We need to get to their CFO, and I think he's a friend of yours."

"That's right, I spoke to him last month," Jack said.

"Would you mind setting up a call for me? I can't get the guy to return my calls."

Jack didn't always agree to these favors, but he knew that Dirk was a good guy and King-Con generally did good work, even if it was pricey. "Done," he replied.

"You need anything? What's new with you?" Dirk inquired.

"I'm working on an interesting project. It's a turnaround. Typical Reality Check. The usual stuff. They got so caught up in the forest, they forgot where the trees were."

"Cool. That's your sweet spot, Bluto. What else is up? You seem off."

"Frankly, I'm wrestling with a chick thing."

"Ah, another sweet spot. Who is it this week?" Dirk asked.

"This one is fantastic. She's smart, hot, and fun, and I feel relaxed and at ease around her. A salad of many tasty fruits."

"What's the problem?"

"Well, commitment stuff, I guess…" Jack stammered.

"Pop the question yet?" Dirk interrupted.

"What, after two weeks?" said Jack, feigning shock.

"Sounds like you like her. Are you going to spend your life in Drive-Thru mode or are you going to stop and build something?"

"Maybe you're right," Jack said.

"Listen, Jack, I've got to go. Good luck with the relationship. Call me over the weekend if you want to talk more." Dirk hung up.

I like this guy, Jack thought. Dirk was faithfully married to a very cool woman and had two young kids. He wasn't one of those guys who broadcasted a veneer of stability and then when he went to Atlanta, Dallas, or Vegas on a business trip, spent all his free time getting lap dances in the VIP room. *The problem with the corporate world is that the fabric of trust that our economy is based upon has many small tears. How could I trust someone in business that was admittedly untrustworthy with his own spouse? Trust takes so long to establish but a moment to break. Once broken, it may be mended, but never without a visible seam. Is anyone truly trustworthy? Maybe trust is the core component of true love, just as clarity is at the core of effective technology.*

"God, I'm losing it," he said aloud.

The food arrived and it looked better than Jack had expected. *Maybe it will all work out,* he thought. He picked up his smartphone and pressed the voice-dial button. "Dial Annie Wu," he said, as his mind became focused on PNP.

☆ ☆ ☆

WEDNESDAY, JULY 20TH 7:10 AM

Jack drove to the plant and headed to Biff's office. Biff, Rona, and Meyer were waiting for him. Rona nodded without a hint of a smile. Her chilly gaze left a pit in Jack's stomach. Jack noticed that the circles under Biff's eyes had darkened.

"Jack, come in," Biff said.

Both Meyer and Jack nodded their greetings.

"We may be stabilizing somewhat," Biff said. "I don't know if we're getting on track, but people seem to be more spirited around here."

"When you get into Fail-First mode, those high spirits will be challenged," Jack predicted.

"What do you mean?" Biff asked worriedly.

"The beginning of a turnaround always requires the most energy, like the braking of a landing jumbo jet," Jack explained.

"I'm sure. Listen, I brought you folks in this morning because PNP's board has called a special meeting. They want me to report on the project and they want to know its long-term impact on the company. I can relay to them the changes we're in the midst of, but I need a better sense of how these approaches fit in with our long-term business strategy."

"I'm not completely sure what you mean. I think the consultant-speak has rubbed off on you," Jack responded, smiling.

"You're right," Biff replied, expressionless.

Manage Technology Like A Stock Portfolio

"Biff, have you heard of the portfolio approach to technology management?"

"No, what is it?"

"It's a useful tool for understanding the value that technology brings to an organization. A medium-sized company like yours tends to have many technology projects underway simultaneously. All your technologies, whether active or in-development, comprise your portfolio."

"Okay, go on."

"Managing a technology portfolio is like managing a stock portfolio. Each technology or project has a probability of success and a potential economic impact. Ideally, you have a diversified portfolio, like a diversified portfolio of stocks: with high return, high risk projects balanced by lower risk, more predictable, lower reward projects. If you're a good IT portfolio manager, you select projects that will maximize your potential return for the level of risk that your company deems acceptable. Also, if technology has a bad year at PNP, that good portfolio manager will make sure that failed projects don't dramatically impair the organization."

"Go on," Biff requested.

"A balanced stock portfolio has assets that are relatively uncorrelated so that a bad year for some asset classes will likely be offset by a good year for other asset classes. You can apply the same thinking to your portfolio of technology projects," Jack explained.

"Sounds like rocket science, and also pretty undoable," Rona snorted.

"Perhaps. It's a combination of art and science, but you can deploy the 80/20 rule here to get value out of this approach without having perfect technique."

"How's that?" Rona asked, still irritated.

"Technology budgets may range between five and ten thousand dollars per employee per year. This varies widely, but it's a good rule of thumb. IT dollars are dispersed throughout the portfolio to get the highest return for a planned amount of risk. Budgets may vary considerably from year to year depending on revenue, profitability, whether major new initiatives are underway, or if the company is in maintenance mode."

"But, Jack," Meyer said, "how do you know when to vary the budget?"

"You remember when we talked about planting years and harvesting years?" Jack said, turning to Biff.

"Sure. You invest heavily during the planting years to reap value during the harvesting years. Also, planting years may contain hidden costs that have to be closely managed," Biff recounted.

"Right on," Jack said. "The costs for consultants and the technical people are usually rolled into the analysis but the cost of the time spent by your non-technical people is rarely tracked properly."

"Okay," Meyer said.

"PNP is over-planting this year – your budget is thrice the level it ought to be. You can't possibly farm all that you're planting. Stanley has too much going on. The company is attempting to transform itself overnight, and this never works," Jack said.

"We all know that now," Biff replied.

Growth, Profitability Improvement, And Expansion

"It sounds trite, but remind yourselves that technology is a means to an end. Losing sight of that perspective bodes trouble," said Jack.

Meyer jumped in, adding, "Jack, you're preaching to the choir now. I've been saying for years that technology strategy must flow from business strategy. Our customers really don't give a damn about what technology we have inside of our four walls as long as it enables them to do what they need."

"But in this case, Meyer," protested Biff, "we have to connect to Broadway."

"Yes, but that's all Big-Box cares about. As long as our systems give their systems what they need, they don't care whether we have a Rolls Royce or a Dodge Dart."

"Hey, I thought I was the consultant here," Jack interjected, grinning. "The key point is that you have to leverage technology as a platform for growth, profitability improvement, and expansion. Good technology helps you make better business decisions; bad technology increases the number of decisions you need to make to keep above water."

Meyer leaned forward. "That's why it's so critical that we balance our portfolio," he said.

"Right," Jack agreed. "The current portfolio is over-leveraged, and your margin interest expense is crushing. Sell your losers immediately, get back your cash, and let the winners run. Get all of your eggs out of that fraying wicker basket."

Meyer nodded.

"Your biggest winner is the project to connect PNP to Big-Box's Broadway. Anything that interferes with that project should be eliminated or pushed to a lower priority in the portfolio. Remember, technology must be managed like an asset. Assets are designed to help produce revenue and lower costs. If a manufacturing machine wasn't producing any value, you'd scrap it," Jack said.

"And we should do the same with technology?" Biff asked.

"Yes. Technology assets are similar to any other asset used to produce value. When possible, seek to convert ongoing variable costs to fixed costs, because doing so unbinds your growth potential," Jack said.

"Because it allows us to lower our per-unit cost at higher volume levels?" Meyer asked.

"Assuming we can get a reasonable payback," Biff added, cutting in.

Switch From CBA To ABC Thinking

"Exactly," Jack began. "But let's talk more about spending. It's not something I'll mention in the Reality Check Assessment Letter but I think it would be helpful for you to hear," Jack said.

"Go on," Biff prompted.

"Recall the five to ten thousand in spending per employee rule of thumb. Now, in certain industries such as banking or insurance, technology spending can be much higher. In your industry, basic manufacturing, spending is at the lower end of the range. Good management makes a huge difference in the returns a company earns, and executives of the best companies have a tight rein on both the level and nature of technology spending."

"Stop talking theory. What returns should we be getting on technology if we manage it properly?" Rona asked.

"You mean ROI's?" Jack said.

"Yes," Rona exclaimed impatiently. "For every million we invest, what should we get back?"

"It depends."

"That's an empty answer, Jack," Rona said, turning to Biff. "These guys are all the same," she muttered softly but audibly.

Biff ignored the remark, keeping his eyes on Jack. "Can you give us a better answer?" Biff asked.

"I wish I could. Many organizations measure returns on technology investments, but I would argue that when it comes to measuring the value of a major IT transformation like the one underway here, measurement isn't possible, except perhaps tying back overall profitability."

"That's double-talk, Jack," Rona said.

"Maybe so, but when you plant and harvest the best crops, you have a fitter, more effective environment. It would be unwise to rely too heavily on any single metric to gauge effectiveness, because none are comprehensive."

"So how do you evaluate a prospective technology investment?" Meyer inquired.

"First, most companies rush their cost-benefit analyses. Costs are usually easy – you add up all the technology and implementation estimates and multiply by three," Jack quipped.

Biff had heard this before. It made him mistrustful of technology people.

Jack continued, "Second, after deciding how much Return on Investment or ROI you need to get the project approved by your CFO, you figure out the revenue impact. Then, you manufacture a bunch of made-up benefits to ensure the numbers work out. You know I'm not joking when I say this is the way business works."

"How should we do it?" Biff asked.

"Aim for a competitive edge. Rather than the shopworn Cost-Benefit Analysis, think of it as Analysis of desired Benefits with associated Costs, or ABC. ABC thinking focuses on the upside and how to get there versus gaining meaningless precision on the downside. Get your people to brainstorm all the possible benefits to your business that can be unlocked by properly implementing the right technology."

"But, Jack," Biff protested, "Budgets are so tight…"

"Then why would you ever consider a cost before a benefit? Jack responded, "It doesn't make sense. In your current project, you're not focused on either!"

"That's not true," Biff replied. "The benefit to our project is that we stay in business and continue to serve our largest customer. The cost is too high for me to think about. If I consider the real costs, I would be sicker than I already feel."

Benchmark Goal And Role Models

"There's a better way to think about it. Remember our portfolio analogy. Your portfolio consists of benefits and costs. Balance the benefits with the costs. Let's look at these four projects but remember that if you listen to me, you probably won't have four projects by the end of this week. This is the time when it makes the most sense to come up with incremental ABCs, in other words, incremental improvements to your overall business and its underlying systems.

"What's the best way to do that?" Biff asked.

"By benchmarking your Goal Models and Role Models."

"What do you mean?" Meyer asked.

"A Goal Model is an organization with which you share similar goals. Maybe your methods and markets are different from theirs, but you can both learn by collaborating with each other. Wouldn't it be great to find another manufacturer in a non-competitive industry that is presently implementing the same technologies as PNP?" Jack said.

"Makes sense," Meyer agreed. "Why pay Pro-Con when we can learn from our friends for free?"

"And I assume a Role Model is an organization that already has a track record worth mimicking?" Biff asked.

"Precisely. They've achieved the goal and are now playing the role," Jack replied. "You've got to benefit from the investments others have made in their learning curves. It's not always easy, and you have to be skeptical when someone is too interested in sharing information, but valuable wisdom can be gained from your Goal Models and Role Models."

"I should talk to my peers in other companies about what they are doing."

"It won't cost you anything," Jack said.

"That's what you think," Biff replied. "There'll be a lot of scotch and steak money spent to get that information."

"Biff, you read all the time. Surely you must come across success stories of organizations that do technology right," Jack said.

"Sure, but after meeting you, I doubt I'll take these stories at face value."

"Ha," Jack said. "Now you're learning."

Biff grimaced, pained by the biting reality of his situation. "Let's not go there," he muttered unhappily. He knew this project had knocked him off his lifeguard stand at PNP and into the shark-filled ocean.

Be A High-Priced Leader Or An Economy-Class Follower

"PNP has to decide where to position itself technologically. For a company that sells non-technology goods or services, then a rule of thumb is that it costs ten times more to be a high-priced leader than an economy-class follower."

"You mean a laggard?"

"No, laggard implies that you were late to the party and additional spending is required to catch up with the pack. An economy-class follower sits back, waits while the technology stabilizes, and then seizes upon it. In some businesses this would be a terrible strategy: Amazon.com's selling tool is technology even though they are a retailer. By being a first mover, technologically, they reaped enormous value. Bezos saw an opening, drove a truck through it, and his billions are a testament to his foresight."

"But what about all those other .com retailers that failed?"

"Exactly my point. The 10X leader-premium also includes adjusting the investment return to reflect the probability of a total loss or a DELETE error."

"I want to talk about that some more," Biff said.

"In a moment. There's controversy about whether IT has any strategic value for non-technology firms," Jack said.

"Does it?" Meyer said.

"Again, it depends. Some argue that corporate IT has become commoditized, making it difficult to use it to gain a competitive advantage. In many cases, I agree. What matters is how well the technology is implemented, and of course you can't evaluate this without taking into account total cost and risk."

"So it's unlikely that any particular brand of a technology will either increase the inherent value of a company's equity relative to its competitors as indicated by its P/E, or Price to Earnings ratio?" Rona asked.

"Yes, but a company could get a value premium or a positive P/E bump if it did a great job implementing its technology," Jack explained, recalling Rona had told him about her days as a stock-broker. *God, she is smart*, he thought.

Rona nodded her head. *He seems so surprised by my question*, Rona observed. *He must think that I'm a simpering idiot.*

"But you said earlier that most technology from the large vendors is the same," Meyer noted, addressing Jack.

"Exactly. The technology industry's goal is to perpetuate itself. It does that by avoiding transparency, maintaining mystique, and continuing to scare non-technology executives into buying technology that they don't need, in other words, new versions of the same old songs," Jack said.

"Okay," Biff said. "But you know Wall Street values these guys based on tomorrow's growth prospects, not yesterday's track records. I can't risk letting their 'grow or die' mentality impact us."

"Right, so if you're in a mature industry like yours," Jack said, "stay with the pack and leverage proven technology to streamline and speed up your organization. Then you'll be better positioned to respond to new, potentially game-changing market, product, or service opportunities. Why pay for a first class ticket when economy will get you there and leave you money left over to cut prices, market more effectively, or enhance quality?"

"That makes sense. PNP should learn to run in the middle of the pack. For now, we need to get that right," Biff said.

"Agreed," replied Jack.

Measure <CONTROL>, <ALT>, And <DELETE> Errors

"It's so easy to fall off track and not recognize it," Biff lamented.

"Remember we spoke about the errors that tie together the PC reset sequence?" Jack asked.

"Yes."

"Use the <CONTROL><ALT><DELETE> framework to classify and attack your problems," Jack said.

"Okay, go on," Biff said.

"CONTROL errors are common when your project consists of medium and large triangles. Simply stated, these errors occur when your project runs out of control and the value of the error is the cost of the unplanned deviation or overrun. Say a project that was supposed to take six months now takes nine, but the project is completed successfully so that the original scope is preserved. If the monthly run rate on the project was $100K, then the value of the error was $300K or fifty percent over plan."

"For technology projects, a CONTROL error of fifty percent doesn't seem bad," said Meyer.

"True, because most projects come out of the gate over-scoped and under-staffed," Jack replied.

"Under-staffed or staffed by people low on their learning curves?" Biff said.

"Exactly Biff," Jack said, nodding. "ALT or ALTERNATE errors are trickier to value because they are akin to opportunity costs. An ALT error occurs when an organization fails to choose the best alternative when making a technology selection or implementation decision. Let's say that a municipality wants better control over its parking meter revenues and decides to invest a year to implement a wireless control system that alerts a repair crew when a meter malfunctions. It seems like a good idea because the municipality ought to be able to improve the yield of its assets. They buy the right technology platform, retain qualified experts to implement it, and roll it out on time. Sounds good, right?" Jack said, looking at Rona, trying to ascertain whether she was still upset.

"Not if they missed out on a better alternate project," Rona responded coolly.

"Exactly. This same municipality has old systems for keeping track of its scofflaw's balances. Those systems often fail to collect the largest fines from repeat offenders. By hiring a database expert and a programmer for a couple of months, the municipality could correct the old technology and achieve the same level of collection increases, so which project makes more sense?"

"I see," said Biff. "They should clean up their collections systems first, so the value of the ALT error is the money spent on the wireless project minus the money that could have been spent on the database project."

"Yes, but when evaluating ALT errors, you have to make a lot of assumptions. In this case, we assumed that both projects achieve exactly the same revenue recovery in the short-term and then also contribute equally to long-term value. We also ignored the time value of money. In the second project, the revenue recovery would start sooner. It can be confusing to be too precise when evaluating ALT errors, but one should strive to fully understand the logic, risks, costs, and timeframes associated with each alternative."

"So every time we look at a business project, we should consider whether we are making ALT errors and attempt to value those errors?" Meyer said.

"Yes, and in the process your people will hone their thinking skills."

"And DELETE errors?" Meyer asked.

"Ah, DELETE errors are the catastrophic errors that obliterate you from existence. In this case, the value of the error is the value of the organization prior to the decision that caused it to fail. Biff, how much is PNP worth?"

"It depends who's asking. If this thing collapses, the private equity firm will value the DELETE error at around $80 million."

"Only if PNP goes under because of the decision," Jack noted. "CONTROL, ALT, and DELETE errors are all tied to decisions. If an organization shuts down because of an unforeseeable force or the market changes dramatically, and the shutdown can't be specifically tied to either decisions or failure to make such decisions, then there are no relevant CONTROL, ALT, or DELETE errors to measure."

"I see," Biff said.

"Striving to measure these errors will enable you to reduce the cost of future errors, and you'll become a better decision maker in the process," Jack said.

"Makes sense."

"When you think carefully about what could go wrong before you embark on an endeavor, you are likely to improve your outcome," Jack added.

☆ ☆ ☆

The meeting broke up. Biff walked out his office door and felt his smartphone vibrate. Amelia had forwarded an email from Constance commanding Amelia to stop asking about whether she could travel to Kansas City this coming weekend with a friend to see Justin Bieber in concert. Amelia added to the message:

"Dad, why does Mom have to be such a pain? This is really, really important to me. Bye for now. Love, Amelia."

Biff knew that when his stepdaughter called him Dad, she wanted something that she knew she was not supposed to get.

WEDNESDAY, JULY 20TH 10:30 AM

Jack walked to the cafeteria, waving to the production workers enjoying their break. Earl invited him to sit, but Jack smiled politely and declined, heading straight for the coffee machine.

As he stirred in creamer and sugar, Jack noticed a dimly familiar face at a nearby table. The man noticed his gaze, and the man's face lit up with recognition. As the man approached him, Jack racked his brain trying to remember from where they knew one another. Jack held out his hand and said, "Jack Bluto."

"Fred Namath."

Jack recognized the name from Princeton.

"How are you Fred?"

"Great, and you? Boy you look like you never left the gym since I saw you at our reunion. I think you were still working for our New York office at the time."

"Yes Fred, thanks, you're too kind." Fred had added a pound per year since college.

"Hey, I thought you were losing your ha…" Fred then noticed Jack's corny row.

Jack fidgeted and said uncomfortably, "Do you work here?"

"No, I was brought in from Pro-Con to help out on this job. I heard you're doing one of your Reality Check projects, right?" Fred said.

"You got it. What a small world. I didn't know you're still at Pro-Con."

"Can we talk? I'd love to get your insights into what's happening," Fred said.

"Sure," Jack replied.

"Frankly, Jack," Fred spoke, lowering his voice, "we're in the process of blowing up and anything you can do to help get this mess sorted out would be greatly appreciated."

"Let's go."

Fred led Jack down the hall to the consultants' work area. One consultant was present and he straightened up when he saw Fred. The work area was a thousand square feet and contained a dozen PCs and two high-speed printers. Fred asked the consultant if he would work elsewhere so Fred could speak privately with Jack.

In the consulting business, Fred was known as a delivery guy, a good consultant but one who was ineffective at selling consulting work. At Princeton, Fred was ambitious, hardworking, and speedy with numbers. Today, Fred sported a pre-smartphone suit, and a white shirt with a too-bright yellow and purple striped tie. His socks were anklers, and as Fred sat back and crossed his legs, his pants crept up and exposed his hairy legs. *Maybe if he makes partner in charge, his socks will get longer? Which would happen first? The chicken or the egg?* Jack ruminated silently.

"Jack, this is a lousy project," Fred began. "We're billing several good people and can't make headway. The progress that's being reported at the status meetings is illusory. We have a plethora of technical problems. The software vendor is working hard to solve them and the client's IT team seems focused, but we're dead in the water. The software was delivered buggy, but we're used to that. PNP is using an offshore consulting team to write reports, build interfaces, and handle configuration. We didn't like this at first because it's money out of our pocket, but they're doing a good job."

"And they also deflect blame for you guys," Jack pointed out gently.

Fred sighed and replied, "You're right. My big concern is the CIO; he's a megalomaniac. His vision is laudable but it's impossible to execute. Unless we make radical changes within the next few weeks, Broadway will fail, Pro-Con will be out of a job and we'll have trouble collecting our money."

Jack nodded.

Fred's voice quieted as he continued, "PNP is seventy days late on one of our invoices and forty days on another. We haven't billed them for last month yet. The Executive VP in charge of our office is a step away from pulling our whole team out of here, and then we open ourselves up to a huge lawsuit, especially if Big-Box drops PNP."

"What are you doing to fix this?" Jack asked.

"I don't know what to do. We're flailing. Yesterday I met with Stanley and today I'm meeting with our team. Morale is poor. We're flying in five senior guys in from Dallas next week. They're our strongest SWAT Team of ThickWare consultants in the United States."

"Why didn't they come sooner?" Jack asked.

"Maybe they could have helped," Fred said, "but our problems run deeper. Stanley wants three signatures every time my guys want to test a new procedure or program and this is forcing us to run with our feet stuck in the mud. We must simplify—"

"Rather than complexify," Jack finished.

"Yes. We have too many balls up in the air."

"How has Biff reacted?"

"He hasn't. He's been stonewalling me. I think Roscoe & Lauer has imposed such an onerous timeframe on modernizing the technology that Biff feels hamstrung," Fred said.

"If he doesn't lead, he'll lose," Jack said.

"We'll all lose."

Would Biff make the manly decisions and do what needed to be done? Jack wondered. *Would he push Roscoe & Lauer to shut down the other projects? Fred's presence was no coincidence. The brass at Pro-Con had heard that PNP hired Reality Check, so they sent in their fixer.*

"What else can you tell me?" Jack asked Fred.

"You have some reputation, Jack. I know Pro-Con made it difficult for you at a couple of your former engagements. You were seen as an antagonist who was interfering with our people and, frankly, with our clients. At first I agreed, but I would have never voted to authorize that lawsuit."

"No worries," Jack said. "The judge threw it out."

"Now that I've seen the results that your efforts have produced at other companies, I am on your side. This project needs a Reality Check and PNP needs a wake-up call. Only an unbiased auditor can legitimately make the case for greatly modifying the scope of our activities. I'll support you in whatever recommendations you make."

Audit, Really Audit, Or Expect To Fail

"Fred, I appreciate that."

"No sweat. It's amazing how the impartiality of the financial audit function has disappeared and the scandals of the past few years have ensnared our business. Even Pro-Con messed up," Fred confided. "Our guy that sells financial audit services shares introductions with the executive who sells management and technology consulting services."

"The risk for impropriety is pretty high there," said Jack.

"You bet it is. If our consulting guy is trying to close a consulting contract, he may try to pressure the audit guy to go easy on the client. When that happens, the validity of the audit is compromised. The company, its employees, and its investors all suffer. I've seen it happen," replied Fred.

"Can you say where?" asked Jack.

"I'll just say that I was at a clothing manufacturer in the Midwest. It was an audit client for several years until it got involved with a major technology implementation, and the tech project generated twenty times the annual fees of the financial audit. The CFO was pressuring the auditor to recognize revenue early so they could meet Wall Street's expectations. From what I heard, in a closed door meeting with our audit guy, the CFO told him that we would be replaced as the lead consulting firm on the technology implementation if we didn't look the other way on the audit."

"Fred, how often does that happen?"

"I don't know, but when it does, it's dirty business."

"Yes, and difficult for anyone to prove. It's impossible to be an impartial referee and an implementation consultant at the same time," Jack declared emphatically.

Fred nodded. "You're right and clients need to be wary of all the relationships that consultants have with vendors. It's difficult to use a consulting firm to perform a project audit, even if that consulting firm doesn't sell any other services to that particular client. At the next account that same consulting firm may be partered with your vendor on an implementation project. In order to do an impartial audit, you ought to be just an auditor."

"Can you give me an example?" Jack asked.

"Sure, look at ThickWare. All the major consulting firms have symbiotic relationships with it. Although ThickWare does its own consulting, it doesn't have the expertise to run big projects. They need the major consulting firms like us to supply the implementation expertise and staffing. You know all the consulting firms are ThickWare authorized implementation partners? There are platinum levels of partnership, gold levels, silver levels, and so on. The higher your level, the better support you get from Thick-Ware and the more likely they'll send a hot prospect your way," Fred explained.

"So if Big Consulting Firm 2 is brought in to audit the work of Big Consulting Firm 1 on a ThickWare project, Firm 2 may back off being too critical of Firm 1 because it doesn't want to cause the client to become too upset with Firm 1?" Jack asked.

"Exactly, Firm 2 won't come down hard on Firm 1 because at the next client, Firm 2 may be running the implementation and Firm 1 may be asked to do the audit," Fred said.

"I see. These companies are all part of the same back-scratching sub-economy. No member of the sub-economy would be willing to damage the good thing that they all have going by publicly attacking another member. It would sabotage the entire 'old-boy' network," Jack concluded.

"That's putting it strongly Jack, but I agree that the checks and balances aren't there," Fred said.

"And no sub-economy member wants to piss of ThickWare, because ThickWare supplies the leads," Jack added.

Fred nodded in agreement.

"Fred, what do you think about internal auditors in business, you know, like the Internal Affairs unit at a police department?" Jack asked.

"Seems like a sensible role, until you look closely. You take a team of people that does nothing but spends its time scouring the various internal operating units for out-of-bounds behavior. This is the concept used by the General Accounting Office (GAO) of the federal government. I don't like it," Fred said.

"Why not?" Jack asked.

"Because it's not always fully independent and it doesn't enable the auditors to become experts in a subject area. The internal audit or the internal auditor can always be corrupted by an internal political agenda. Also, how can an internal auditor understand a complex project without proper training?" Fred said.

"Suppose the internal auditor was an SME?" Jack asked.

"That could work, but an internal person doesn't have the exposure that an outside person has to other companies, processes, and techniques."

"So an internal SME wouldn't remain an SME very long?" Jack asked.

"Probably not," Fred agreed.

"Fred, you're a straight shooter. Reality Check hasn't always been easy or fun. When I first started, a Pro-Con partner on a job in Chicago convinced the CIO to call security and have me forcibly removed from the premises when my questions became too probing. Remember *Trading Places* with Dan Ackroyd and Eddie Murphy?"

"I think so."

"Dan Ackroyd went from being on top of the world to underneath it. The guards at the bank where he was a major customer threw him out on the pavement in the shadow of Philadelphia's famed Clothespin sculpture. That same scene was replayed in my life and I was Dan Ackroyd. Mr. Pro-Con claimed I was disrupting the client's project team."

"Were you?"

"Of course not. I was in the process of uncovering malfeasance and Mr. Pro-Con was covering his flank."

"That's very serious Jack," Fred said in a monotone.

"Fred, when I stood up and brushed myself off, I felt vindicated. I knew my ideas made sense and that Reality Check would be successful. The consultants on that job were afraid of having a bright light shone upon their activities. They were stealing the client's time and creating tremendous waste, while billing for massive consulting hours."

"I didn't know that happened. I'm sorry. Who was Mr. Pro-Con?" Fred asked.

"It doesn't matter, but he's one of the top guys in your firm today," Jack said.

Fred remained silent.

"Look, Fred, I'm committed to making this work for everyone. Your people will deserve credit when we win this thing. Realize that your team may have to be scaled back but you'll be arm in arm crossing the finish line with Biff."

"Thanks, Jack, that's all we want," Fred said, beginning to turn away.

"Fred, have time for a beer tonight, after we get out of here?"

"I don't drink," said Fred slowly, "but good to see you, Jack."

Fred walked away quickly. It took Jack a moment to realize why. Fred could never be seen fraternizing with the enemy. If Flynch found out, Fred would lose face. *How foolish,* Jack thought.

WEDNESDAY, JULY 20TH 11:30 AM

Jack had just finished adding PNP's powdered creamer to his second cup of coffee when he noticed Annie sitting with three ladies from PNP's Quality Control department. Jack sat down next to Annie and motioned for her to continue.

"That's okay, Jack, we just finished our discussion about how ThickWare will be used to improve quality," Annie said.

"That's a stretch," drawled Hattie, the lady in charge of the department.

"We'll get there," Jack replied. "It may take a while, but all the work you've done won't go for naught."

"Okay," Hattie replied slowly. "We'll hang in there."

WEDNESDAY, JULY 20TH 11:40 AM

"Annie, if you're done here, let's go back to the BigEight's business center and finish the material for tomorrow's seminars," Jack said.

"Sounds good. We can video with Marcus and the production department back in New York."

"Good. Annie, how are you feeling?"

"Fine Jack. I'm in my fourth month now, so I'm not throwing up anymore."

"Good, how's Charlie doing at home with the triplets?"

"They just turned two, so he's got his hands full."

"Is he happy?"

"No, but he's less unhappy taking care of the boys than he was working as a corporate lawyer."

Jack nodded.

✭ ✭ ✭

THURSDAY, JULY 21ST (THE NEXT DAY) 1:20 PM

Jack and Annie stood in front of the Frying Pan room for the second Reality Check seminar of the day. The participants ambled in and sat down. Jack looked down at his notes, but his mind wandered and he suddenly realized that the audience was waiting for him to begin.

Jack began, "In technology and in life, there are no guarantees, only probabilities. A wise person seeks to raise his probability for success. It's about weeding out independent variables that throw us off the critical path. You may conclude that we are merely cutting scope, but I don't view it that way. Instead, we are drilling through the old project plan to find the rich wells of value versus uncovering the...."

Rona entered the Frying Pan and sat at the far end of the room, maximizing the distance between herself and Jack. Rona wore a thick, bright turquoise necklace – even from across the room, Jack could tell it was exotic and elegant. Her tailored dress and cropped jacket were a deep gray, and Jack wasn't sure but thought the outfit was another Chanel. Jack squinted as he focused upon Rona's well-defined collarbone, sixty feet away.

"...empty wells of distraction," Jack finally stammered, as Rona began pounding away on her smartphone. During the next ninety minutes, she didn't look up once.

Jack soon found his stride. He and Annie tagged-teamed as they addressed a variety of information technology best practices. Jack hammered home the notion of Fail-First. The class had several questions, mostly about whether they would lose their summer vacations during Fail-First.

"Vacations are always a touchy issue, but I know Biff is very concerned about not inconveniencing the people who have already given their all on this project…"

The shift whistle sounded and the audience members rose and hurried back to their posts.

"How do you think they took it?" Annie asked.

"I'm not sure," Jack replied, moving toward the door of the Frying Pan with Annie close behind him.

Rona moved to the doorway.

"Rona," Jack began, looking uncomfortably at Annie, "I want to speak with you more …about…my Fail-First plan. The model tells us that implementation should be back-end loaded more than front-end loaded. I know that is counterintuitive and that you want to see the path before you travel on it, but part of the problem is that until a system is in place, it's often hard to understand how much value it can bring," Jack said.

"Big deal," Rona answered.

Jack used his eyes to say "take a hike" to Annie. She understood and moved away.

"Rona," Jack said, quieting his voice, "We got off track somehow. I really want to talk with you. Can we get dinner tonight?"

"I'm not sure I have anything to say to you. You were very candid. You're a player and," she paused, looked him straight in the eye and whispered, "I'm sorry I slept with you."

Jack remained silent. The room had emptied. Rona continued, "I get plenty of one-night stand offers. That's not what I am looking for."

"Rona, please meet me tonight. You're misreading me."

Rona hesitated. "I can meet you for a few minutes," she allowed.

"Okay, great. Le Maxwell?"

"No, just a quick drink. I have a friend coming over at 8:30, so we have to be done by then."

"But, umm," Jack stammered, "I want to spend some time with you. I'm flying back to New York tomorrow night."

"I said I have plans later," Rona said. "Stop pushing."

"It's just that—"

"Jack, forget it. I can't do this," Rona said, whirling around. In a moment, she was gone.

I do not understand this woman, he realized, dejected. From the hallway, Annie looked at Jack and shrugged her shoulders. He slunk to the parking lot and meandered the Tapir's snout through traffic, back to the BigEight.

✳ ✳ ✳

FRIDAY, JULY 22ND 2:15 AM

Jack tried to purge Rona from his mind as he pored over the copy of the Reality Check Assessment Letter. Annie had long since retired to her room for the evening, leaving Jack to handle the final tweaks.

He looked up at the vanilla walls of the BigEight's business center for the hundredth time in the past four hours. *Like writing that big check for technology, the sex part was easy. But making relationships work is so much more difficult,* he told himself. "I'm no SME," he said softly. "Will I ever find High Value?"

Jack stood up, walked into the lobby men's room and filled his hands with cold water. He looked at himself for a long moment in the mirror before splashing the water on his face. He walked back to the business center, sat down in the still-warm green leather chair, and shifted into drive.

KEY 7: CHANGE – THINK DIFFERENTLY AS YOU TURN THE SHIP

FRIDAY, JULY 22ND 6:15 AM

Jack arrived early in Biff's office. Biff was at his desk; his eyes red and framed by dark semi-circles.

"Where's your letter?" he asked, trying to shift into wartime mode.

Jack handed Biff the nine page Reality Check Assessment Letter. Biff read through it, pausing and nodding several times. The recommendation to slice out the other three projects, a Fail-First plan for Broadway, Flynch's lack of objectivity and the "Bill At Will" situation he created for Pro-Con...it was all there. Biff frowned as Jack guessed Biff was studying Reality Check's findings regarding the reuse of the work from Stanley's former employer, but Biff remained silent.

"Jack, send me an electronic copy so I can forward it to Roscoe & Lauer. They're waiting for it now."

"It's in your inbox," Jack said.

"Thanks. Give me a half hour and then I'll find you."

Jack went into the empty consultants' work area and promptly fell asleep, his head on his clasped hands. These were the first moments in days that his mind was clear. He slept like a baby until Biff tapped him on the shoulder, barely thirty minutes later.

FRIDAY, JULY 22ND 7:20 AM

Simplify, Don't Complexify

"Come on, Jack, let's go. It's going be a busy day. I have a call with Roscoe & Lauer at 10:00 AM to talk about your letter. I can't shut down the other projects without clearing it with them. It's too big of a decision."

"I know," Jack said, following Biff toward his office.

"To tell you the truth, Jack, all I care about now is getting those backorders shipped tonight."

"I understand," Jack replied. "Will you make it?"

"By the skin of our teeth," Biff replied. "The freight company is going to make a special pickup tonight."

"Okay, good luck."

"Since we're stuck until 10:00 AM, let's talk through those simplification tools first," Biff said.

"Good. My associate and I covered these yesterday in the seminars, so your team will be better able to execute its projects in the future."

"Okay," Biff said.

"The best way of reducing risk on your project is to streamline before you technologize. Complexity creates a double-whammy because not only do you have the obvious costs associated with more complex processes, you have the non-obvious ones that result from the increased variability."

"I'm not sure what you mean by that," Biff said.

"Simplify the critical path as much as possible in order to have the best chance of sticking to it. Some companies are able to redesign their business processes on a whiteboard and then program software to support those redesigned processes, but at most companies this doesn't work."

"Suppose we need to radically change to keep up with our customers?"

"In that case, you may have to re-engineer what you're doing, but keep in mind that you will be complexifying and riskifying your project."

"How do you get away with making up so many words?" Biff asked.

"Sorry, I don't mean to be a wise guy. I want to change the language we use to think about the roadblocks to corporate effectiveness. It may be a vain attempt," Jack sighed.

"Keep going, but how do we do it?"

"No standard best approach exists. Do what works best for you and for your people. Think of a process as a series of tasks needed to accomplish an objective. Scope the process tightly, so that no task gets particularly onerous. Remember that grand process map in Stanley's office?"

Biff nodded, "It's gibberish to me."

"Biff, a single process should be clear enough so that it can be written as a list of steps on the back of an envelope."

"Give me an example."

"Look at accounts receivable, specifically the process of applying customer cash to old invoices. You receive a check or an electronic payment, match it with the invoice, record the cash, and close the open receivable."

"Jack, that's the back of the envelope version, but it's not always so clear cut."

"True. Those nasty special cases complexify the process. When there's no invoice number referenced on the customer's check, how do you apply it? You could post to the oldest invoice, or post based on nearest dollar match, assuming we recognize the payer on the check. Maybe the company changed names recently and our system doesn't know this yet. How do we apply the cash properly?"

"This seemingly easy set of tasks is starting to mushroom into confusion," said Biff.

"That's right. Remember, the best approach is to solve one problem at a time. Sometimes we will have to backtrack and change the solutions to earlier problems. But the linear approach allows for problems to be fully solved. You know I'm a big believer that the mind can only focus on one thing," Jack said.

"But if we focus on the micro, how do we deal with the macro?" Biff asked.

"By taking together all of the process maps, you'll have a wiring diagram of the way the entire system is supposed to look, irrespective of how large the system is. Of course, the larger the system becomes and the more complexity it contains, the harder it is to build. It's useful to lay out the entire wiring diagram before you begin a project because by stepping back and looking at the whole forest, you can identify and cut areas of repetition. Pre-Engineering and Design should be exercises of reduction, not of expansion," Jack said.

"I see," Biff replied, "so when we cut the pizza, we may be able to toss out a few of the slices."

"Yes, you want to reduce complexity, not capability," Jack explained.

"But what about those special cases?" Biff asked.

"At some point, you have to ask yourself whether the special cases are worth computerizing. You can consider making certain manual entries to the system."

"Can't that corrupt the integrity of the data?"

"Yes and no. Most systems have provisions for manual entries so that the data integrity is preserved. It may be inelegant, but in my opinion it's better to get something on-line quicker than it is to complexify a system. Also, special cases are the most costly to computerize."

"Where do you draw the line?"

"Think about it the same way that you would when you are deciding whether to automate a work station on your production line. For example, I saw how your guys hand-pack the shipments to Big-Box before the cartons go to the glue station. Would it make sense to buy a packing machine that automatically combines the right styles and sizes in the carton? I heard that each Big-Box store gets a different combination."

"We looked at that. It would take three years to get a payback on the labor savings, assuming that our business doesn't fall off with Big-Box," Biff replied.

"Excellent," said Jack. "Apply the same thinking to technology. If you're considering technologizing a portion of your process, you want to go ahead only when you are confident that it will pay off. You can't do that without understanding the risks that may ruin this investment."

"But what about data the customers see?"

"I assume you mean your real customers, not those spurious internal customers."

Biff nodded and Jack continued. "Yes, if customers have access to one of your internal systems or if you are rolling out systems for the benefit of your customers, you want to present them with that Transcendental Experience, even if that means complexifying the development –"

Biff interrupted, "But if it's an internal system, then we shouldn't do extra work by overbuilding."

"Exactly, because for every piece of additional functionality that you add into the system, you have to test that functionality, and then you have to retest the entire system to make certain that the additional functionality doesn't have any unintended ripple effects on other parts of the system. And don't forget you have to train people on the new functionality. These are the risky gotchas that no one ever wants to pay attention to during the pre-project euphoria."

Reduce Risks

"I don't like risk," Biff said. "Whenever I take risks that I don't understand, I get hosed."

"Perhaps more than anything else we have discussed during the past two weeks, a healthy respect for risk and how to manage it is what differentiates organizations that run technology projects well from those that run them into the ground. Risk management is more important than hardware, software, or the consultants you choose."

"How can you get us into that top fifth?" Biff said.

"It's not that easy," Jack replied.

"Try me...but give me the ten minute summary. I'm pretty fried."

"I can do it in five, because I know you already understand it, but you need to train everyone who touches a project like this about risk management."

Biff nodded.

"There are three components to risk management: identification, impact analysis, and control," Jack began.

"Go on," Biff urged.

"All complex projects are rife with risk. Looking at a project from an altitude of twenty thousand feet, the risks that come to mind are missed deadlines, budget overruns, and poor scope definition. Refocusing the lens at the five thousand foot level reveals different contours of the problem, like we spoke about with the Little-Triangles," Jack explained.

"Okay," Biff agreed.

"Now, say the risk of missing a project's deadline is built upon the risks of the software testing missing its deadline, the hardware not arriving in time, and so on. Descending to a thousand feet, and looking even deeper at missing the software testing deadline, we see that it may be due to a complex piece of computer code that the consultants haven't finished. Maybe the code isn't finished because the consultant who knew the most about it left yesterday to start his own business? I don't know. Maybe the code is just too complex and it makes sense to slice this work into Little-Triangles," Jack continued.

"So drilling down we see that the entire deadline of the project may be at risk because of one small piece of code?" Biff said.

"Yes, you're starting to look at this in terms of impact analysis. Do you remember when we spoke earlier about expected value with respect to the total cost of an investment?"

Biff nodded in agreement.

"And you understand the basics of probability and expected value?"

"I think so. Probability is the likelihood that an event will occur, and you assign a percentage to that likelihood from zero to one hundred percent."

"Great. What about expected value?"

"I thought I did, but I can't explain it, so I guess I really don't understand it."

"Your candor becomes you," Jack said, smiling. "The expected value of an event is the economic benefit or economic harm you will experience if that event occurs, multiplied by the probability that the event will occur."

"Give me an example."

"Let's put some numbers on the example we just spoke about. Let's say that the consultants you have are great and there's a ninety percent likelihood that they'll get the code finished and tested so that PNP won't miss its Broadway deadline. We have the alternative to go live on the system without this piece of code and the likelihood of Big-Box coming back to us and asking us to put it in is thirty percent."

Biff said, "I might be tempted to have the consultants finish the code."

Jack said, "You may, but not once you look at the economics of the problem. In the first case, if we miss the deadline and Big-Box shuts us down, you are out $60 million in annual business. In the second case, let's say Big-Box penalizes us by shifting twenty percent of our business to a competitor, but agrees to give us time to finish that piece of code. So we lose $12 million in revenue. Your decision boils down to a simple impact analysis: do you want to have a ten percent chance of losing $60 M or a thirty percent chance of losing $12 M?"

"I see, so I am comparing an expected loss of $6 M versus $3.6 M?"

"Exactly, so what would you do?"

"I would leave out the piece of code and hope."

"Yes, and a big hairy no," Jack said, his voice rising. "Never hope! Hope is a fool's tool. You must engineer failure out of the problem to the extent possible and that is all you can do. Hope implies an abdication of responsibility and I don't like that."

"Okay, Jack, get off you high horse," Biff said, clearly annoyed.

"Risk control is about minimizing the number of risks you're exposed to and their impacts. Once you choose to leave the code out, you need to figure out how to reduce the probability of the event happening and its potential economic impact. Perhaps your programmers create a simpler, but less feature-rich version of the code that will lower the probability of Big-Box rejecting it. Also, you could ask Rona to communicate PNP's approach to Horace in advance so maybe he won't penalize us as much when he shifts some of the business to the competitor."

"Okay, so we have to control and mitigate our risks."

"Right, and you should teach these practices to everyone on your team. Annie Wu and I introduced these concepts to your people during yesterday's seminars."

"Jack, I like it. It's intuitive and simple, but it's almost too simple. Does it work?"

"Absolutely. It may be less elegant than the executive MBA management techniques, but this freeware gets the job done. If you can't explain this to a team member in ten minutes, consider throwing him overboard."

"What about variability?" Biff asked.

"Don't you need a break yet?" Jack inquired.

"No, let's keep rolling," Biff said. "I'm picking up steam."

"Okay, Biff. A close cousin of risk management is variability management."

Stamp Out Variability

Jack continued, "Variability is inherently confusing, and it's the most insidious destroyer of value. It's more harmful than buggy software, a bad project plan, or even nefarious vendors. It's imbued into every part of every business process and is the least understood source of organizational ineffectiveness."

"Like the variability in our manufacturing processes?" Biff asked.

"Exactly. Variability is the omnipresent force that pushes you off the critical path."

"Give me an example."

"That's easy. I like to look at variability in terms of fitness. Remember we talked earlier about weight loss goals?"

"Yeah, I used to think about that. Lately, fitness is barely an afterthought," Biff said wistfully.

"Think about all of the pain people suffer through to maintain a certain weight. You're an athlete and my guess is that you still know about keeping fit. What do you normally weigh?"

"For years I was at 180, now I'm at 185."

"So you're really saying that your weight is around 185, give or take five pounds. Do you ever get more than ten pounds out of bounds?"

"No."

"Then you control your weight well, but it still varies. Maybe a major supplier wines and dines you, so you pack on a few. Or, you visit an angry customer and take him to all of his favorite places and you are so sick from thinking about the bill that you have no appetite and lose a few pounds."

"That's pretty accurate," Biff said.

"Do you know anyone who usually weighs 180 but sometimes he is 160 and other times he is 200?

"Stanley, but add twenty pounds to your numbers," said Biff. "I hate to pick on him but he's the fat kid in the room. And the skinny kid. His weight runs all over the place. He has a terrible time controlling it."

"Can you imagine how hard it must be on Stanley's body to have his weight swing back and forth like that?" Jack said. "He pendulums around his goal and rarely steadies at his target weight. Interestingly, the pendulum travels fastest as it's passing its midpoint. Ever see a meandering river from an airplane? If you made a graph of Stanley's weight and plotted it over time, you would see a similar pattern."

"He always tries new diets, loses weight, then loses control, and eats like crazy. I almost feel sorry for him," Biff paused, and continued, "So Stanley is working a lot harder to keep up his average weight of 180 than me?" Biff asked.

"It seems so," Jack responded. "Think about it. If your swing is greater than ten pounds, you need to have three wardrobes. So the costs rise geometrically with variability."

"I see. So far I've gotten by with one wardrobe, but you're right. Stanley has a fat one, a thin one, and the transitional one," said Biff.

"Remember that car trip from Chicago to San Francisco. You're taking the straight route, maybe getting off at a rest stop or a roadside McDonald's now and then. Stanley is stopping at every outlet mall within 150 miles of the interstate."

"And will require a lot more gas to complete the trip," Biff added.

"You got it," Jack said, looking out the window behind Biff. A throaty rumbling noise was coming from outside. A moment later Stanley drove his Harley-Davidson past Biff's office window on his way into the parking lot.

Biff didn't notice. "It's like our manufacturing processes," he said. "We can never get our glue machine to apply the right amount of glue on our boxes. The control system is screwed up and the customers complain. The glue leaks into the boxes and we have to rework the shipment and clean, re-sort, and repack the pots, or the boxes go out without enough glue and they open up during handling in the stores. It costs us thousands in reprocessing every month."

"Consider a similar example with respect to technology. Think about Broadway. It's a small part of what PNP is looking to accomplish. We all agree that it's the most critical of your critical paths. Then think about the other projects underway. They are all intertwined around the Broadway project—"

Biff cut him off, "Making it harder for us to identify a variability problem on any single pathway."

"Right, the projects are muddled together. Look, in reality you don't have the luxury of doing all your projects in sequence. You have multiple priorities. But make sure that you understand and control those sources of variability. If you can't identify and control the variability in a multi-task effort, you're better off single-tasking. Managing variability properly will dramatically improve your success," Jack said, adding, "All that Six Sigma stuff that you hear about is designed to identify the critical path, shorten it, and engineer out the variability."

"Just how do we do that?" Biff asked.

"Here's the million dollar secret, Biff. Picture an apple tree. Think about the apples hanging on the ends of the branches. These apples are the greatest drivers of variability. The low hanging fruit are what causes the branches to sway the most," Jack said emphatically.

"So they drive the most variability?"

"Yes," said Jack.

"So by first picking the low hanging fruit, we'll get the greatest reduction in variability?" Biff asked.

"Exactly," Jack said.

"I love it!" Biff exclaimed.

"Biff, the process for identifying and reducing variability starts with data and ends with creative thinking. You could add a worker in packing to inspect each box as the glue is applied. He can rework any problems on the spot before the boxes are shipped."

"But that's expensive, Jack. I'd like to avoid that."

"Try it for a month and I bet whomever you assign to that job will figure out how to fix, or substantially reduce, the variability in the gluing process."

"Makes sense," Biff responded. "That's a reasonable investment."

"Biff, the greatest challenge in identifying true variability is teasing apart the tentacles of interdependency within an organization's various processes. Once key processes are isolated, we can estimate both the probability and economic impact of the variability. Multiplying these together produces an expected risk rating."

"Jack, I'm losing the flow," Biff protested.

"Maybe we are getting more complex than we need to. I bet your intuition will tell you where the greatest variability is eating up cost and time. Pick off the low-hanging fruit and watch the business improve."

Under-Train And Avoid Ill-Timed Training

"Jack, forget process for a minute. Let's talk about people. The way we train them embeds a huge source of variability into everything we do," said Biff.

"Biff, you've done this before," Jack said, nodding approvingly and continuing, "Technology training is critical, but companies waste enormous amounts of money on it. Most training fails because it's ill-timed. You need to immerse people in the knowledge and then immediately task them to apply that knowledge. There can be no delay. Your people have lots on their minds. They're thinking about their home lives, their kids, politics, who knows what else. Don't expect them to keep technology training information fresh in their minds for more than a few hours after it's taught to them."

"You mean a few seconds, don't you, Jack?"

Jack was about to reply when Rona entered Biff's open door. Biff motioned for her to sit down beside him at the conference table. The irony of the moment was not lost on Jack. Biff and Jack were two once-ripe pieces of fruit that had fallen off her tree. *Am I that piece of low hanging fruit that is now rotting on the ground?* Jack wondered.

"We were speaking about training," Biff explained.

Rona nodded.

"What has your experience with technology training been?" Jack asked Biff.

"Usually negative," Biff said. "Training classes contain way more detail than I can absorb. In twenty years of using computers, I have never once opened one of those manuals that we paid the consultants to develop for us."

"I agree," added Rona. "Training is usually a waste of time and money. It's only beneficial effect is team building. When we visit a vendor's training center, we drink, party, or do whatever, but the knowledge souvenirs are, at best, chintzy tokens and trinkets."

"How would you do it, Jack?" Biff said, nodding at Rona.

"Your experiences are typical. Training on the fly works best. The A players and SuperUsers on the project team should handle most of the training. You must work through problems in real time with an expert guiding you past the rough spots. You learn by narrowing down your perspective—by scoping what you want to learn, focusing on acquiring the knowledge, rehearsing what you've learned by applying it, and then repeating the process."

"Those who want to learn will practice what they were taught," Biff added.

"Right. A user should never have to wait to attend a training class a month from now to learn how to process a critical transaction today. Conversely, can you imagine reading your smartphone's training manual two weeks before the phone arrives? Would you remember how to operate the thing?" Jack said.

"Probably not," said Biff.

"Narrow down the training to reduce variability and provide users with a common experience. When there is variability in the way that users are taught to use the system, the likelihood of that variability propagating and metastasizing across the organization increases exponentially, and your fixed cost dream unwinds into a pile of site-specific variable costs. This is why training must be thin, simple, timely, and uniform."

"Okay," said Biff. "We get the point."

"I'm not sure. When you use most Internet sites, no training is needed. What to do becomes intuitive. The less training that is required, the easier it becomes to move people in and out of your organization and on and off your teams without the variable cost of training and the pernicious cost of variability."

"Jack, that's a mouthful. Let's not talk about that now," requested Biff.

"Agreed," said Rona.

Conduct Decision Oriented Meetings

Meyer entered the room, nodded hello, and sat down unobtrusively.

All eyes turned to Jack. "How would you structure the work day?" Biff asked.

"I like the idea of daily status meetings. They get the team together and allow it to attack critical issues," Jack replied.

"I disagree, Jack, especially in light of your earlier comments about meetings," Biff said.

"Those idiotic status meetings are like watching re-runs of bad sitcoms," Rona said. "You already know what's going to happen."

"All true," said Jack. "Bad meetings sap everyone's motivation. You should hold DOMs, or Decision Oriented Meetings. DOMs are tightly choreographed interactions designed to bring the best thinking to bear on an issue and raise the probability that the ideal solution will emerge. Decision-less meetings waste everyone's time. To get things done, you need only the right people at the right time armed with the facts they need to make decisions."

"I want to avoid more meetings with the technology people. I don't understand what they do and I don't want to get bogged down in their details," Biff stated.

"Biff, the technology people are critically important. If you're not willing to learn their language, how can you expect other business people to stay in touch with the project?"

"Fine, but I need to figure out how to not lose my time," Biff said.

Throw Back The Fish Until The Problem Is Caught

"Biff, I understand," Jack said. "Good leaders don't give out food, they teach people how to fish. Conflict resolution training and productivity training are important supplements to that good leadership—"

Rona cut Jack off, saying, "The problem that people have with projects, and in life, is that they don't know where the fish are. Fishing is a two-step process, and teaching them how to fish misses the first step."

"What do you mean?" Biff asked, picking his vibrating smartphone out of its holster. Biff hit the thumbscrew, read the message and left the room quickly. Rona, Jack, and Meyer all stared. Silence filled their ears. *It must be Stanley,* each thought.

"You have to know *where* to fish," Rona began emphatically, after a long pause. "You have to be certain that you're solving the right problems first," she continued, her face reddening and her voice rising.

"So how do you do that?" Jack prompted.

"By knowing how to prioritize," Rona said with a noticeable tinge of sarcasm in her voice. You know the 80/20 rule. Use it!"

Meyer, not recognizing the undertow of angst dragging on the conversation, jumped in, adding, "Of course! The 80/20 rule forces you to focus your fishing on where the big fish are, the high value targets."

"Exactly," Rona said triumphantly.

"But we can't lose sight of *how* to fish," said Jack. "Very few people know how to fish out the solutions from the muck of problems that big projects decay into. They don't understand that the tug on their line is often just a symptom of a deeper problem and not the problem itself.

Meyer nodded.

"Rona, say your Bimmer doesn't start," Jack said. "Is that a problem or a symptom?"

"Sounds like a problem to me," Meyer quipped.

"It's a problem, Jack," Rona said flatly, her countenance becoming more combative with Biff out of the room.

"You're right, but if you want to fix the situation you have to recognize that the car not starting is a symptom of a deeper problem. Maybe the battery is dead? Maybe there's a blown fuse? Maybe there's a loose wire?"

"So those are the problems?" Rona asked.

"They may be, or they may be another layer of symptoms belying deeper problems. Probe further. Maybe the battery is dead because the alternator failed to recharge it? Maybe the fuse is blown because there is a short in the electrical system and the blown fuse is an expression of that electrical short?"

"That sounds challenging to do, Jack, but it makes sense," Rona said, begrudgingly.

"Search until you find the real problem and then solve it," Meyer added.

"Right, keep fishing until you land the problem on the end of your hook, reel it in, and deal with it directly. Too often, the project team members will falsely assume that the symptom they've hooked is the real problem. They'll treat the symptom and leave the problem untouched," Jack said.

"Like a doctor who prescribes a pain reliever without taking the time to figure out what's causing the pain," Meyer added.

"You got it," Jack replied. "Keep digging until you uncover the core. Then you can find the cure. That's why most projects are two to five times over budget. The team spends hours, months, even years casting at symptoms without hooking the problems. Throw back the symptoms and fish until the problem is caught. If Rona merely replaces the battery and it's an alternator problem, she'll have another dead battery in two or three days."

"That's another reason to use Little-Triangles, I guess," Meyer said. "The problems are less complex and easier to see."

"Meyer, you're the man," exclaimed Jack happily. "It's much easier to spot the fish in a shallow pond."

Meyer beamed.

Manage Change Or Change Management

"That's why it's critical to recognize that Change Management takes place throughout the project," Jack continued.

"My friend at the University of Chicago told me that when an organization begins a Change Management program, it's time to change management," Meyer said dryly.

"Replace management?" Rona prompted, not expecting a wisecrack from Meyer.

"Of course!" Meyer declared.

Rona and Jack snickered cautiously.

"Meyer, I like that," Jack said. "Change Management is all about recognizing where your people are now, identifying where they need to be, and devising a plan for getting them there. That's the change you have to manage."

"Go on," Rona requested.

"A good start is a motivating speech by the leader of the troops. It's much easier to manage change when there's an inspiring reason to change. But Change Management is not about a speech. It's about encouraging people to align with a more productive set of beliefs, objectives, and behaviors. Encouragement should be nurturing," Jack paused and looked at Rona. Her look softened. *My ploy worked,* Jack thought. *Whenever a woman hears the word nurturing come from a man's mouth, she lets her guard down.*

"It's important to ensure that all the team members are singing off the same song sheet," Jack continued. "The project newsletter, the website, and whatever else you use as a broadcast mechanism must showcase accomplishments in order to maintain the energies and spirits of the team members."

"The players will play harder when they know the score," Meyer said.

"Well said, Meyer," Jack responded.

✵ ✵ ✵

FRIDAY, JULY 22ND 10:25 AM

Biff stood outside the plant. Buck Roscoe's voice rang out loudly from the speaker on Biff's smartphone.

"Biff, we liked Bluto's letter, but shutting down the other projects is your call. Play this right or find another place to play," Buck said.

"You saw the part about Stanley?" Biff asked.

"That's your problem. Take care of it. I don't give a damn what you do as long as you do it right. You've got no runway on this," Buck declared.

"Okay," Biff replied.

Buck hung up.

Biff walked inside and rejoined the group, looking haggard.

"What's wrong?" Rona inquired.

"Nothing to discuss now," he said with a faint smile. "Why does everything have to happen at once?"

"That's life," said Jack.

The group disbanded. Rona avoided Jack as she left the room. Jack's eyes followed her shapely figure. "She is so fine," he muttered to himself.

"What did you say?" prompted Meyer.

"Oh, only that I know we'll do fine."

✳ ✳ ✳

FRIDAY, JULY 22ND 1:07 PM

Stanley's group was readying itself for a visit from Big-Box's Business Continuity team. Biff was returning to his office with a hot cup of coffee, and Ahmed and Park walked rigidly by him. Once they passed Biff and turned the corner they broke into a run toward Stanley's office.

Stanley was inspecting a new Coach leather portfolio and a Mont Blanc pen he had just received from ThickWare. 'SUC' was emblazoned in the lower right portion of the portfolio's cover.

He gently rubbed his manicured thumb across the snowcapped tip of the pen. *This is no imitation,* he realized proudly.

Stanley heard the running steps and looked up as Ahmed and Park burst into his doorway. "Yes?" Stanley asked, surprised.

Ahmed started, "I don't know how to tell you this, but…."

"Just say it," Stanley said, impatiently.

"I, I mean we," Park began, looking at his shoes, "we accidentally must have erased all of the data files, or at least I think we did."

"What the hell are you talking about?" said Stanley, rising from his chair.

"Well, you know the fix we came up with the other day? We figured that we could tweak it more to improve the response time," said Park.

"It was supposed to organize the data, but instead it corrupted the data, so we lost all of the order history from Big-Box," added Ahmed, anxiously biting his lip. "We lost the list that tells us which backorders ship to which stores!"

"Restore the backup!" Stanley ordered loudly. "No big deal."

"We haven't been doing the backups for three months," said Ahmed. "The vendor that makes the backup system that you ordered after we lost the Homemaker's Club data still hasn't shipped us the servers."

Stanley gulped loudly. That vendor was funded by an elder at the House of Worship. The elder promised Stanley stock in another of his companies if Stanley would steer business toward the new company. Stanley had never expected any problems. After all, when had he ever had to restore a backup before?

Stanley fell back into his seat. There was a loud whoopee-cushion sound as the chair's air bladder ruptured, dropping Stanley's seating surface to its lowest level. Stanley's chin was suddenly at the height of his desktop. He looked up at Ahmed and Park, who now seemed so far away. "You guys can't be serious," he wailed. "I never told you to refine the approach."

Ahmed and Park remained silent.

Stanley turned his broken chair toward his window. A tar truck had parked outside, belching dirty, black smoke all over his once-gleaming Harley-Davidson. He turned toward Ahmed and Park. They were already gone. Moments later, Stanley was on the phone with a recruiter. Within fifteen minutes, Stanley accepted a job offer with CompuSquat in Lisle, a town located a few miles from Naperville and closer to his church.

News of the lost data reverberated quickly within PNP's walls. Biff's anger was palpable when he marched toward Stanley's office thirty minutes later. *I am going to call him out on the We Love Ewe deliverables too,* Biff decided. *This is the last straw. Once I get control of his department, he's outta here.*

Biff walked through the door and saw that Stanley was packing his awards, photos, and plaques. *What's going on? Is he sabotaging me?* Biff had never spent time with the technical team and had few relationships with the consultants. *I can't believe that I let him get this far. This fuck has me over a barrel,* Biff thought furiously.

"I'm resigning from PNP. I can work until next Monday," Stanley said.

"You're what?" Biff responded, his red eyes widened with incredulity.

"Yes. And not that I need to tell you, but I'm going to work at CompuSquat to run their consulting division for western Chicago."

Biff paused for fifteen seconds, fighting to understand what was happening. "You can't leave. I need time for the transition, and you need to fix these data problems. If we can't ship tonight, Big-Box will shut us down," Biff said anxiously.

"That's your problem now, I already accepted," Stanley responded. *I finally one-upped the pretty boy CEO,* Stanley thought.

"You and I both know that leaving on such short notice is totally unprofessional and irresponsible. Can't you call them and postpone?" Biff pleaded.

"I can, but I won't."

I have to act, Biff realized. *What did Stanley crave?* Biff had no feel for Stanley. They never connected on any level.

"I need a 100% bonus for every week I remain," Stanley began, sensing Biff's predicament. I also want a glowing reference letter attesting to my valuable contributions to this company," Stanley said.

Biff stood there quietly, absorbing the tension. After a few moments his eyes narrowed and focused tightly on Stanley. *Fuck this asshole. But I have no choice. I have to say yes,* he concluded. *Giving Stanley a good reference hurts more than the extra cash. He may be bluffing about CompuSquat, but I can't afford to take the chance.*

Stanley is irreplaceable, at least in the short run; I haven't spoken two words to either Ahmed or Park since they joined PNP. As Jack might say, Stanley was at the peak of his learning curve and despite his failings, his time now was worth several thousand dollars per hour. Big-Box will hold up payment if PNP doesn't ship tonight, and Stanley is the only PNP employee who knows all the passwords and unlock codes for PNP's systems.

"Okay, expect to remain until October 1**st**. Your reference letter will be forthcoming," Biff said.

"Wise choice," Stanley grunted.

Biff walked away. *How could I be so stupid,* he wondered. *This guy can shut us down any time he wants, and we would never know what hit us. How could I have taken so much risk? Now I have to deal with his extortion.*

Biff looked at his watch and then hurried out the plant's back door. He had a doctor's appointment at 1:45 PM. He popped two pink pills into his mouth while running toward the parking lot.

✲ ✲ ✲

Meanwhile, in her office, Rona took a call from Gladys, still at the hospital.

"I can't believe I fell for the jerk," Rona began. "You were so right! He seemed so smart, so focused, but he's just out for the milk, like most guys."

"Mmm," Gladys said.

"What a nothing! But I feel so unsettled. I never expected it to go this way...we had such chemistry...I thought this one was different. I am just so discouraged now. Maybe I'll have a child by myself," Rona lamented.

"You're too good for him. Get a massage and hit the Oak Street Beach tomorrow. It's going to be a hot day. The guys will all be after you, I guarantee it. You'll forget about that putz."

Rona laughed weakly. "You get better quickly so we can both go next weekend. By the way hun, Myron confirmed for a week from Saturday for your sister's bachelorette party. The girls will love his dancing show."

"Myron's such a sweetie pie. Thanks so much."

"Glad you're feeling a little better. Okay, bye." Rona hung up.

FRIDAY, JULY 22ND 3:45 PM

Exhausted, Biff sank into his office chair after returning from the doctor's appointment. His blood pressure had risen to 155/105. The doctor insisted that Biff power down his smartphone before probing about Biff's rapidly declining health. Biff remained tight-lipped. After recommending more exercise and a healthier diet, the doctor doubled the potency of Biff's blood pressure meds and sent Biff on his way.

FRIDAY, JULY 22ND 4:45 PM

Biff called a meeting for five o'clock in the Frying Pan room with the intention of announcing his plan for bringing Broadway back on track, though he had yet to formulate a plan. He began drafting a short email to all his employees and cc'd several of the Big-Box people on it. His mind was racing, but his concentration was failing. Frustrated, he saved the email to his Drafts Folder. He took a deep, shaky breath, trying to calm himself.

He looked around, desperate for a diversion. He typed cnn.com into his computer, and soon became entranced by the live audio feed. The anchor gravely reported that an explosion had occurred on a MidPoint Airways flight to Kansas City, damaging the nose gear. A retired airline captain provided expert commentary, but after listening for several minutes Biff realized that he had learned nothing. *My god,* he thought, *today was the day Amelia wanted to go to Kansas City. But I saw her leave for school this morning, right? There's no way she flew to Kansas City without telling us.*

Biff stood up and then sat back down. *My mind must be playing tricks. There can't be another problem with MidPoint. After the last incident the FAA must be taking extra precautions. They must be. Why is CNN ending this feed now?*

I can't call Constance, he decided. Fingers shaking, Biff texted his stepdaughter, "Hi, honey, hope your day at school is great. How are you doing?"

FRIDAY, JULY 22ND 5:00 PM

The worried murmurs of the fifty-three people from the project team wafted out of the Frying Pan. They were all waiting for Biff, wondering how he would guide them to ship Big-Box's backorders that evening without the store-by-store data, while also putting forth a plan to get Broadway live. Rona was seated alone in the front row, nervously sifting through e-mails on her smartphone. Meyer leaned over to her and said, "Jack told me what you said about business travel. It's not true. I used to travel because I couldn't handle taking care of my girls. Work is easy compared to those two!"

Rona laughed. "Someday I'd like to experience that problem myself," she said wistfully.

✷ ✷ ✷

As Biff pushed back from his office desk, Gertrude rushed in. Biff started to wave her away. "Your mother is on the phone – she's crying – you'd better take it," Gertrude said.

Biff picked up the phone.

"Biff, Biff, oh my god, your father had a stroke and the ambulance just took him away."

"Mother," Biff said without losing his composure, "is he—is he okay? Where are you?"

"They did CPR and he was breathing. Your sister is meeting me at the hospital."

"Did you tell the EMTs about his allergies?"

"Yeah, but I can't remember the names of the drugs he's allergic to and he lost the thingamajig with his records, you know that thing that plugs into the computer."

"Mother, don't worry. I'll get on a plane as soon as I can."

"Okay. I should go meet your sister."

"Bye, Mom," Biff said, hanging up. "Love you," he mouthed, but the line was already dead.

He sat back down in his chair, the color draining from his face. His eyes focused on Gertrude, who remained standing in the doorway.

"Shall I cancel the meeting?" she asked tentatively.

"No," Biff replied slowly.

Biff stood up. He tried to gather his thoughts while walking carefully down the hall, but images of his father kept flashing into his head. With a sense of reeling out of control, he entered the Frying Pan, and walked slowly to the lectern. Focusing on the moment, he cleared his mind and then his throat. "Thanks for coming," he began.

"I want to recognize the hard work that you've all put in... the...the long hours and time away from your families..."

"We are at a crossroads," Biff continued, his voice throaty. He paused for a second and lost his train of thought. Fortunately, it always takes the audience an extra second to realize that the speaker is messing up, and Biff remembered what he was going to say before that second passed. He continued, "Our next actions will impact you, our customers, and our shareholders. It pains me to say that we've bitten off more than we can chew. I take full responsibility for this...."

Eunice whispered to Myron, "why is it when the boss takes full responsibility for something, nothing happens to him, but if I take full responsibility for anything, I get fired? That ain't right."

Myron nodded, smiling, but kept his eyes trained on Biff.

Biff had been on autopilot, but he knew he had to address the specifics of the project and he wasn't sure how to. His voice started to shake as he continued. "By tackling too much in parallel, we haven't made enough progress in several critical areas. We must now turn our full attention to Big-Box. It's no secret that they'll cut us off if we can't get our computers to work with theirs by the end of this year. Now I find out that our database is...is...is corrupted and we can't ship tonight." Biff felt the stress building up in his body, and tried to calm his rapid breathing.

Venkat raised his hand. Biff nodded at him, relieved at the reprieve.

"Do you know how long will it take us to retrieve the data? And does Big-Box know about the situation yet?"

Biff stared at Venkat. Biff's mind went blank as he gasped for air. "PNP is midway through a major upgrade…" Biff stopped, his face white. Everyone focused on their leader. His voice weakened. "PNP is midway through…" Biff stopped again. "I'm sorry.…"

Rona stood up, "Are you okay?"

Biff ignored her. He started again, "PNP is midway through.…" He paused and clutched the lectern. It shook as he leaned heavily upon it.

Deathly silence filled the room. Biff looked down as he reached into his pants pocket with his right hand. In slow motion, he raised his head to look at his employees.

"Fuck!" Biff suddenly yelled. Stupefied, the people in the room watched him take the pill bottle from his pocket and then throw it hard to the floor. The safety cap split open and pink pills spilled under the feet of the participants sitting in the first two rows. No one moved. Biff grabbed the lectern, hunched over, and looked up.

He began to speak but stopped again. A moment later he opened his mouth. Many of the workers looked down, embarrassed for Biff. Rona tried to establish eye contact, wondering if she should take over.

He stopped again and flinched as though a sharp pain passed through his body. He straightened up and let go of the lectern. Several seconds passed.

"I'm gay," Biff said softly, followed by a muffled, queasy giggle.

Everyone looked up. Silence suffocated the room until Biff spoke again.

"I'm gay," he repeated, more loudly.

He stood, shaking, in front of the room, suddenly realizing what he had done and feeling lost and unsure of what to do next.

Rona walked toward him and put her hand on his arm. "Let's sit down, babe," meanwhile saying to herself, *I knew it, I knew it, I knew it, I knew it.* The crowd murmured. Jack stared, wide-eyed.

"No. No, I'm okay. Biff straightened up and like a dissipating cloud, his eyes became sharp and clear. He could feel his blood pressure dropping. He felt his jaw relax. He spoke firmly. "I can't lie any more. I can't lie to you, to Big-Box, to my family. I can't lie to myself!"

Biff laughed nervously and leaned forward. For a moment it looked like he would fall over, but he righted himself. He stood in front of the crowd silently, surveying their response.

"Cool man, that's cool," Earl said softly. "Way to go."

Eunice leaned across the lap of an expressionless Myron. "Damn, what a sissy!" She muttered back to Earl, shaking her head.

"Come on woman, get outta yesterday," Earl replied scornfully.

Biff took a deep breath. Finally, he spoke. "I can't lie to myself anymore, and PNP can't lie to itself anymore. We're hip deep in a major IT upgrade and it's been a miserable failure," Biff declared. "That's right, a miserable failure. Now we're in the Black Hole, on the verge of becoming a DELETE error." Biff paused, and looked into the center of the crowd. "We believed that our investments in these four projects would enable PNP to cement our dominant position in our industry. We were wrong."

Those in the crowd exchanged confused, shocked glances, but Biff ignored them as his voice became louder and clearer. He continued, "As of this moment, I want you to suspend all your work on ERP, CRM, and Supply Chain. Put all of your efforts toward connecting to Broadway, and I don't care if we have to yank out all of the ThickWare software upgrades we've made so far. We'll get back to 3.5 when we're ready."

"Many of you who have helped with this have been led to believe that the finish line is in sight. It is not. Broadway is our first stop along this trip to automation. There will be other stops, but they will occur one at a time. I will no longer tolerate confusion. Clarity must reign, and we will have accountability."

He's gathering steam, Jack observed with a sense of pride, realizing that this was Reality Check's first coming out party. *Our clients have succeeded in many ways, but never like this,* Jack thought.

Biff continued, the pace of his speech accelerating, "PNP has these strategic objectives: Maintain our market leadership position for quality and innovation. Shorten new product-to-market cycle times. Reduce inventory investment and storage costs. Leverage information technology to create barriers between PNP's customers and competitors. Involve every PNP employee with customer satisfaction and double sales while maintaining existing overhead. We have an obligation to be our best with all of our partners, up, down, and across the supply and demand chains." Biff paused and looked at the attendees. They were rapt.

Biff continued, "These are our long-term objectives. For now, everything is on hold until we can prove to ourselves that we can do technology right. Next Monday we'll be kicking off a Fail-First project to get live on Broadway. I will lead this project."

Work To Win

"We will hold project status meetings every Tuesday, Wednesday, and Friday morning at 9:00 am here in this room, starting immediately. We're turning up the heat in the Frying Pan and renaming it the War Room. It'll be our base of operations for all project activities. This will be a tense time for us, and I want to now outline what will be our four Rules of Engagement for our project. The rules are designed to allow us to function more effectively as we organize ourselves into a fighting battalion."

On his best day, Harry had never projected the clarity and sureness that Biff was showing now.

Too bad he's gay, Rona thought. *Wow, is he sexy!*

Biff continued, "We are all guilty of wasting too much time talking and waiting to talk. This breeds conflict—not major conflict, but the kind of conflict that turns a productive meeting into an unproductive one.

First, no one should hold a meeting unless there is a clear purpose for it. Meetings are diabolical time toilets. The One-Hour Rule limits the meeting time. Meetings longer than an hour degenerate quickly. The Three-Minute rule tells us that no one should ever take more than three minutes to make a point. If you can't make your point in three minutes, you didn't think it through properly before you began to speak. The No Interruptions Rule gives everyone an opportunity to contribute his or her three minutes. The speaker must monitor his own time.

Second, we don't have the luxury of wasting energies on the Re's. The Re's are Rework, Retalk, and Rethink. By tightly scoping meetings, you avoid Re'ing everything. You may not always get it right the first time but sometimes it's better to make bad decisions quickly than good decisions slowly. Why? Because when you decide and act, you will see a result. If it's not a result that you wanted, then you can adjust your course or backtrack. Don't get caught in the spider's web of analysis paralysis. Keep moving.

Third, we all know each other on this team. If you need to communicate, do it in person or on the phone. Don't waste time on email unless you're using it to schedule a meeting. It's a huge source of unproductivity.

Fourth, and most importantly, remember that we're all in this together. We must win this fight by bringing out the best in each other, or we'll surely fail. Collaborate today so we won't have to commiserate tomorrow. Be optimistic, take charge, focus on the critical path, and don't get off it. If you see your teammate wandering, help him back on track. If you need a jolt of optimism, my door is open."

Biff held the lectern closer, pushing his square jaw slightly forward. "We're in a new world. Information matters. When we have the right information at the right time, we can make the right decisions. When we are unable to get the right information, or worse, when we don't know what information we need, we start drowning. Once we start fighting against those riptides, we're as good as dead. The way to stay alive is to avoid a losing fight in the first place.

We are under a mandate to ship the 8 – 10 –12s out tonight, and at this moment we lack that right information I just mentioned. Big-Box's frying pan sets are built and waiting on our shipping dock. I have full confidence that the people in this room can quickly reconstruct the shipping information and I look forward to seeing your creative solution in action later this evening."

Biff paused, and then continued, "I should never have begun these technology projects without having understood what I was getting into, but I know that if we all work hard and stay focused, we'll get through this. As we hunker down and focus on Broadway's go-live date, the project team will be working more long hours. We're going to have the most rockin' holiday party you've ever seen once we light the lights on Broadway," Biff added, his voice rising. A few people laughed.

Earl leaned forward into the next row and touched Otis' shoulder. Otis turned his head slightly. "Whatcha think, Otis? Will it work?" Earl asked in a quiet voice.

"Depends on his commitment. Remember, people get optimistic slowly and pessimistic quickly," Otis whispered.

"Where'd you learn that?"

"From the stock market. It goes up twice as many days as it goes down but moves almost twice as far on a down day as an up day. People's spirits move the same way."

"Hmmm." Earl nodded, leaning back, "For a guy with one eye, you sure see good."

"This is truly a team effort and each of us has an oar," Biff continued. "We're all equally important in rowing this ship into port. It's time to perform, not to panic. Remember, mark that Broadway coming out party down on your calendars," he said, beaming. "Now let's get to work!"

Biff walked in front of the lectern. For a moment he stood there and then there was silence. The applause began but Biff didn't stay long enough for it to finish. He left the room with the spry step that his people had missed. He stopped in the consultant's work area and noticed that CNN was still covering the circling flight.

Ahmed approached Biff nervously.

"Come here," Biff said.

"Yes Mr. Harper," Ahmed said.

"What's on your mind, son?"

"Mr. Harper, I have something to tell you, but I can't tell you."

"What does that mean?"

"I don't know what to do."

"Just say it. That's what I did. Just let it go."

His voice cracking, Ahmed told Biff why the backup servers weren't operational.

"Thank you, son. You did the right thing. I won't forget it," Biff said, walking away. He dialed his mother from his smartphone. Harry had been admitted to Booth Hospital in New York and the doctors treated him without being aware of his multitude of medication allergies. Neither Harry nor Biff nor the doctors knew that Harry's life depended on the outcome of a roulette wheel of imperfect information. Everybody won on that spin. None of the lifesaving meds administered by the doctors was red-listed on the lost USB drive containing Harry's health records.

FRIDAY, JULY 22ND 5:20 PM

The last few stragglers were leaving the newly named War Room. "Finally, this nightmare is starting to make sense to me," exclaimed an accounts payable clerk.

"I don't like meetings three times a week. It's waste of time," said a second.

"What do you care? We get paid for showing up. This thing will never work anyway," chimed in a third.

Jack overheard this comment and smiled. *Maybe she's right,* Jack mused, *but I don't think so.*

Ahmed and Park adjourned to the Double Boiler to work on a theory that Park had formulated to uncorrupt the data. Without noticing each other, both Rona and Jack tried to leave the War Room at the same moment. They bumped hips.

"Excuse me," Jack said. "Oh, Rona, can we talk for a...." Jack's voiced trailed off.

Rona shook her head. In a moment, she turned a corner and was gone.

FRIDAY, JULY 22ND 5:30 PM

Damn, Jack thought as he made his way toward the parking lot. *What does she want, a marriage proposal? After two weeks? I'll never understand how women think. Why can't they be logical like Biff? He fought hard and found clarity even though he was drowning in confusion.* "He's the man!" Jack said aloud. *Why can't I be?*

Jack grumbled as he got into his Tapir and began creeping toward the Fox Valley Mall in Aurora. The Friday afternoon traffic was miserable. He crawled past the quarter-mile long entrance for Big-Box, watching its long bold pink sign inch by. He shook his head, exasperated. It reminded him of Rona. *What else can I do? Surprise her with an engagement ring? What kind of ring did her polo-playing first husband buy her? No way, this is crazy. But I don't want to lose her,* he said to himself, eyes wandering.

He pulled out his smartphone and began fumbling with the keys. Glancing back and forth between the road and his phone, he struggled to compose a text to Rona. The message was only two lines long, but Jack kept backspacing and editing. He reached for the thumbscrew to finally send the text when Jack was rocked back to attention by an object floating in the air before him. Reflexively, Jack slammed on his brakes.

A marauding plastic grocery bag headed straight for the Tapir's grille. He swerved and punched the accelerator to move out of its way, but the bag's heat-seeking ability kept it on target. Jack muttered to himself, "go ahead, creep, make my day." The bag flew under the car and instantly melted around Jack's tailpipe, creating a choking stink inside the Tapir. He opened the window, gasped for air, and dropped the smartphone on the car's floor, without sending the message. Trying to hold in his breath as he entered the mall parking lot, he recalled what Gary Gibson had once told him, before Gary's arrest:

"Parking at the mall is a great metaphor for making life choices. Say the mall is crowded. You drive down the aisle toward one of the main entrances and you see a parking space. You begin to pull into the space and then you hesitate. Maybe there is a closer space, you wonder. So you pull out and drive farther down the aisle, hoping to find a better space but hoping just as strongly that no one takes the first space, in case you still need it. Tension fills in the divide between two points of clarity. Even when a better choice may exist, it's often best to park in that first space and accept it. When you go for it all, you may get nothing."

I believe this, and I want Rona, Jack decided. *Maybe there is a better woman out there, but why wait?*

He saw his space. It was near the front of the aisle between two minivans. He parked and stepped from the Tapir. His left foot landed squarely into a steaming pile of beige-colored dog dung, left by a bull mastiff's owner who didn't want to put down her smartphone long enough to scoop the poop. As if on a banana peel, Jack's foot slid through the pile, forcing him into a partial split. He fell over, his left leg landing right in the pile.

"Shit," Jack screamed. *This is the real Mudslide. I wish I'd had the one at Dante's instead,* he thought, shaking his head in disgust.

Jack walked into a department store. A mother pushing a strollered baby and wearing an 'I Love My Mastiff' sweatshirt sniffed, whirled around, and exclaimed, "You're disgusting!" Jack ignored her. Three more dirty looks and several held noses later, Jack finished buying a pair of jeans and changed into them. He put his soiled trousers into the shopping bag and tossed the bag into a trash can.

Jack walked past the food court and into a jewelry store. He noticed diamond rings priced from eight hundred to twenty thousand dollars, but he didn't stop walking. He went to the toe ring display and found the most expensive item. He plopped down his credit card and the clerk rang up $379 for the gold toe ring, encrusted with tiny diamond chips.

FRIDAY, JULY 22ND 7:07 PM

Unknown to anyone else at PNP, Biff called the Naperville police after his speech to tip them off about Stanley's dirty deal. Congressman Chmeat was known for being a skinflint with the Illinois police budgets, so the cops were all too happy to arrest his son on a fraud charge that they believed would stick.

Stanley had missed Biff's speech. Stacey had picked Stanley up for dinner three hours earlier and was now dropping him off at PNP. The STANSTAC1 vanity license plate gleamed on her bright yellow Hummer H1.

From his office window, Biff watched the cops drive up in their patrol car. Stanley and Stacey thought nothing of flipping the middle finger to the ozone layer as they laughed together, refreshed by the frigid blast of the Hummer's powerful air conditioner. The patrol car moved slowly and parked next to the Hummer, sandwiching it against PNP's building. The officer tapped his horn and Stacey looked down at him from the Hummer's highly perched passenger seat. The officer motioned for Stacey to roll down her window. Unalarmed, she complied.

"Stanley Chmeat!" the officer barked.

Stanley leaned over his wife and looked down at the officer. "Yes…Yes sir," he yelped.

"Step out of the car," the officer commanded. A burly second officer got out of the patrol car, and with his hand on his holster, moved quickly toward Stanley, who was now standing beside the Hummer.

"You are under arrest for fraud. Put your hands behind your back!"

Stacey looked terrified as the officers manhandled Stanley. "What's happening?" she screamed. "Somebody help him!"

Meyer, Otis, Earl, and Rona and several other workers began to gather near PNP's main entrance, thirty feet from the chaos.

Stacey opened her door. She tried to step down but missed the running board, and her foot dropped heavily to the ground. Her large ankle rolled and gave way. She collapsed between the Hummer's and the patrol car's rear wheels. Her face hit the curb between the wheels, splitting the flaccid skin of her third chin wide open. She rolled over and sat up, dazed, the blood from her face soaking her spring-weight fox coat.

"My god, she looks like the bloody carcass of an animal that got its head caught in the jaws of a trap," Eunice said.

"Or the deer I shot last week," Earl remarked.

Biff watched from his office window as the first officer handcuffed Stanley while the second officer read the Miranda card as Stacey wailed, "He's innocent. He didn't do anything. He never knew what the technology was supposed to do…."

They flipped on the siren, drowning her out. Stacey pulled off her orthopedic shoe and threw it at the police car is it pulled away. The shoe banged into the rear window. The police car slowed for a second and then raced toward the Cook County Jail. Stacey turned her corpulent body back toward the PNP crew who looked at her with pity. Rona whisked off her expensive suit jacket and tried holding it under Stacey's chin to stop the bleeding. Stacey pushed her away, screaming, "What are you looking at, bitch!?"

Biff looked on, concerned for Stacey but satisfied that Stanley was in handcuffs. After calling 911 from his desk phone, he felt his smartphone vibrate. He drew the weapon out of its holster with the alacrity of an Old West gunslinger, and clicked the thumbscrew.

"Hi Dad. Driving to Kansas City with Kyle. Please, please don't tell Mom. Also, forgot my credit card. Can you FedEx me some cash to the BigEight? Don't worry, we got two rooms. Promise to be back by Monday before school starts. Love you Daddy, Amelia."

Biff sat down and looked at the smartphone, sighing with relief. Constance never knew what was happening. Biff clicked on the CNN bookmark in his News folder. The plane to Kansas City had landed safely. Biff rose and went toward the window. He saw three EMTs strapping Stacey into a gurney. They struggled to lift her.

Biff turned, picked up his office phone and dialed Flynch's smartphone.

"Hello," Flynch answered.

"Flynch, you're out. I want to hear from the CEO of Pro-Con by 9 AM tomorrow concerning whom you're sending to clean up this mess. Namath won't do."

"But..."

"No discussion. By Monday morning our lawyer will be putting into motion a lawsuit against Pro-Con for fraudulent billing, and we will speak with the Cook County attorney general regarding criminal charges."

Biff hung up. He looked out the window at the waning light. It was a cool, cloudless summer evening. For the first time in months, Biff heard birds singing.

FRIDAY, JULY 22ND 8:45 PM

Biff dialed Jack's smartphone. Jack was eighty feet away, alone in the War Room.

"Jack, you've done a great job here. The Reality Check Assessment Letter was dead-on. There are no rebuttal points worth mentioning."

"Thanks, Biff, I'll tell my team. They'll appreciate the feedback."

"Now it's up to us. I know you were planning to leave tomorrow, but if you can still fly out tonight on the eleven o'clock Mid-Point flight, go for it. We'll see you again after Fail-First."

"Are you sure?" Jack said, hesitating, hoping to see Rona one more time.

"Yes."

Biff escaped his Black Hole, Stanley fell into his, and Jack teetered on the rim of his own. Rona didn't return his texts or phone calls, so Jack flew back to New York, feeling as if he were retreating rather than returning home.

✣ ✣ ✣

Venkat realized that the data was never lost, but somehow the columns and rows of the database had become transposed. Ahmed wrote a short program to flip the data into its proper position and Meyer and Rona assigned a team that used last month's shipping reports to validate the recovered data.

The backorders were loaded on the trucks and shipped to Big-Box that evening. The shipments arrived in the stores moments before the July 31st issue of *Gassy Vegans* hit the newsstands. The PNP team solved the problem without Big-Box ever realizing how close its supplier had been to the edge of the abyss.

Before leaving the office that evening, Biff dialed Myron's extension. The two agreed to meet for a late dinner. At six the next morning Biff told Constance that he was leaving her. Three days later, Biff and Myron left on a hastily planned weeklong vacation to South Beach. Biff's mother called Biff poolside at the Delano to let him know that Harry was making a good recovery. Biff was relieved and Myron's strong hands comforted him as they celebrated with a bottle of champagne. It was a lovely time.

EPILOGUE

Fail-First worked. Big-Box and PNP successfully processed test transactions through the Broadway interface during the week of August 24th. Lars called Biff to congratulate him and to reinforce PNP's importance as a supplier. Biff asked him to record a video message to PNP's employees. Lars did so, and emailed the link to everyone at PNP. Eight weeks later, Broadway officially went live, sixty-three days early. Biff scheduled ERP's restart for December 1st while CRM and Supply Chain remained on indefinite hold. Roscoe awarded Biff a handsome five-year contract that included a multi-million dollar options package and generous same-sex partner benefits.

Biff worked at recovering his athletic physique. He hadn't taken another oxycodone since he threw the bottle away, and other than enjoying an occasional strawberry daiquiri with Myron, he stayed on the wagon. Biff rented a condo in Chicago's hip Lakeview neighborhood and Myron moved in a week later. Rona came over after work to help decorate and Amelia brought a gift basket from The Body Shop.

Biff didn't return to Hollow Hills. Myron switched to a two-days-per-week schedule at PNP, and enrolled them both in a salsa dancing class. Biff reciprocated by accompanying Myron to Toastmasters' Lincoln Park chapter meetings.

Several lobbyists were indicted on ethics violations, but Congressman Chmeat was not among them. Stanley was free on bail awaiting trial. CompuSquat withdrew its job offer while Stanley was under indictment. To help pay for Stacey's upcoming plastic surgery holiday to Rio, Stanley began writing articles at a dollar per word for *Tektanic*.

Jack had been checking in with Meyer and Biff by telephone. Jack, Marcus, and Annie participated in weekly videoconferences with the project team. That summer he wrote four letters to Rona. He didn't want to send emails to her PNP address, and figured that the old-fashioned approach would charm her. It didn't work. The first two letters were returned to him unopened, sealed in larger envelopes. The toe ring sat in his top drawer on the top floor of the Greene Street condo.

✳ ✳ ✳

MONDAY, OCTOBER 30TH 3:30 PM

Jack pulled a maroon Tapir into PNP's driveway on his way to O'Hare. He had spent the weekend teaching at Northwestern. He was due back in New York the following day for his last scheduled hair transplant procedure. Finally, he would have full coverage.

Gertrude ushered Jack into Biff's office. "He'll be back in five minutes," she said.

"Thanks very much."

Jack took out his smartphone, muttering, "Nothing ventured, nothing gained." He texted Rona:

"I got the job done at PNP....maybe I can get us back on track as well.....give me one more chance, one little triangle. Come on, put your toe in the water. Jack."

Biff strode into his office. Jack noticed he was tanner, more muscular, and the circles that had been under his eyes were now gone. His stride seemed almost buoyant.

"Jack, thanks for all you've done for us. We're escaping DELETE and positioning ourselves for High Value," Biff said, firmly shaking Jack's hand.

"Feels good to be out of the Black Hole, doesn't it?"

"Yes. By the way, did you hear that Rona has been promoted to Executive VP? She's now the number two at PNP."

"That's great," Jack gulped. "Have you filled the CIO's role?"

"No, and we're not going to. Instead, we hired a technology savvy guy to take over Rona's job and we've moved Ahmed up to run all the infrastructure activities. We're committed to providing our customers with that Transcendental Experience, and we're changing our compensation structure to support these efforts."

"More great news," Jack noted approvingly.

"How's Reality Check going? What are you doing now?" Biff asked.

"I'm taking a sabbatical. The President called me last month and asked me to join a new cabinet position in Washington, Undersecretary for Lean Technology. He's concerned that the Big Data tsunami will drown us," Jack responded. "He wants me to help set policies to keep us safe."

"Wow!" Biff said excitedly.

"It'll be publicly announced next week," Jack said.

"Fantastic, and thanks a million," Biff said.

"Is that my bonus?" Jack asked, eyes widening.

"Don't you wish," Biff responded, smiling. "Don't worry. I suspect you'll be pleasantly surprised in about seventy-five days."

"I'm not worried. Thanks again for everything," Jack said, firmly shaking Biff's hand.

✳ ✳ ✳

Jack walked out the door of the plant, toward the Tapir. As he grabbed the door handle, he felt a vibration at his hip. He reached for his smartphone, clicked the thumbscrew and read Rona's reply,

"Maybe we needed to Fail-First and we're 98% of the way to High-Value :) Have time for a drink?"

PART III – THE SEVEN KEYS TO ESCAPING DELETE (SUMMARY)

KEY 1: PROJECT – COMPLETE SMALL, SHORT-TERM, HIGH VALUE PROJECTS

1.1   Paradigm Paralysis
1.2   50/50 Properties Of The Law Of 98/2
1.3   See The Critical Path
1.4   Beware: The Fully Integrated Enterprise
1.5   Little-Triangles
1.6   Strive For Clarity And Forget Multi-Tasking
1.7   Fail-First
1.8   Be Lean & Stay Fit
1.9   <CONTROL>, <ALT>, And <DELETE> Errors
1.10 Get High!

KEY 2: CUSTOMER – DELIVER A TRANSCENDENTAL EXPERIENCE TO YOUR CUSTOMERS

2.1   Eliminate The Oxymorons
2.2   Focus On The Business Details, Not On The Technical Details
2.3   Excite Your Customers
2.4   Tirelessly Measure Satisfaction

KEY 3: TEAM - USE THE RIGHT TEAM

KEY 4: TECHNOLOGY - LEVERAGE TECHNOLOGY TO ENABLE BUSINESS, NOT DISABLE IT

KEY 5: USER – EMPOWER USERS TO CREATE VALUE, NOT WASTE TIME

5.1   Free Your Users To Work Everywhere

5.2   User Community Extends Traditional Boundaries

5.3   Expect To Be Amazed By New Technology

5.4   Don't Allow Personal Technology To Get Too Personal

5.5   Avoid The Email Unproductivity Trap

5.6   Slim That Computer-Ass!

5.7   Users Will Only Use What's Usable

5.8   The Path To Tomorrow Does Not Go Through Yesterday

KEY 6: VALUE – HARVEST VALUE FROM IT INVESTMENTS

6.1   Manage Technology Like A Stock Portfolio

6.2   Growth, Profitability Improvement, And Expansion

6.3   Switch From CBA To ABC Thinking

6.4   Benchmark Goal And Role Models

6.5   Be A High-Priced Leader Or An Economy-Class Follower

6.6   Measure <CONTROL>, <ALT>, And <DELETE> Errors

6.7   Audit, Really Audit, Or Expect To Fail

KEY 7: CHANGE – THINK DIFFERENTLY AS YOU TURN THE SHIP

7.1   Simplify, Don't Complexify

7.2   Reduce Risks

7.3   Stamp Out Variability

ABOUT THE AUTHOR

Jon Bellman fixes broken IT projects.

Before founding Reality Check LLC, Jon worked for the investment banks Donaldson, Lufkin & Jenrette, and Kidder, Peabody & Co. Prior to his Wall Street career, Jon worked for the management consulting arms of three major accounting firms: Coopers & Lybrand, Ernst & Young, and Price Waterhouse.

He graduated from the MMM Program at Northwestern University, earning an MBA from the Kellogg School of Management and an MEM from the McCormick School of Engineering.

Jon also graduated from the Jerome Fisher Program in Management & Technology at the University of Pennsylvania, earning a BS from the Wharton School and a BAS from the School of Engineering and Applied Science.

Jon may be contacted via:

www.jonbellman.com

www.ingramcontent.com/pod-product-compliance
Lightning Source LLC
Chambersburg PA
CBHW060541200326
41521CB00007B/444